Commanding Generals
and
Chiefs of Staff

COMMANDING GENERALS

—— AND ——

CHIEFS OF STAFF
1775–2005

Portraits & Biographical Sketches
of the
United States Army's Senior Officer

William Gardner Bell

CENTER OF MILITARY HISTORY
UNITED STATES ARMY
WASHINGTON, D.C., 2005

Library of Congress Cataloging-in-Publication Data

Bell, William Gardner.
    Commanding generals and chiefs of staff, 1775–2005 : portraits &
biographical sketches of the United States Army's senior officer / by William
Gardner Bell.
        p. cm.
    1. Generals—United States—Biography. 2. United States. Dept. of the Army.
General Staff—Biography. 3. United States. Army—Biography. 4. United
States—History, Military. I. Center of Military History. II. Title.

E181.B53 2005
355'.0092'273–dc22
[B]

                                                                    2005047145

First Printed 1983—CMH Pub 70–14

For sale by the Superintendent of Documents, U.S. Government Printing Office
Internet: bookstore.gpo.gov   Phone: toll free (866) 512-1800;   DC area (202) 512-1800
Fax: (202) 512-2250 Mail: Stop SSOP, Washington, DC 20402-0001

ISBN 0-16-072376-0

Foreword

Leadership is of surpassing importance to the profession of arms. Judgment, competence, and courage often count for more than armed might alone in achieving success. Generalship is carefully studied by Soldiers who will lead men in combat, whether or not they aspire to general-officer rank themselves. Over time our comparatively young army has developed an impressive list of senior officers who have ably demonstrated the importance of leadership in trying circumstances.

This volume offers a unique glimpse of the commanding generals and chiefs of staff who have led the United States Army in peace and war. Their rise through the levels of leadership to the pinnacle of their profession reveals both striking parallels and fascinating contrasts. As the author's introductory analysis makes clear, their responsibilities have evolved over the last two hundred and thirty years. Although the essential elements of leadership remain unchanged, the complexity of technology and staff organization has increased radically over time.

The format of this volume combines biographical sketches with the officially designated portraits of the commanding generals and chiefs of staff, accompanied by brief accounts on the artists. As an aspect of the art of official portraiture that has continued for more than three centuries, these portraits add an interesting and revealing dimension to the biographer's words.

This volume not only celebrates the legacy of dedication and patriotism left by these leaders but also enhances our understanding of military leadership at the highest levels. I commend it to the attention of all students of our profession.

JOHN S. BROWN
Brigadier General, USA (Ret.)
Chief of Military History

The Author

William Gardner Bell was inducted into the Army in August 1941, was commissioned through the officer candidate course at the Cavalry School in 1943, and served as a platoon leader, company commander, and battalion staff officer with the 350th Infantry in the World War II Italian campaign and on the regimental staff during the occupation of Venezia Giulia. He was associate editor of the *Cavalry Journal* from 1947 to 1950 and editor of *Armor Magazine* from 1950 to 1953. From 1956 to his retirement from military service in 1962 he was a historian in the Office of the Chief of Military History. From 1963 to 1984 he was a historian in the U.S. Army Center of Military History, where for a dozen years he prepared the Annual Report of the Secretary of the Army and the annual *Department of the Army Historical Summary*. As staff specialist on the frontier army, he wrote the Indian wars chapter of the Army's historical volume *American Military History*. Mr. Bell is the author of *Secretaries of War and Secretaries of the Army: Portraits and Biographical Sketches* (1982), *The 350th Infantry in Occupation* (1947), *The Snake: A Noble and Various River* (1969), *John Gregory Bourke: A Soldier-Scientist on the Frontier* (1978), *Quarters One: The United States Army Chief of Staff's Residence* (1981), and *Will James: The Life and Works of a Lone Cowboy* (1987).

Preface to 1st Edition

From earliest times one might have expected to find at departmental headquarters a uniformed commander of the whole Army. Such ruling considerations as structure, organization, discipline, and leadership—the very essence of military operation—ordained commanders at every level and invested them progressively with advancing rank, expanding numbers of subordinates, and increasing measures of responsibility and authority. Yet logic, for a number of reasons, stopped short of the top, and over the early course of American history the role of the United States Army's senior officer was often uncertain, frequently shifting, and variously perceived by the incumbent, his service, and his superiors. The long road to regularization of the title and function, and to final acceptance of the official as a chief of staff rather than a commanding general, was marked by passion and controversy as well as by statesmanship and good will.

It is understandable that some measure of experimentation and revision in military command, staff, and structural relationships occurred in the early years of the Republic as the young nation developed the organization, methods, and means that would permit it to function effectively. But the War Department's search for the proper role for its uniformed leader extended well beyond a reasonable trial period, the more surprising because of the intimate executive, legislative, and constitutional involvement in the process. From 1775, when the Continental Congress elected General George Washington as the first commander of the Army, until 1903, when Congress legislated Secretary of War Elihu Root's reforms and Lieutenant General Nelson A. Miles retired taking the designation of commanding general with him, the senior officer's title fluctuated, the office lay vacant for two extended periods, the incumbents absented themselves on occasion, and a lively controversy rattled along,

rising and falling with the play of events and personalities.

Even the introduction of the Root reforms, the designation of the senior officer as a chief of staff rather than a commanding general, and the installation of Lieutenant General Samuel B. M. Young under the new title, did not still the differences over the assignment of functions and the lines of authority. Pulling and hauling continued as the chief of staff sought to consolidate his position at the center of power, the General Staff strove to establish control over planning and policy, and the technical services fought to retain their traditional control over special functions and fields and their direct access to the departmental secretary. It required sixty years, periodic legislative spurts, subordination of the military departments within the Department of Defense, and some culminating reforms by Secretary of Defense Robert S. McNamara to resolve the fundamental problems and place the Army and its senior officer on a sound institutional and functional footing.

By and large, the Army's top soldiers have been able men who worked their way up the career ladder to reach the summit of their profession. As in any walk of life, they moved in a competitive environment. Strong-willed and ambitious soldiers have vied for the title, responsibility, authority, honor, and opportunity for service embodied in the senior officer's position. As William Shakespeare pointed out, "'Tis deeds must win the prize," and indubitably those who succeeded invested a lifetime of dedicated and distinguished service on the way to the top. Yet so did many of their fellows, and to such qualifications as seniority, longevity, and accomplishment must be added the kinds of considerations that inspired President John Quincy Adams to bypass Generals Winfield Scott and Edmund Gaines to select General Alexander Macomb to command the Army; President Theodore Roosevelt to jump General John J. Pershing over 862 more senior officers for promotion from captain to brigadier general; and President Jimmy Carter to move General Edward C. Meyer around 17 more senior officers to be his Army chief of staff.

It is not the purpose of this book to provide a history of the Army, the War Department, or the General Staff; those subjects are dealt with in such existing works as *American Military History* edited by Maurice Matloff, *From Root to McNamara: Army Organization and Administration, 1900–1963* by James E. Hewes, Jr., *National Security and the General Staff* by Otto L. Nelson, Jr., and *History of the United States Army* by Russell F. Weigley.

The present work focuses upon the Army's senior officer. Although this generic designation has been used throughout in alluding to incumbents of all periods and dates irrespective of formal or informal practices at any given time, the titular line of succession also has been divided arbitrarily into two categories that are nicely descriptive of the contradictions that dogged the senior officer position for many years. Thus incumbents of the early period (1775–1903) are called commanding general, even though two of the officers were not generals and the title was not formalized until 1821; those of modern times (1903–1995), generals all, are merged under the title chief of staff, the designation formalized in 1903 and still in use today. An introductory essay traces the development of the position, highlights the organization and operation of the office, and reviews some of the associations and connections of a unique body of military figures.

The central element of the book is the catalog of senior officers in the line of succession, each represented by a color portrait and a concise biographical sketch. Considerations of style and format have dictated the approach used in the biographies, which have been scaled roughly to uniform size despite variations in the terms of office, substance of service, and celebrity or distinction of the incumbents. The treatment is telegraphic and factual rather than narrative and analytical; seniority in rank and position is the common denominator.

A word should be said here to explain the inclusion of an acting chief of staff in the line of succession. As the book's introduction makes clear, executive military continuity was highly irregular in the early period of Army history, and

there is little purpose in assessing the acting officials for a time when formal patterns of primary progression, much less secondary, were erratic. On the other hand, there has been increasing formality in this regard since the inception of the chief of staff era early in the twentieth century. Obviously, the Army's senior officer will be absent on occasion—on a peacetime tour of inspection, on a wartime visit to a battlefront, on a well-earned vacation. In such instances it has been standard practice for a second-level official to act in his behalf. General Bruce Palmer, Jr., vice chief of staff under General William C. Westmoreland, served frequently in an acting capacity during the chief of staff's absence. Under different circumstances, however, he served as acting chief of staff during the period from General Westmoreland's retirement on 30 June 1972 until the delayed confirmation of General Creighton W. Abrams, Jr., on 12 October 1972. His status therefore differs from that of two other officers who served as acting chief of staff: Brigadier General Thomas H. Barry, who covered the central office in the closing weeks of 1906 while the chief of staff, Brigadier General J. Franklin Bell, was in the field with the Army of Cuban Pacification; and Major General John Biddle, who presided for six weeks in late 1917 and a similar period in early 1918 while the chief of staff, General Tasker H. Bliss, was in Europe attending meetings of the Supreme War Council. In both of these cases there was a sitting chief of staff, whereas General Palmer acted in his own right during the Westmoreland-Abrams interregnum. Thus his inclusion in the line of chiefs of staff.

For readers who wish to probe more deeply into the history of the United States Army, the Department of the Army, the General Staff, and the lives of the respective senior officers, a select bibliography is supplied. It is by no means exhaustive, but will serve as a starting point. The material available on the commanding generals and chiefs of staff is as uneven as the careers of the individuals involved. Some wrote personal memoirs, and multiple biographies exist on the more prominent figures, while little coverage is available on others of less conspicuous service.

For ready reference, two appendices are provided in chart form. Appendix A displays, in dated chronological order, the presidents of the United States and the Army's parallel senior civil and military officials in each administration.

Appendix B is a chronological list of the Army's senior officer line of succession, including dates of birth and death, period of incumbency, tour length, and age at time of entry into office and, as appropriate, at death.

Readers primarily interested in the paintings reproduced in this work should note that dimensions are given in inches, with height preceding width, and are sight measurements in the frame.

In the Army's historical office the author has benefited from the intersection of the military and historical professions; perceptive comments and constructive suggestions were advanced by several readers with both backgrounds and perspectives. On the military side the manuscript was reviewed by Brigadier General James L. Collins, Jr., Chief of Military History, and Colonel James W. Dunn, Chief, Histories Division; on the historical side the material was read by Dr. David F. Trask, Chief Historian, and Mr. B. C. Mossman, Chief, Staff Support Branch.

In addition to this internal review, several outside authorities took time out from busy schedules to read the manuscript and bring their expertise to bear. The author expresses his thanks and appreciation to Dr. Edward M. Coffman, Professor of History at the University of Wisconsin; Dr. Maurice Matloff, former Chief Historian of the Army, Fellow of the Woodrow Wilson International Center for Scholars (1981–1982), and Visiting Professor (1982–1983) at the United States Military Academy; and Dr. Robert W. Coakley, former Deputy Chief Historian of the Army.

Other members of the staff of the Center of Military History furnished valuable assistance. In the preparatory stages the support provided by Miss Carol I. Anderson and Mr. Joseph K. Mosley of the Center's library, and by Miss Marylou Gjernes, Curator of the Army Art Collection, was especially helpful. In the publication process the finished product testifies to the high quality of the professional services rendered by Mr. John W. Elsberg, Chief of the Editorial Branch, and his staff, including Miss Joanne M. Brignolo who edited the manuscript. Also deserving of mention is Lieutenant Colonel Adrian G. Traas, Assistant Chief of the Histories Division, for coordinating numerous and complex administrative details within and between agencies.

Externally, essential support and assistance was provided by the staffs of the National Museum of American Art, the National Archives, the Library of Congress, the Defense Audiovisual Agency, and the Army Audiovisual Center. Numerous libraries, galleries, and historical societies also responded affirmatively and productively to requests for materials and specific pieces of information. Finally, acknowledgments would not be complete without a recognition of the work of the Government Printing Office in the important fields of typography, design, and printing. The completed book owes much to its talents.

Despite the contributions of a wide array of agencies and individuals, the ultimate responsibility for any faults in this book rests with the author. Errors of omission or commission are mine alone.

William Gardner Bell
Washington, D.C.

Army Portraits

The Army has long been interested in pictorial representation of its top officials—the senior civilian and the senior officer. In the early 1870s Secretary of War William Worth Belknap began the tradition of engaging prominent artists to paint the individual portraits of the departmental secretaries to record the line of succession. Since then, the secretarial portrait collection has been carefully nurtured and continues today. The portraits are reproduced in color in the author's companion volume *Secretaries of War and Secretaries of the Army: Portraits and Biographical Sketches*, published and periodically updated by the U.S. Army Center of Military History, most recently in 2003. A number of the portraits are on permanent exhibit in the Secretarial Portrait Gallery at the Pentagon in Washington, D.C.

Due in part to the shifting nature of the senior officer position in the period from 1775 to 1903, the portraits of the Army's senior officers are not as complete as that of its senior civilians. Although the Army has portraits of a few of its early commanders, they were acquired, in many instances, for reasons other than the individual's senior role in the uniformed line of succession. Thus, to represent the senior officers of the first 128 years of Army history, reproductions of suitable portraits were located and obtained from other organizations, galleries, institutions, and individuals. Each is acknowledged in the respective brief accounts on the artists that accompany the portraits and biographical sketches.

Unlike the early years, the Army has a formal collection of chief of staff portraits extending from the inception of that title and office in 1903 to the present. The Chiefs of Staff Portrait Gallery, also at the Pentagon, was made possible through the generosity of former Secretary of the Army and Mrs. Robert T. Stevens, whose substantial gift enabled the Center of Military History to commission contemporary artists to execute the portraits of the officers of the modern period.

The portrait element of the book thus represents and blends the work of some of America's most noted and accomplished artists of the past—William Cogswell, Daniel Huntington, John Wesley Jarvis, Charles Willson Peale, James Peale, and Thomas Sully—with that of established and gifted contemporary portraitists like John Edward Bannon, Joyce Ballantyne Brand, Cedric Baldwin Egeli, Everett Raymond Kinstler, John Boyd Martin, Margaret Holland Sargent, and Christine Conniff Sheahan.

Contents

	Page
Introduction	1

Commanding Generals, 1775–1903

George Washington (first tour)	52
Henry Knox	54
John Doughty	56
Josiah Harmar	58
Arthur St. Clair	60
Anthony Wayne	62
James Wilkinson (first tour)	64
George Washington (second tour)	66
Alexander Hamilton	68
James Wilkinson (second tour)	70
Henry Dearborn	72
Jacob Jennings Brown	74
Alexander Macomb	76
Winfield Scott	78
George Brinton McClellan	80
Henry Wager Halleck	82
Ulysses Simpson Grant	84
William Tecumseh Sherman	86
Philip Henry Sheridan	88
John McAllister Schofield	90
Nelson Appleton Miles	92

Chiefs of Staff, 1903–2005

Samuel Baldwin Marks Young	96
Adna Romanza Chaffee	98
John Coalter Bates	100
James Franklin Bell	102
Leonard Wood	104
William Wallace Wotherspoon	106
Hugh Lenox Scott	108
Tasker Howard Bliss	110
Peyton Conway March	112
John Joseph Pershing	114
John Leonard Hines	116
Charles Pelot Summerall	118

		Page
Douglas MacArthur	. . .	120
Malin Craig	. . .	122
George Catlett Marshall	. . .	124
Dwight David Eisenhower	. . .	126
Omar Nelson Bradley	. . .	128
Joseph Lawton Collins	. . .	130
Matthew Bunker Ridgway	. . .	132
Maxwell Davenport Taylor	. . .	134
Lyman Louis Lemnitzer	. . .	136
George Henry Decker	. . .	138
Earle Gilmore Wheeler	. . .	140
Harold Keith Johnson	. . .	142
William Childs Westmoreland	. . .	144
Bruce Palmer, Jr. (acting)	. . .	146
Creighton Williams Abrams, Jr.	. . .	148
Frederick Carlton Weyand	. . .	150
Bernard William Rogers	. . .	152
Edward Charles Meyer	. . .	154
John Adams Wickham, Jr.	. . .	156
Carl Edward Vuono	. . .	158
Gordon Russell Sullivan	. . .	160
Dennis Joe Reimer	. . .	162
Eric Ken Shinseki	. . .	164
Peter Jan Schoomaker	. . .	166

Appendices and Bibliographies

Appendix A. Chronological List of Chief Executive Authorities, Departmental Secretaries, and Senior Officers	. . .	171
Appendix B. Chronological List of Senior Officers of the United States Army	. . .	178
General Bibliography	. . .	180
Bibliography of Senior Officers	. . .	183

Illustrations

George Washington	. . .	2
Facsimile of Washington's commission	. . .	2
Washington in the field	. . .	4
Benjamin Lincoln	. . .	5
Henry Knox	. . .	6
Andrew Jackson	. . .	10
John C. Calhoun	. . .	11
Winfield Scott	. . .	12
Edmund P. Gaines	. . .	12
Alexander Macomb	. . .	12
Abraham Lincoln	. . .	17
Andrew Johnson	. . .	20
Edwin M. Stanton	. . .	20
William T. Sherman	. . .	22
Philip H. Sheridan	. . .	22
Nelson A. Miles	. . .	22

John M. Schofield 25
Elihu Root 28
General Staff Selection Board 30
Members of the General Staff 32
Fred C. Ainsworth 33
Leonard Wood 33
Peyton C. March and Newton D. Baker 35
Henry L. Stimson 37
George C. Marshall 37
George Washington 38
Ulysses S. Grant 38
Dwight D. Eisenhower 38
The Joint Chiefs of Staff, 1950 40
Matthew B. Ridgway 41
Maxwell D. Taylor 41
Robert S. McNamara 42
William C. Westmoreland 43
Peter J. Schoomaker 44

Introduction

On 14 June 1775 the Second Continental Congress, meeting in Philadelphia, adopted a resolution under which ten companies of expert riflemen would be immediately raised, six in Pennsylvania, two in Maryland, and two in Virginia. The "compleated" companies were to "march and join the army near Boston, to be employed . . . under the command of the chief Officer of that army." On the following day the Congress elected George Washington, Esq., of Virginia to be general and commander in chief "of the forces raised and to be raised in defence of American Liberty." In these two conspicuous legislative resolves the United States Army was born and its first senior uniformed officer appointed.[1] Neither the Army nor its commander sprang full-blown into being upon congressional cue. The institution would begin to take shape only in the fires of the war of American independence, while the individual would pass to his successors the problems inherent in the development and perpetuation of the senior military office.

From their earliest appearances on the North American continent, Europeans had found it necessary to defend themselves, first against the native inhabitants, later against each other as well as against the American Indian. As England and France developed footholds in the New World their interests clashed, and both dispatched military forces and cultivated indigenous allies in their attempts to prevail on the colonial frontier. By the time the English colonists along the Atlantic Coast of North America had become disenchanted with the mother country, they had participated as British subjects in colonial extensions of four world conflicts: the War of the Grand Alliance (1689–1697), known in America

as King William's War; the War of the Spanish Succession (1701–1714), identified in the colonies as Queen Anne's War; the War of the Austrian Succession (1740–1748), called King George's War in the New World; and the Seven Years' War (1756–1763), distinguished in North America as the French and Indian War.

Colonial units carried the burden of operations in the first three of these conflicts and joined British regulars in the fourth. The colonists were thus well indoctrinated in British concepts of military and civil affairs, modified by their requirements and experiences in colonial life, as they moved down the road toward separation from the parent country and creation of their own. Their problem was to disengage from an armed, tenacious, and authoritarian monarchy; mold a group of highly independent colonies into a common government under new national authority; and bring a variety of colonial elements into a unified force under central command and control. Much of the burden would fall initially upon the new commander's shoulders.[2]

George Washington was the unanimous choice of his fellow delegates to command the Army of the United Colonies (later designated the Continental Army). A youthful surveyor of frontier lands, he became interested in things military as a member of the Virginia militia, and the colonial governor, Robert Dinwiddie, selected him to carry a message to the French on the Ohio frontier to warn them that they were encroaching upon lands claimed by England. When the French rejected the imputation and expanded their intrusion, Dinwiddie in 1754 commissioned Washington as a lieutenant colonel and sent him with a small force to secure a British outpost at the forks of the Ohio River (near present-

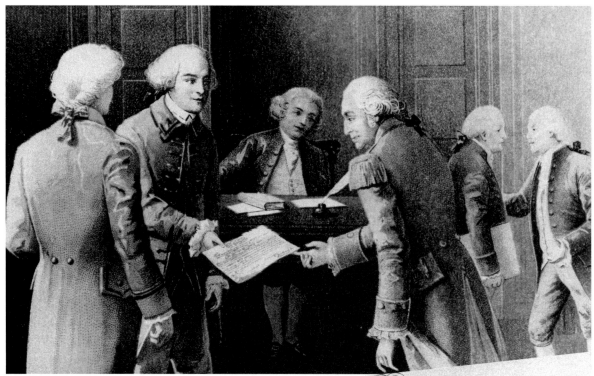

George Washington received his commission as general and commander in chief of the Army of the United Colonies (later designated the Continental Army) from Second Continental Congress President John Hancock at Philadelphia on 19 June 1775. *From the collections of the Library of Congress.*

Facsimile of Washington's commission. *From the collections of the Library of Congress.*

day Pittsburgh). Unfortunately, the French had captured it and had established Fort Duquesne there before Washington arrived, and although Washington defeated a French scouting party, he was then besieged in his fortified camp—Fort Necessity at Great Meadows, Pennsylvania—and forced to surrender.

In 1755 the British sent General Edward Braddock with a force of regulars against Fort Duquesne, and Washington went along as the commander's aide. The French defeated the British in the Battle of the Monongahela, inflict-ing heavy losses, mortally wounding Braddock, and putting the Redcoat remnants to flight. Washington was a tower of strength in getting the survivors back across the mountains to Virginia.

Dinwiddie next appointed Washington commander of all Virginia forces with the responsibility of defending 300 miles of frontier with a like number of men, an assignment that embodied on a regional level the multiform difficulties he would face on a national scale in the future. He joined a second expedition against Fort Duquesne, but when the French withdrew before the British reached the site, erasing a central problem of frontier defense, Washington resigned to take up private life once again.[3]

As a prominent Virginian and concerned citizen, Washington moved easily from military to civil affairs even as he pursued his private interests, and between 1758 and 1774, both as a member of the Virginia House of Burgesses sitting at Williamsburg and a justice of Fairfax holding court in Alexandria, he came to understand the negative influences of British colonialism. As the Second Continental Congress convened at Philadelphia in May 1775, George Washington of the Virginia delegation was recognized for his wide experience in military, civil, and business affairs; his sound ability and common sense; his scrupulous sense of honor and duty; his innate dignity and impressive bearing; and, above all, political and geographical contours with enough appeal to overcome sectional rivalries. All of this combined to ordain his selection as commander in chief.

Washington's stewardship as the Army's senior officer was unique and, by its nature, could not have been duplicated by his successors. He took office as the head of the forces of a budding nation whose government was still in its formative stages. Already at war, the country had no national army with established civilian leadership, no departmental military organization, no administrative rules and regulations, no supply system, no senior officer structure, no institutional seasoning. Much of this would have to be developed by the left hand as the right hand fought the war.

In the days following Washington's appointment the Congress moved quickly to give substance to its plans, requirements, and intentions, authorizing two major generals and eight brigadier generals to serve under Washington; establishing the offices of adjutant general, quartermaster general, commissary general, paymaster general, and chief engineer, as well as some other positions; setting pay scales; and adopting Articles of War for the governance of the military establishment.[4]

Washington took command of the Army in the field at Cambridge, Massachusetts, on 3 July 1775. On the following day he issued the general order that formalized the American Army as a national institution under the authority of the central government: "The Continental Congress having now taken all the Troops of the several Colonies . . . into their Pay and Service . . . they are now the Troops of the United Provinces of North America."[5] To bring "a mixed multitude of people" under order and discipline, he gave his personal attention to such matters as strength returns, roll calls, health and sanitation, efficiency, distinctions in rank, obedience to orders, and punishment of offenders. And as he kept the British Army bottled up in Boston, he dealt with such major problems as short-term enlistments, senior officer rivalries, scarcity of powder, inadequate military intelligence, and deficiencies in both organization and training.[6]

As the country fought for and edged toward true yet distant autonomy, it moved also, albeit slowly, toward the organizational and managerial arrangements that would provide for direction and control over the military forces of a free people. In the absence of a chief executive the Congress created boards and committees to carry out its policies, and one of its first moves along this line—antedating by three weeks the Declaration of Independence—was the establishment in June 1776 of the Board of War and Ordnance to see to "the raising, fitting out, and despatching [of] all such land forces as may be ordered for the service of the United Colonies."[7] Among other things, the board was to keep a register of officers in the service of the colonies; maintain a record of the state and disposition of troops; account for arms, artillery, and other supplies; oversee the exchange of military correspondence between the Congress and the United Colonies; and preserve original letters and papers.

Development of a true war office and delineation of the responsibility and authority of the senior officer of the American Army came slowly, for there was a government to establish, a war to be fought, and experience to be gained through a long process of trial and error. Initially, the government was weak and the board became bogged down in minutiae, leaving General Washington, under the exigencies of field operations, to fill a void and make decisions on his own. This independence was consistent with Congress' mandate to Washington. As supreme commander, he had been "vested with full power and authority to act as you shall think for the good and welfare of the

General Washington assumed command of the Army in the field at Cambridge, Massachusetts, on 3 July 1775. *From the collections of the Library of Congress.*

service."[8] Congress had been quite explicit in its reasoning, for

whereas all particulars cannot be foreseen, nor positive instructions for such emergencies so before hand given but that many things must be left to your prudent and discreet management, as occurrences may arise upon the place, or from time to time fall out, you are therefore upon all such accidents or any occasions that may happen, to use your best circumspection and (advising with your council of war) to order and dispose of the said Army under your command as may be most advantageous for the obtaining of the end for which these forces have been raised, making it your special care in discharge of the great trust committed unto you, that the liberties of America receive no detriment.[9]

It was only natural that this broad mandate be curtailed as the central government broadened its knowledge of military matters and increasingly assumed its legitimate responsibilities. Step by step the composition of the war office was modified from five legislators to three nonlegislators, then to a mix of two congressmen and three outsiders. But there was a weakness in the committee process, and in February 1781 the Congress created the post of secretary at war to replace the Board of War and appointed Major General Benjamin Lincoln as its first occupant in October of that year.[10]

Lincoln picked up the reins of a war office with fairly well-defined powers and responsibilities. The secretary at war was directed by the Congress "to examine into the present state of the war-office [and] the returns and present state of the troops, ordnance, arms, ammunition, cloathing, and supplies of the armies of the United States . . . , to obtain and keep exact and regular returns of all the forces . . . , to prepare estimates for paying and recruiting the armies . . . , to execute all the resolutions of Congress respecting military preparations . . . , to transmit all orders and resolutions relative to the military land forces . . . , to make out, seal, and countersign all appointments . . . , [and] to report to Congress the officers necessary for assisting him in the business of his department."[11]

By and large, the parties primarily responsible for military matters in these formative years of the Republic found their terms of reference in

Benjamin Lincoln, the nation's first secretary at war (1781–1783), and George Washington worked out the delicate operational relationship between the Army's senior civilian and senior officer. *Portrait by James Harvey Young from the Army Art Collection.*

their respective operational spheres in the field and at the seat of government, and although their functions were by no means mutually exclusive, the individuals were reasonable and dedicated men who saw what must be done and did it. Accumulating experience suggested, and the secretary at war and commander in chief worked out, a successful division of authority. Military business was conducted by correspondence and in personal visits to each other's headquarters, and cooperation, not competition, was the order of the day.

Inescapably there were differences. In the period after the Cornwallis surrender at Yorktown, Virginia, Washington disagreed with Lincoln over the new secretary's estimate of remaining British strength and intentions and his assessment of American force requirements and general prospects, thus prompting him to bypass Lincoln in correspondence with Major General Nathanael Greene, the commander in the South. Again, while both the secretary and the commander in chief were responsible to Congress, the lines of authority were blurred, and on one occasion Washington asked that reports of inspectors be sent to him in order to secure his responsibility and ensure that the inspectors remained subordinate to rather than independent of the commander in chief. These were relatively minor frictions compared with some that would develop later between other secretaries and commanding generals.[12]

The British defeat at Yorktown in October 1781 ended major active campaigning in the Revolutionary War and opened a static period for the patriot forces facing remaining enemy troop concentrations at New York in the North and Charleston in the South. While lengthy peace negotiations proceeded an ocean away, American thoughts turned to consideration of the form and composition of a postwar Army. Since regulars and militia had shared in the fighting and would share in the victory, sharp differences developed over the question of whether the future security of the nation should be entrusted to a standing Regular Army or to militia that would be called up in emergencies. This was only part of the larger question of whether the country would have a strong central government or a loose federation of states; whether, indeed, the citizen would assume not only the privileges of freedom and equality envisioned by the Declaration of Independence but the obligations and responsibilities, including military service, associated with a democratic system. As events unfolded, opinion came to favor a centralized government but for a long time shunned a standing Army.[13]

The transitional period from war to peace left the Army at its lowest ebb. After the signing of the Treaty of Paris on 3 September 1783, Washington, at congressional direction, began to demobilize the Army, a process that was completed after the British evacuated New York in November. On 23 December, the war concluded and his mission accomplished, George Washington resigned his commission and returned home to Virginia. He left Major General Henry Knox, the next senior officer, to preside over an Army reduced to one regiment of infantry and one battalion of artillery—about 600 men. The decline did not stop there.

Despite the conclusion of a peace treaty, a dual threat continued to hover over the young

Henry Knox had the distinction of serving as both the senior officer (1783–1784) and the senior civilian (1789–1794) of the Army. *Portrait by Charles Willson Peale from the Independence National Historical Park Collection.*

nation in the Northwest, where the British, in contravention of peace terms, continued to garrison a chain of posts along the inland waters bordering Canada and where frontier lands ceded by the states to the central government saddled the Congress with the problem of Indian defense over a wide region. Obviously the United Colonies must have an Army, but of what form and nature? To deal with a complex set of circumstances that involved politics, land, money, manpower, and deployments, the Congress, as a first step, on 2 June 1784 directed General Knox to discharge all but 80 of the 600-man force and to station the remnant at West Point (55), New York, and Fort Pitt (25), Pennsylvania, to guard military stores. There being no need for a major general to command a company-size force, Henry Knox was retired and nominal command of the Army passed on 20 June 1784 to the next senior officer, Captain John Doughty, a veteran of Revolutionary War service and head of the detachment at West Point.[14]

Doughty's seniority was necessarily short-lived, lasting only about seven weeks, and had an organizational rather than institutional complexion. Despite postwar disarray, sectional differences, Lincoln's retirement, and deficiencies in the Articles of Confederation under which the government was operating, the Congress saw the need for action in the field of military affairs. Only one day after it reduced the Army to 80 men, and on the very eve of the current session's adjournment the legislators passed an act calling upon four states—Connecticut, New York, New Jersey, and Pennsylvania—to furnish a total of 700 men from their militias for the national army. Pennsylvania, with the largest quota (260 as opposed to 165 each from Connecticut and New York and 110 from New Jersey) and with an exposed position on the frontier, filled its assessment promptly, and, as a result, command of the new force went to a Pennsylvanian. Lieutenant Colonel Josiah Harmar, who had served with several of his state's regiments during the Revolution, became the Army's senior officer on 12 August 1784.[15]

As had been Doughty's situation on a smaller scale, Harmar, despite his status as the ranking officer of the Army, became a field rather than a staff and institutional commander. With the war office vacant and with military concerns among the more pressing matters before it in the spring of 1785, the Congress appointed Henry Knox as the second secretary at war and issued a call to the four states of the previous year for new troops with longer enlistments to man the First American Regiment. Most of the Army was posted in detachments along the western frontier, and Harmar, far removed both organizationally and geographically from the seat of power, had all he could handle as the field commander. On top of that, the authoritarian Henry Knox was in the secretary's chair, fully assured that his powers as secretary at war embraced those of commander in chief—a role for which he was, by experience and inclination, well prepared to exercise.[16]

The secretary's task was not an easy one, and in its way represented the problems of the government as a whole. To the existing Indian peril, British presence, and state dissension connected with the western lands were added the difficulties of raising, supplying, and funding military forces. The government, lacking the power to tax and

operating in a period of depression, faced serious fiscal problems that were reflected throughout the colonies. Discontent finally escalated into an open unrest among debtors that took its most organized and violent form in Massachusetts, where an insurrectionist band led by one Daniel Shays attacked the Springfield Arsenal.

Although Shays' Rebellion was unsuccessful, it challenged both state and federal government, coalesced a gathering concern over the need for a national army and stronger central government, and lent impetus to a movement to convene a Constitutional Convention. In 1787 the government entered a two-year period of transition from the Confederation to a constitutional system, and the war office, the active focus of a variety of state functions, served as "the chief connective element."[17]

In formulating and refining the new nation's system of government, the framers of the Constitution assigned to Congress the functions to raise and support armies, make rules for the government and regulation of the land forces, and declare war. They created what had been lacking under the Confederation—an executive branch of government—and made the president the commander in chief of the Army and Navy, thereby ensuring that this important command function would be entrusted to a civil rather than to a military official.

On 30 April 1789 George Washington, who had been the nation's first senior military officer, became its first senior civil official under the new Constitution: president of the United States. Three months later, on 7 August 1789, the Congress established the Department of War, changed the title of the department head from secretary at war to secretary of war, and made that official directly responsible to the president rather than the Congress. Henry Knox remained in office to become the first secretary of war, and Josiah Harmar, who had been brevetted brigadier general in 1787 and was still on the frontier, remained the Army's senior officer.

If from the beginnings of constitutional government the role of the secretary as the minister charged with running the War Department—acting with the president's authority and in his behalf in the conduct of military affairs—was codified, accepted, and understood, that of the senior officer of the Army was not so clear. During the century and a quarter from George Washington's installation as commander in chief to Samuel B. M. Young's induction as chief of staff, uncertainty, misunderstanding, and controversy swirled around the office, involving from time to time some of the leading figures of their day. The title as well as the authority of the incumbent seemed in a constant state of flux.

The inception of constitutional government ensured not only that "a politically responsible President replaced the hereditary monarch as Commander in Chief" but also that Washington's historical standing as the only uniformed commander in chief of the American Army was assured. After Washington resigned in 1783, fluctuations in the strength of the Army, the rank and location of the senior officer, the viewpoint of an incumbent secretary, and usage in government circles all influenced the designation and mode of operation of the senior officer. Commander in chief, general in chief, major general commanding in chief, commanding general of the Army, lieutenant general of the Army, General of the Army—all were applied at one time or another and in one way or another to the senior officer of the Army.

As with George Washington and Benjamin Lincoln, the senior civil and military figures of the early years of the Republic went about their business with little friction; the complexities of government, inexperience of officials, geographical separation, limitations of communications, and field operational requirements kept them absorbed in their respective spheres. Harmar, who served as the senior officer until March 1791 before returning to Pennsylvania to become state adjutant general; Major General Arthur St. Clair, who succeeded him for a one-year tour between terms as governor of the Northwest Territory; and Major General Anthony Wayne, the late Georgia congressman who occupied the Army post up to his death on 15 December 1796, were all involved in Indian warfare on the northwestern frontier—Harmar and St. Clair disastrously, Wayne successfully—and could not have jousted with the secretary of war about lines of authority and separation of powers even had they been so inclined. Brigadier General James Wilkinson, at home with controversy and intrigue, might have relished confrontation, but he, too, served in the western arena, where he led a force of volunteers against Indians north of the Ohio before being assigned to Wayne's command. Upon the latter's death, Wilkinson ascended to the ranking position in the Army for an eighteen-month stint, to July 1798, with duties that kept him on the frontier as a field rather than institutional commander.[18]

Throughout this period the Army commanders conducted their operations with inadequate strength and supplies, poorly trained troops, and imperfect logistical support. The Congress, prompted by the Harmar and St. Clair reverses, gradually increased the Army's strength until Anthony Wayne was able to train a respectable force along legionary lines and, with some 3,000 men, redeem the Army's reputation in the Battle of Fallen Timbers.[19]

External forces now intruded upon the young nation as French and British contentions spread across the Atlantic to involve American shipping and raise the possibility of war with France. George Washington, only sixteen months out of the presidency, received his country's call once again as, early in July 1798, President John Adams dispatched Secretary of War James McHenry to Mount Vernon with Washington's appointment as "Lieutenant General and Commander in Chief of all the armies raised or to be raised for the service of the United States. . . ." Unfortunately, Washington was sixty-six, the call was to some extent politically inspired, and a general controversy developed over which officer among three candidates—Alexander Hamilton, Charles Cotesworth Pinckney, or Henry Knox—should be the senior major general and, in effect, second in command to the aging Washington. Although Knox outranked the others, Hamilton, at Washington's behest, was elevated to the ranking position.[20]

Washington had informed the secretary of war that he would accept the new charge with the understanding that he would become fully active only if his presence should be required in the field. This stipulation kept him in the mold of his predecessors—a field rather than an institutional commander. As things turned out, his presence in the field was not required. Except for a visit to Philadelphia to work with

McHenry and Hamilton on an organizational plan for a Provisional Army to meet the putative emergency, Washington exercised his command function principally from his Mount Vernon home, while the influential and ambitious Major General Hamilton, in combination with a weak secretary of war, carried the burden of day-to-day details at the seat of government under President Adams' watchful and suspicious eye. Adams, in appointing Washington to the Army command, had acted not only to neutralize a strong sentiment for Hamilton's selection to the post but also out of concern, however justified, for what uses Hamilton might have found for an Army he controlled.[21]

As 1799 unfolded, the French threat and the perceived need for Washington's name and services receded, and the general's death on 14 December brought the century and an era to a close.

As he had foreseen the possibilities, Alexander Hamilton was ideally positioned to succeed Washington as the Army's senior officer, and on the day of his predecessor's death he picked up the reins for an abbreviated tenure. Hamilton presided over the preparation of new drill regulations and the discharge of those Provisional Army soldiers already mobilized—about 4,100 of a planned 50,000—before departing military service on 15 June 1800.[22] The evaporation of the emergency and the reduction of the Army to peacetime strength erased all prospects for the martial glory that might have held him in the service. Yet, as Washington's aide, a former member of the Continental Congress, and the nation's first secretary of the Treasury, Hamilton remained an influential citizen up to his death in 1804 in a dual with his bitter political rival, Vice President Aaron Burr.

Brigadier General James Wilkinson now returned to the scene for a second tour of nominal military seniority. In almost twelve checkered years spent principally on the southern frontier, he negotiated with the Indians, fraternized with the Spaniards, consorted then broke with Aaron Burr, served as governor of Louisiana Territory, and survived several courts of inquiry and a court-martial inspired by his excessive use of authority and private commercial dealings. His

stewardship, if such it might be called in view of its organizationally disconnected and militarily incoherent character, was of a piece with the trials of the first decade of the nineteenth century when the nation and the Army were groping for policies and procedures to make government and institutions work. Regrettably, as the threat of war with France faded, the menace of renewed conflict with England increased. By the time the Congress declared war against England in June 1812, Wilkinson had reverted to a subordinate position and Major General Henry Dearborn had become the Army's senior officer.[23]

Like many of the nation's potential military leaders, Henry Dearborn had acquired more than enough campaign experience and reputation during the Revolutionary War to mark him as a candidate for recall in emergencies. After his discharge in 1783, he had maintained a tenuous military connection through militia ties, and from 1801 to 1809 he operated in the mainstream of military affairs as President Jefferson's secretary of war. But like many veterans, he had turned sixty, and he was on the eve of his sixty-first birthday in January 1812 when President Madison made him the Army's senior major general. With the outbreak of the War of 1812 he became, not the professional uniformed head of the Army posted in Washington, but a coordinate field commander—and one of a number of aging officers not well equipped mentally or physically to deal with the rigors of campaign, a worthy enemy, and deplorable deficiencies in manpower, supply, and administration.[24]

After an inept performance on the northeastern Canadian front, and with recurring health problems, Dearborn, still the senior major general, was transferred in July 1813 to command at New York City, where he served until his discharge on 15 June 1815.

Seniority among the Army's uniformed leaders passed next to Major General Jacob Jennings Brown. As commander in western New York in the late war, he had added much-needed luster to American arms in operations at Chippewa and Lundy's Lane on the Niagara front. Unlike his predecessor, Brown was of a younger, post-Revolution generation; only forty, the vigor and zeal he brought to the ranking position were not

Andrew Jackson was one of the first Army field commanders to challenge the War Department on the proper use of the chain of command after one of his attached technical service officers was reassigned without his knowledge. *Lithographic portrait from the collections of the National Archives.*

a general staff concept, created by the Congress in 1813, to deal with the Army's housekeeping functions. But his fourteen-month tenure was too brief for a concerted effort to strengthen the peacetime Army. That fell to his successor, John C. Calhoun.

Before Calhoun took office in October 1817, however, and while Acting Secretary George Graham was in charge, an incident occurred that brought to a head some long-standing questions concerning the operation of the chain of command, the responsibility and authority of senior officials, and the relationships between staff and line.

Secretary Crawford had ordered Major Stephen H. Long to New York. Although Long, a topographical engineer, was assigned to General Jackson's Division of the South, the field commander was not informed of the transfer, and when he learned of it he wrote the department asking for an explanation. When Acting Secretary Graham replied testily that the department assigned officers "at its discretion," Jackson complained to President Monroe, questioning a practice under which Washington could move officers without a field commander's knowledge. Upon learning that Jackson had instructed his attached officers to obey no departmental order that did not come through the commander, Monroe informed Jackson that the orders of the War Department were those of the president. As the case evolved, the central issue—proper use of the chain of command—became sidetracked in favor of a discussion of the president's role as commander in chief.[25]

Despite the fact that he was the loser on the constitutional side of the question, Jackson was partially vindicated in the practical aspects when Calhoun, while sustaining the presidential prerogatives, announced that future orders would be issued through field commanders to the maximum extent possible. But the matter was far from settled. Jackson had raised the nagging problem of the distribution of authority between staff and line; should communications between the heads of the technical services (Engineer, Quartermaster, Subsistence, Medical, etc.) in Washington and their assistants in the field, and from those subordinates back to their chiefs in

to be dedicated to war so much as peace. His extended tenure carried him more than halfway through an era characterized as "The Thirty Years' Peace," a period free of general conflict and marred only by occasional Indian troubles to the South and West, notably the First and Second Seminole Wars and the Black Hawk War.

On the heels of the War of 1812 the Congress passed the act of 1 May 1815 fixing the peacetime strength at 10,000 and establishing two geographical regions, the Division of the South commanded by Major General Andrew Jackson, and the Division of the North headed by General Brown. Some important evolutions occurred at the upper levels of the War Department during Brown's incumbency.

Secretary of War William H. Crawford, who entered office in August 1815 with the conviction that the country should have in place in peacetime the kind of headquarters organization required in war, consolidated and enlarged upon

Although Secretary of War John C. Calhoun established the office of and formalized the title of commanding general in 1821, the action failed to resolve constitutional and organizational problems. *Portrait by John Wesley Jarvis from the Army Art Collection.*

Washington, be direct or through field command channels? Strangely enough, the senior officer of the Army, who might well have been at the center of the controversy, especially in light of his dual role as a division commander, was little more than a bystander. Yet the moment had come when that would change to some degree.[26]

The War of 1812 had demonstrated the need for more centralized control over the scattered elements of the Army. The creation of two main geographical divisions had answered this in part, but an apparently logical next step—that of establishing a single uniformed head of the whole Army—was left in suspense. Only George Washington had served in this capacity, first in 1775 during the Revolutionary War when the Congress elected him general and commander in chief, again in 1798 during the anticipated crisis with France when the president, with congressional authorization, had appointed him lieutenant general and commander in chief. In the

first instance the country was at war, lacked a chief executive, and was desperately in need of an all-powerful field commander. In the second instance, the Congress and the president knew their man; knew that, as one who had served at the pinnacle in both military and civil capacities, he subscribed fully to the principle of separation of powers and knew his place. But without a Washington, what would a strong-willed figure in uniform—an Alexander Hamilton, for example, or an Andrew Jackson—make of the position of commander as opposed to senior officer, and despite the constitutional role of the president as commander in chief? How would the functions, the powers, the responsibilities be distributed? A partial answer was soon forthcoming.

Secretary Calhoun acted in conjunction with the reorganization of 1821, which cut the Army to about 6,000 men. The Divisions of the North and South were abolished, and were replaced by Eastern and Western Departments, commanded respectively by Brigadier Generals Winfield Scott and Edmund Pendleton Gaines. At the apex, a possible dilemma was negated when Major General Andrew Jackson left service to become governor of Florida. Calhoun then brought Major General Jacob Jennings Brown to Washington as commanding general of the Army.[27]

Both the formal establishment of the position of commanding general and the title given Brown raised more questions than were answered. Hovering over the arrangement were a number of uncertainties: if the president was commander in chief of the Army and the secretary of war was his direct agent in the administration of the Army, what was the role of the commanding general? As his position was not defined constitutionally or by statute or regulation, what was his relationship to the president, to the secretary, to the bureau chiefs, and to the field commanders? Was he simply a professional military adviser to the secretary?

Jacob Brown seems not to have been disturbed by these considerations. Despite his energy and dedication, he appears to have been more interested in making an anomalous arrangement work than in making himself an agent of challenge or an instrument of disruption. What effect a wartime wound and an apparent stroke

President John Quincy Adams bypassed his quarreling generals, Winfield Scott (*left*) and Edmund P. Gaines (*center*), to pick the more junior Alexander Macomb (*right*) to replace the deceased Jacob Brown as commanding general of the Army. *Scott portrait facsimile of a T. R. Welch engraving from the collections of the Library of Congress; Gaines photographic portrait by Matthew Brady from the collections of the National Archives; and Macomb portrait by Samuel L. Waldo from the New York City Hall Collection.*

in late 1821 may have had on his efficiency is also unknown. In any case, his service under Secretaries of War Calhoun and Barbour up to his death in February 1828 was unmarked by crisis, and many of the procedural questions went unanswered.[28]

Brown's death left the Army with no major generals and opened the way for selection of a successor from among the regular brigadiers. At the moment, Winfield Scott and Edmund Pendleton Gaines, the department commanders, were the only two in that grade. Properly positioned in the chain of command, they were the logical candidates, except that, proud, ambitious, and arrogant individuals both, and highly sensi-

tive to considerations of relative rank and General Brown's mortality, they had long been locked in a public dispute over seniority that not only shook the Army to its foundations but also escalated into a national scandal. So far as the record was concerned, the choice was a difficult one. Both had been promoted to colonel on 12 March 1813 and both to brigadier general on 9 March 1814. Gaines was the senior at the lieutenant colonel level, but Scott was senior in a brevet major generalcy.

Ultimately these considerations became academic, for President John Quincy Adams had had his fill of the spectacle of two of the country's senior military figures publicly denouncing each other and making constant claims for preferment. He called a cabinet meeting to hear the views of his departmental secretaries on the subject, found a general consensus with his own impressions, and on 29 May 1828 reached down below the troublesome pair to appoint the chief of engineers, Colonel and Brevet Major General Alexander Macomb, as commanding general of the Army.[29]

A protégé of Alexander Hamilton, and with an excellent record in the War of 1812 and later in special assignments, Macomb wisely stepped aside to let the president and the secretary of war deal with Scott's insubordinate announcement that he would ignore the new commander's orders as those of a junior officer. Such fulminations led to Scott's suspension from his departmental command and placement on a list of officers awaiting assignment. His representations to both houses of Congress fell upon unsympathetic ears, and only after a change in national administrations was the suspension lifted. Scott then went abroad on a six-month leave of absence, and time and the counsel of friends finally prompted him to accept the facts of life and preserve his great abilities for future crises. Meanwhile, Macomb, to distinguish his preeminence over other two-star brevet major generals, resorted to the simple device of inserting in the Army Regulations of 1834 a provision that the insignia of the major general commanding in chief should be three stars. Thus in image if not in true rank, Macomb placed himself on a par with a distinguished predecessor, the General Washington of 1798.[30]

It was only natural that the basic considerations of leadership and chain of command—the essence of military operation—should suggest a permanent establishment of a uniformed commander of the Army. If there were uniformed commanders at every other level, then why not at the top? It might also have been assumed that the duties of the senior uniformed officer were so self-evident as to require no regulatory expression; only Washington, serving at the outset of nationhood, had been issued formal terms of reference by the civil authority, and these had related principally to the conduct of field operations. In the intervening years until Jacob Brown's specific designation as commanding general, the senior officer seemed to see himself, and to be viewed

by others, more as a field than an institutional figure. Even Brown did not depart noticeably from that mold despite his titular designation and station in Washington.

But now a statement of functions appeared in the Army Regulations of 1834—the same edition that sewed a third star on General Macomb's epaulettes. Article XLI, titled "The Commander of the Army," delineated the top uniformed official's responsibility and authority thus:

1. The military establishment is placed under the orders of the major general commanding in chief, in all that regards its discipline and military control. Its fiscal arrangements properly belong to the Treasury Department, under the direction of the Secretary of War. While the general in chief will not interfere with the concerns of the Treasury, he will see that the estimates for the military service are based upon proper data, and made for the objects contemplated by law, and necessary to the due support and useful employment of the army. The general will watch over the economy of the service, in all that relates to expenditure of money, supply of arms, ordnance, and ordnance stores, clothing, equipments, camp equipage, medical and hospital stores, barracks, quarters, transportation, fortifications, military academy, pay, and subsistence, in short, every thing which enters into the expenses of the military establishment, whether personal or material. In carrying into effect these important duties, he will call to his council and assistance, the staff, and those officers proper, in his opinion, to be employed in verifying and inspecting all the objects which may require attention. The rules and regulations established for the government of the army, and the laws relating to the military establishment, are the guides for the commanding general, in the performance of his duties.

2. All estimates, exhibits, and reports, of the several branches of the military service, required annually to be made, with a view to their transmission to Congress, will be addressed to the commanding general of the army, who, after examining them, and fixing with the officers concerned, the amounts required for the service, will present them to the Secretary of War, for his consideration.[31]

In these paragraphs and two more in Article XLIV fixing the responsibilities of inspectors general to the commanding general, the central authority of the Army's senior officer and the subordination of the staff were well established. Indeed, the provisions of the second paragraph appear to have been so objectionable to the bureau chiefs that it was dropped from the 1835 edition of the regulations, and the first paragraph was amended to shift fiscal control back to the staff bureaus, stipulating that the Army's "fiscal arrangements properly belong to the administrative department of the staff and to the Treasury Department, under the direction of the Secretary of War." Despite the modification, the "General-in-Chief" still was directed to "see that the estimates for the military service are based upon proper data, and made for the objects contemplated by law, and necessary to the due support and useful employment of the army."[32]

It was the perceived intrusion of the commanding general into their operations and his presumed interdiction of their direct access to the secretary of war that disturbed the bureau chiefs. Their case, and the nature of the controversy over lines of authority and separation of powers, was set out by Colonel Roger Jones, the adjutant general of the Army, on 24 January 1829. In a beautifully engrossed paper addressed to Secretary of War Peter B. Porter under the title, "Analysis of the theory of the Staff which surrounds the Secretary of War," Colonel Jones noted that the Adjutant General's, Ordnance, Quartermaster, Subsistence, Pay, and Medical Departments and the Corps of Engineers "constitute [the] many avenues through which the various acts and measures of the Executive . . . are communicated and executed, and such is the symmetry in this organization, that whilst each member of the military staff of the War Department is confined to the sphere of his own peculiar functions, all regard the Secretary as the common superior, the head of the harmonious whole."[33]

The adjutant general went on to point out that everything relative to military commissions, under the secretary of war, had been conducted in his office since 1797; that these were administrative duties under the secretary "in contradistinction to . . . Military Staff duties under the General in Chief. . . ." He wondered if these or similar executive functions had ever been assigned to any general officer of the line; whether, indeed, they were compatible with the high military duties of a commander of the Army? Ought a general in chief aspire to these comparatively subordinate responsibilities, and could it be to the interest of the Army that he assume them and virtually relinquish "the glories of the field?"[34]

If it did nothing else, Colonel Jones' paper exposed some of the complexities inherent in the question of whether the Army's senior officer was, or should be, a commander or a chief of staff. It was not a simple matter to resolve. Bureau chiefs were reluctant to surrender the authority and prestige of their independent jurisdictions; senior officers were proud and ambitious individuals, jealous of hard-won rank and status and fiercely protective of honor; and secretaries were transient civilians often uninitiated in military affairs and usually not in office long enough to come to grips with complicated military organization, procedures, and personalities. Accommodation among such disparate interests was not easy to achieve, and apart from competition and bias, it was not that clear in 1829 just how the senior officer of the Army should function. It would take three-quarters of a century and further clashes before the problem would be resolved.

After General Macomb died in office on 25 June 1841, Major General Winfield Scott, who had been waiting in the wings for thirteen years and had more than redeemed himself in official and public eyes in a series of skillfully conducted and eminently successful peacekeeping missions for the government, was appointed commanding general of the Army and took office on 5 July. The Second Seminole War was coming to a close, and the only cloud on the horizon was possible trouble with Mexico over its lost province of Texas. When James K. Polk won the American presidency on a platform that included annexation of Texas by the United States, and that process occurred in mid-1845, Mexico declared war on her northern neighbor.

President Polk, a Democrat and well aware that three of his predecessors—George Washington, Andrew Jackson, and William Henry Harrison—had been helped into office by battlefield achievements, saw further possibilities along this line as Brigadier General Zachary Taylor, a member of the Whig opposition, won a series of victories over the Mexicans along the Rio Grande. When it became apparent that the war could not be won in that northern theater, Polk turned with great reluctance to Winfield Scott, also a Whig and a former presidential contender in that party, to conduct a landing at Vera Cruz on Mexico's east coast and drive inland against the enemy capital of Mexico City. The president, it may be noted, had been left with no alternative when the Congress rejected his proposal to create the rank of lieutenant general and place Senator Thomas Hart Benton of Missouri, no soldier but a Democrat, in the post as commander of the coming expedition.[35]

The wartime emergency and the employment of the commanding general as a field commander perpetuated the ambiguities of the position. President Polk, in effect, vacated the office by assigning Scott to command the Vera Cruz expedition; by limiting him, upon his departure from Washington, to control over the field force; and by appointing no successor in Washington. The Army thus went without a commanding general from 24 November 1846 to 10 May 1849, raising questions as to the need for such an office. The president, the secretary of war, and the bureau chiefs operated as the headquarters of the Army, and in the absence of a uniformed professional head, President Polk and Secretary William L. Marcy served as their own general staff. Despite some mastery of military detail they had neither the time nor the training, much less the responsibility, for carrying out the planning and programming function of a general staff. How their successors might have met the challenge was yet another question. In 1848 the Army's two major generals—Scott, after returning to the United States, and Taylor—were assigned to coequal divisions, Eastern and Western. Scott assumed command of the former, with headquarters in New York.[36]

When Zachary Taylor became president in 1849, Scott was restored to the position of commanding general. A special order of 10 May specified that, "in pursuance of the orders of the President of the United States, Major General Scott will resume the command of the Army. . . ." The order went on to prescribe that the headquarters of the commander of the Army would be "at, or in the vicinity of New York." Apparently the location was agreeable to both Taylor and Scott, although how a commander of the whole Army— even one as small as the 10,000 to 12,000 men of the moment—could possibly fulfill the responsibilities implied by the title when he was so far removed from the executive base in Washington was not explained. It was also apparent that the commanding general was still to be a field rather than an institutional commander.[37]

Scott, who had outlasted Generals Macomb and Gaines as well as President Polk, now survived President Taylor. After Taylor's death in 1850, Scott transferred his headquarters back to Washington, where, at President Fillmore's request, he served for about three weeks as acting secretary of war. In 1852, as the Whig candidate for president, he was defeated by Franklin Pierce. In January 1853 Scott moved his headquarters back to New York to put some distance between himself and the victorious incoming administration. From there he carried on a running battle with the new secretary of war, Jefferson Davis, over the settlement of his remaining outstanding Mexican War accounts and other matters. When he questioned the secretary's authority over the commanding general, he was overruled by the president.[38]

On 15 February 1855 the Congress, in a joint resolution, revived the grade of lieutenant general, and on 7 March the Senate confirmed General Scott as brevet lieutenant general to rank from 20 March 1847, the date of the capture of Vera Cruz. Scott thus became the first officer since George Washington to hold three-star rank. Yet the distinction was an honorary one for a deserving officer's long and distinguished service—temporary elevation for an individual, not permanent creation of an additional echelon that would relieve a grade compression at the upper levels of the Army.[39]

Brevet Lieutenant General Scott spent the final months of a twenty-year tenure—the longest in office of all the senior officers of the Army even deducting the Mexican War hiatus—urging President Buchanan and Secretary of War John B. Floyd to act to protect military installations in the South as the slavery issue began to split the nation. Following President Abraham Lincoln's inauguration in March 1861, Scott brought his headquarters back to Washington and a far more sympathetic administration. But age and infirmity were closing in on him, and on 1 November 1861, at seventy-five and upon his own application, the Army's senior officer retired after half a century of military service.

Upon Scott's retirement Lincoln appointed Major General George Brinton McClellan, forty years Scott's junior, as commanding general of the Army. A graduate of the United States Military Academy, McClellan had served with Scott's forces in the Mexican War, taught engineering at West Point, studied European military systems on the scene, and designed a first-rate saddle. His effective performance against Confederate forces in early operations in West Virginia, coupled with Brigadier General Irvin McDowell's defeat at Bull Run, led Lincoln to appoint McClellan in July 1861 to head the Army of the Potomac. An able administrator who worked wonders in preparing the Army of the Potomac for coming battles, McClellan in the top military post proved to be slow at launching and cautious in executing field operations. Although he might have been more effective as the senior officer at the seat of government than as a field commander, he proved to be flawed in that role as well by arrogating to himself an excessive degree of power, even to the extent of blocking both the president and the secretary of war from his confidence. His methods could not long endure, and on 11 March 1862 President Lincoln relieved him as commanding general so that he could devote full attention to the upcoming Peninsular Campaign.[40]

A second period now intervened when the office of commanding general lay vacant, for no suitable successor to McClellan was readily available. Standing by, however, were two figures ready to exercise the functions in addition to their own larger ones: President Lincoln and his new secretary of war, Edwin M. Stanton. In a four-month period they brought a measure of coordination into the operation of the Union armies, responded intelligently to Major General Thomas Jonathan ("Stonewall") Jackson's Shenandoah Valley threat in May, and sought professional advice by tapping retired Major General Ethan Allen Hitchcock to head an advisory board composed of the bureau chiefs. But both were aware of their limitations and their constitutional obligations, and on 23 July 1862 President Lincoln brought Major General Henry W. Halleck to Washington as commanding general of the Army.[41]

A graduate of the United States Military Academy, Henry Wager Halleck had served in engineer assignments, published an influential book on military art and science, and held responsible positions in California during the Mexican War before resigning in 1854 to engage in railroad and mining enterprises. Seven years later, at the outbreak of the Civil War, he resumed Regular Army service as a newly commissioned major general, with assignment to the western theater. Upon his selection as senior officer in the summer of 1862, he left command of the Union forces in the West with a series of victories to his credit, in which subordinates—notably Brigadier General Ulysses S. Grant—were largely instrumental.

Well fitted by training and experience to fulfill the joint command and administrative responsibilities embodied in the anomalous position of commanding general, Halleck nevertheless became bogged down in detail and buffeted by political pressures, and as events moved on he failed to live up to the command expectations of the president and the secretary of war. Eventually, Lincoln and Stanton resumed active control over military operations. Both used Halleck more as an agent, responsible for translating their directions into military form and issuing them to the field, than as a commander in his own right.[42]

Although Lincoln endured this uncomfortable situation patiently for an extended period, he came increasingly to think about replacing Halleck, and inevitably his attention was drawn to the victor of Henry and Donelson, Vicksburg and Chattanooga—now Major General Ulysses S. Grant.

Like McClellan and Halleck, Ulysses Simpson Grant was a graduate of the United States Military Academy. He had served with distinction in the Mexican War, first with Taylor's forces as a troop officer, then with Scott's as a quartermaster with a combat role. He had resigned from the Army in 1854 to try his hand, with uniformly little success, at a variety of civilian occupations, and returned through Illinois volunteer channels as the Civil War opened in 1861. As a commander under Halleck in the western theater, he gave the Union some badly needed victories, acquiring public acclaim in the process. A bill was introduced in the Congress to revive the grade of lieutenant general and confer it upon Grant in recognition of his outstanding battlefield performance. The

President Abraham Lincoln found himself engaged in a process of trial and error as he searched for the right leader to command the Union forces in the Civil War. When George B. McClellan and Henry W. Halleck fell short of his expectations, he finally found his man in Ulysses S. Grant. *Photographic portrait by Matthew Brady from the collections of the National Archives.*

occasion offered an opportunity to correct, at least in part, an inequity in grade structure that existed in the American Army.

The fact that the Army did not have sufficient separation in rank at the top levels of the uniformed service, a source of vexation during the Scott-Gaines-Macomb discords and on through the Mexican War, had become even more manifest with the major expansion of the Union forces during the Civil War. It led to the unusual, if not absurd, situation under which the Union had a major general commanding a division, a major general commanding a corps, a major general commanding a field army, a major general commanding a geographical region, and a major general commanding all the armies of the United States. Five echelons thus were commanded by officers of the same rank, and the major general who commanded the American armies of more than a million men held no higher rank than the major general who commanded a field division of a few thousand men. Now in the spring of 1864 this logjam might be broken, although not as an official correction of an inequitable system but, as in the case of General Scott, through a personal tribute to an individual officer.[43]

Despite Grant's reputation as a fighting and winning general, not all legislators were in favor of reviving the rank of lieutenant general and assigning it to Grant. In the light of recent experience, went the speculation, suppose the honor had been available to McDowell, McClellan, or Halleck? Why honor one general before the war was over? What could a lieutenant general do that a major general could not do as well? Should a distinguished field commander be sacrificed to the departmental bureaucracy? All of these equivocations were turned aside, and after an extended debate in the Senate as to whether Grant's appointment should be recommended by name in the legislation (it was not), the measure was passed on 29 February 1864.[44]

On 12 March 1864 the Army issued orders of the president of the United States formalizing the new command arrangements. They contained some interesting distinctions concerning the position of senior officer. Major General Halleck, "at his own request," was relieved from duty as general in chief of the Army. Lieutenant General Grant was "assigned to the command of the Armies of the United States." It was stipulated that the "Headquarters of the Army will be in Washington, and also with Lieutenant General Grant, in the field." Here again was that inclination to view the commanding general as a field commander or, put another way, as commander of the armies in the field, and not as a top staff coordinator at the seat of government. But now there was a striking concomitant in the second paragraph of the order: "Major General H. W. Halleck is assigned to duty in Washington as Chief of Staff of the Army, under the direction of the Secretary of War and the Lieutenant General Commanding."[45]

How much of this was a calculated effort to improve command arrangements and how much a propitiary gesture to Halleck who was suffering a demotion it is hard to say. Certainly the action gave Halleck a title and duties more in line with the manner in which he had been functioning all along, and like a good soldier he served out the war in this capacity. Through the general order, the president made it known that he expected Halleck's orders as chief of staff to be "obeyed and respected accordingly," and any blow Halleck may have felt over his change of status may well have been softened by the president's official tender to him of "approbation and thanks for the able and zealous manner in which the arduous and responsible duties of [commanding general] have been performed."[46] Halleck served in his staff role until the war ended in April 1865, then moved on to field assignments.

Grant brought to the role of commanding general the strategic direction and coordination the position had required all along. In Secretary Stanton, General Halleck, and Quartermaster General Montgomery C. Meigs he had an energetic and expert administrative and logistical team to provide the resources for his operational plans, while in President Lincoln he had a commander in chief who respected his abilities and applauded his initiative. He operated in the mode of the modern theater commander, maintaining his headquarters in the field, reporting directly to his civilian superiors, and, unlike McClellan, keeping them informed of his plans.

As lieutenant general and commanding general, Grant presided over four administrative field divisions embracing seventeen subcommands and employing half a million combat soldiers. That some further adjustments were needed in the grade structure was evident in the fact that, under the wartime structure of volunteer rank, Grant was senior to 73 major generals and 271 brigadier generals. The Union could take a back seat to the Confederacy in this regard, for the South had long before solved its grade structure problems by assigning full generals to command separate armies, lieutenant generals to command corps, major generals to command divisions, and brigadier generals to command brigades. And at the apex, General Robert E. Lee was additionally appointed general in chief of the Armies of the Confederate States in February 1865. The Union did not bring its senior officer into line until after the war, when a bill was finally introduced to revive the rank intended for but never bestowed upon George Washington. The title of the grade was modified from the 1799 version—General of the Armies of the United States—to General of the Army of the United States. Ulysses Grant assumed four-star rank on 25 July 1866, and Major General William T. Sherman moved into the vacated lieutenant generalcy. Grant thus became America's first full general under the Constitution, as Washington's rank had been conferred in 1775 by the Continental Congress.[47]

The end of the Civil War, Lincoln's death, and Grant's retention of the top military post during a period when the Army acquired a central role in the reconstruction process, placed the commanding general at center stage on the national scene. His position exposed him to problems that, endemic to the job and present in the best of times, were exacerbated by postwar agitation. President Andrew Johnson's leniency in dealing with the South raised problems for the Army and led to the unusual situation in which the secretary of war and the commanding general found themselves allied with the Congress in opposition to the policies of the commander in chief. The sharp differences between the president and the Congress over how to proceed with reconstruction prompted the legislators to pass a series of acts to assert their supremacy and protect sympathetic executive officials, notably Stanton and Grant, from peremptory presidential reaction.

The Command of the Army Act, attached to the Army Appropriations Act of 1867 and of questionable constitutional validity, specified that presidential orders to the Army be issued through the commanding general, that the headquarters be located in Washington, and that removal from office be approved by the Senate. The Tenure of Office Act denied the president the right to remove cabinet officers—presumably his own appointees—from office without Senate approval, almost a reverse confirmation procedure. The Congress had Secretary Stanton, a Lincoln appointee, in mind in this measure, one that was also of dubious constitutionality. Finally, the First and Third Reconstruction Acts divided the South into five military districts and authorized their commanders, major general in rank, to superintend civil processes and report directly to Washington, essentially free of civil control. The net effect of all of this was to make the commanding general rather than the commander in chief the effective head of the Army, or at least that part of it assigned to reconstruction duty in the South.[48]

Highly sensitive to constitutional prerogatives, angered by congressional attempts to frustrate his reconstruction policies, and indignant over opposition within his executive family, President Johnson on 12 August 1867 suspended Stanton from office and appointed General Grant as secretary of war ad interim. Grant, ill-disposed to be at the center of a controversy between his departmental superior and the commander in chief, yet thoroughly devoted to the Army, accepted the assignment reluctantly and exercised the title while retaining his position as commanding general. When the Congress returned from its recess and resumed its deliberations, the Senate refused to concur in Stanton's suspension, invoking the Tenure of Office Act, and Grant relinquished and Stanton reclaimed the secretaryship in January 1868. Johnson retaliated by dismissing Stanton, by offering the post to General Sherman, who refused it, and by attempting to place Adjutant General Lorenzo Thomas in the office. The Congress then launched impeachment proceedings against the president.[49]

The Senate conducted the trial from March into May, and the final vote of 35 to 19 in favor of impeachment fell one short of the margin required for conviction. With the disruptive issue settled through constitutional processes but with none of the parties—president, Congress, secretary—so substantially vindicated as to revel in victory, Stanton resigned and the turmoil subsided. The president and the Congress, perhaps subdued by the experience, agreed, although for different reasons, upon Major General John M. Schofield as a candidate to pick up the war office portfolio.

Only months later Grant, little damaged by the imbroglio, was elected president of the United States. One day after his inauguration on 4 March 1869 he promoted Lieutenant General William T. Sherman to full general and commanding general of the Army. Major General Philip H. Sheridan was advanced one grade to fill the lieutenant general vacancy.[50]

Like his three immediate predecessors, William Tecumseh Sherman had graduated from the United States Military Academy. Commissioned in 1840, he held various assignments in the southern states and then served as an aide and adjutant in the East and in California during the Mexican War. He resigned in 1853 to try his hand at banking and law, but his lack of success turned him to the more compatible and more successful occupation of superintendent of a military college in Louisiana. Back in the Army in time to command a brigade in the 1861 Bull Run disaster, he was transferred to the western theater and participated in a succession of operations that culminated in his command of the Union forces there and final defeat of the Confederate armies in the deeper South. He was in command of the Division of the Missouri, with headquarters at St. Louis, when he was ordered to Washington in March 1869 to be the Army's commanding general. Sheridan replaced him at St. Louis.

Having been exposed, as the Army's senior officer and secretary ad interim, to the long-standing controversy between the commanding general and the bureau chiefs, if not the secretary of war, President Grant now had it in his power to resolve matters in the general in chief's favor on behalf of his successor. To Sherman's great satisfaction Grant did just that on 5 March 1869, directing through Secretary Schofield that "the Chiefs of the Staff Corps, Departments and Bureaus will report to and act under the immediate orders of

When President Andrew Johnson (*above*) challenged Congress over Reconstruction policies and suspended Secretary of War Edwin M. Stanton (*below*) for siding with the opposition, the legislature brought impeachment proceedings against him. Ulysses S. Grant consequently found himself in the awkward position of serving not only as commanding general but also as secretary of war ad interim until the constitutional process ran its course. *Johnson photographic portrait by Matthew Brady and Stanton portrait by unknown photographer from the collections of the National Archives.*

the General commanding the Army. All official business, which by law or regulation requires the action of the President or Secretary of War, will be submitted by the General of the Army to the Secretary of War; and in general, all orders from the President or Secretary of War to any portion of the Army, line or staff, will be transmitted through the General of the Army."[51]

Sherman's gratification was short-lived. A week later Schofield departed the War Department and Grant installed his principal wartime staff officer, John Aaron Rawlins, in the secretary's chair. From that vantage point it was Rawlins' interpretation, abetted by strong pressures from the bureau chiefs and congressional representatives, that control of the bureaus should be in the hands of the secretary, not the commanding general. Grant deferred to Rawlins' wishes, and only three weeks after the Schofield order a Rawlins directive switched the channels of bureau business away from the commanding general and back to the secretary of war.[52]

Rawlins attempted to ease Sherman's displeasure by routing his orders to the bureau chiefs through the commanding general's office, but the action cooled Sherman's relationship with Grant and represented another setback to a resolution of the War Department's own ménage à trois. Rawlins' death in early September and his replacement by William Worth Belknap in October raised the prospect of even further dissension. Little credit accrued to Sherman for a stint as secretary of war ad interim during the Rawlins-Belknap interregnum.

The new secretary was a strong personality, fully prepared to assume every ounce of power and authority prescribed by law and as much more as imprecise definition, administrative vacuum, and tolerant or irresolute officials might allow. Without hesitation, Belknap took over direction of the War Department bureaus and began to intrude upon Sherman's domain, renewing, as Sherman described it, "all the old abuses . . . which had embittered the life of General Scott in the days of Secretaries of War Marcy and Davis. . . ."[53]

One of Sherman's first encounters with Belknap involved the question of jurisdiction over sutlerships at Army posts. When the secretary infringed upon the commanding general's prerog-

atives in this regard by replacing a sutler at Fort Laramie, Wyoming, Sherman restored the ousted party. Belknap then worked through friends in Congress to secure legislation that removed the authority from the general in chief and gave it to the secretary. He then installed his own man.

Uncomfortable in the political atmosphere of Washington, unlikely to prevail in clashes with his civilian superior, and with his authority largely circumscribed by the secretary, Sherman followed perhaps the only course open to him during the Belknap administration—that of absenting himself from the capital. From April to June 1871 he made an inspection tour on the Indian frontier, visiting Army units and installations in Texas (where he narrowly escaped a collision with a Kiowa war party), Indian Territory, Kansas, and Nebraska. From November 1871 to September 1872 he made the grand tour of Europe, traveling as a private citizen but accorded the highest honors, official and social, in most of the countries he visited. Then in 1874, taking a lead from Winfield Scott, he moved his headquarters to St. Louis.[54]

Sherman remained away from the seat of government until 1876, abdicating to Belknap the running of the Army as well as the War Department. In March of that year the chairman of the legislative committee on expenditures reported to the House of Representatives that Belknap was guilty of malfeasance in office, as a result of having accepted money in return for the award of a post tradership at Fort Sill, Oklahoma. The evidence led the House to vote unanimously to impeach the secretary of war, but Belknap resigned even as the Senate's vote fell short of the two-thirds margin required for conviction.[55]

President Grant then appointed Alphonso Taft as secretary of war, and Taft moved at once to get Sherman and Army headquarters back to Washington. His formal order of 6 April returned a goodly measure of control to the commanding general, stipulating that "all orders and instructions relative to military operations, or affecting the military control and discipline of the Army, issued by the President through the Secretary of War, shall be promulgated through the General of the Army, and the Departments of the Adjutant General and the Inspector General shall report to

William T. Sherman (*left*), Philip H. Sheridan (*center*), and Nelson A. Miles (*right*) took office expecting to command the whole Army. When these proud, ambitious, strong-willed, and distinguished soldiers found that the scope of their power and control as commanding general had been largely circumscribed, they vented their frustrations in part by relocating headquarters, making official trips, and writing personal memoirs. *Sherman/Sheridan photographic portraits by Matthew Brady and Miles photographic portrait by the U.S. Army Signal Corps from the collections of the National Archives.*

him and be under his control in all matters relating thereto." Said General Sherman: "This was all I had ever asked."[56]

Sherman spent his remaining years as commanding general on good terms with the last four of the eight secretaries he served under in almost fifteen years as general in chief: James Donald Cameron, George Washington McCrary, Alexander Ramsey, and Robert Todd Lincoln. He saw the Army through its "Dark Ages," when strength, appropriations, pay, and even rank levels were under legislative assault, and he turned aside active attempts to get him to stand as a presidential candidate. He acted with rare consideration when, faced with the statutory requirement to retire at age 64, he relinquished the title of commanding general in November 1883 so that his successor would have time to prepare the Army's congressional presentation for the coming year.[57]

When Sherman retired from the Army in February 1884, the troublesome constitutional and statutory problems that surrounded the office of commanding general were yet unresolved. That they had not succumbed to the best efforts of a famous, well-connected, able, strong-willed leader suggested that the very nature of the senior officer's job was uncertain. An irascible Sherman had

tried to straighten things out but had failed; now a combative Sheridan would have his turn.

As with his four immediate predecessors, Philip Henry Sheridan had graduated from West Point. He served on the Rio Grande frontier and against Indians in the Northwest before the Civil War drew him into operations in the border states and in the South. His instrumental role at Chickamauga and Chattanooga brought him into Grant's circle, and to command of the cavalry of the Army of the Potomac when Grant took over the main Union forces. A key figure in the final operations in Virginia, Sheridan went on to administer the Division of the Gulf during the external threat represented by Maximilian's suzerainty in Mexico, and was military governor of New Orleans during reconstruction. He followed Sherman to the Division of the Missouri and its Indian campaigns, and to Washington as commanding general, picking up the reins on 1 November 1883.

At the time Sheridan entered office the responsibility and authority of the General of the Army was touched upon in the Army Regulations of 1881. Several of the provisions harkened back to the first published expressions of 1834–1835, and a tenuous trail had appeared in general orders and regulations at intervals down through the years, although the provisions fell far short of the required substance. Article XV of the 1881 edition of the regulations referenced earlier publications for antecedence:

THE GENERAL OF THE ARMY

125. The military establishment is under the orders of the General of the Army in all that pertains to its discipline and military control. The fiscal arrangements of the Army belong to the several administrative departments of the Staff, under the direction of the Secretary of War, and to the Treasury Department.—[G.O. 28, 1876; R.S. 1133, et seq.]
126. All orders and instructions relating to military operations, or affecting the military control and discipline of the Army, issued by the President or the Secretary of War, will be promulgated through the General of the Army.—[G.O. 28, 1869; G.O. 28, 1876.][58]

The dichotomy that placed the military establishment under the commanding general for discipline and control and under the secretary and the staff bureaus for fiscal affairs perpetuated the command problem. "Basic to the controversy was an assertion of the primacy of the line over the staff departments, for which there was a theoretical foundation in the developing conception of war as a science and the practice of that science as the sole purpose of military forces. Since the Army existed only to fight, it followed that its organization, training, and every activity should be directed to the single end of efficiency in combat. Therefore, the staff departments, which represented technicism, existed only to serve the purposes of the line, which represented professionalism. From that proposition it followed that the line in the person of the Commanding General, should control the staff."[59]

Remarking that Sherman "threw up the sponge," Sheridan moved to the attack by announcing it as his interpretation that the president's order assigning him to command the Army necessarily included all of the Army, not excepting the chiefs of the staff departments. To prove the point, he ordered one of the bureau chiefs out on an inspection tour without informing Secretary of War Robert Todd Lincoln. When Lincoln learned that the head of one of his staff departments had departed on a field trip without his sanction, he informed Sheridan in writing that he was sure the commanding general had missed the true meaning of the president's order relative to command of the Army.[60]

Sheridan's lesson in humility did not stop there. When the secretary of war was absent from Washington, the senior bureau chief served as acting secretary. Thus, as General Schofield later described it, Sheridan, "the loyal subordinate soldier who had commanded great armies and achieved magnificent victories in the field while those bureau chiefs were purveying powder and balls, or pork and beans," had to submit to this because of "the theory that the general of the army was not an officer of the War Department and hence could not be appointed Acting Secretary of War." Although this construction did not endure, it lasted long enough for General Sheridan to suffer a situation under which the adjutant general, junior in rank and supposedly a subordinate under the commanding general, served as acting secretary of war, supposedly over the commanding general.[61]

Chafing under the compromise of the general in chief's authority, Sheridan lost no opportunity to raise the problem and press for action to codify the government and regulation of the military establishment and to position the commanding general in the direct line of command at the top of the uniformed service. When General Schofield addressed the subject in his 1885 report to Sheridan concerning developments in the Division of the Missouri, the lieutenant general of the Army was impressed. "I most heartily coincide with the remarks of General Schofield on the need of military legislation," he informed Secretary of War William C. Endicott in his own summary report. "His views are of so much importance that I transfer them bodily to my report":

There is a great need in the military service of legislation under the power conferred by the Constitution upon Congress to make rules for the government and regulation of the land and naval forces.
It is sometimes of supreme importance that the responsibilities of military administration and command be clearly defined by law. And it is important at all times that the rules for the government of the military service be established, like other laws, by competent authority, after due consideration, and under all the

light which experience can bring to the aid of the legislature. Regulations thus established, and subject to change only by Congress, would have such degree of stability as to become the basis of a sound military system which up to the present time has not existed in this country.

Although the regulations have undergone changes almost without number, the most important questions involved in the command and government of the Army which have been the source of constant embarrassment and the cause of much controversy for many years, remain unsettled at the present time. No commanding general, from the highest to the lowest, can know the extent or limits of his authority, and no one can have any staff responsible to him for the faithful execution of his orders.

During the last twenty-five years the country has passed through three momentous crises, wherein these unsettled questions were of vital importance to the nation, and their decision, for the occasion, depended solely upon individual opinions. Another such crisis may not be far distant, when such a decision might not be so fortunate for the country. Hence, while I present the necessity of a considerable increase of the Army, I also suggest, as a still greater necessity, that laws be established by Congress for the 'government and regulation' of the military forces.[62]

If the commanding general's authority was circumscribed, so was his rank. When Sheridan took over the senior officer's position, he retained his three-star rank because of the Army Appropriations Act of 1870 provision specifying that "the offices of General and Lieutenant General of the army shall continue until a vacancy shall occur . . . and no longer. . . ." This stipulation made the ranks of general and lieutenant general personal to Sherman and Sheridan, respectively, with the four-star level lapsing at the time of Sherman's retirement.[63]

Congressional sentiment against upper-level institutional rank, firm during periods of peace and routine operation, had a way of softening to meet special individual circumstances. As noted above, the Congress in February 1855 had revived the grade of lieutenant general, specifying that it could be conferred by brevet only "to acknowledge eminent services of a major general of the army in the late war with Mexico." The honor was tailored for and bestowed upon Winfield Scott.[64] Again in February 1864 the Congress, with Ulysses Grant in mind, had revived the grade of lieutenant general in the Army of the United

States so that it could be conferred upon a major general "most distinguished for courage, skill, and ability."[65] The congressional action of July 1866 reviving the rank of general was intended for Grant as the victorious field commander in the late war rather than as the appropriate rank for the uniformed head of the Army.[66] And now in 1888 the Congress, prompted by Sheridan's rapidly failing health, acted on behalf of the individual rather than the institution by discontinuing the grade of lieutenant general, merging it with the grade of general, and ensuring that the four-star billet go to Sheridan by stipulating that it should continue "during the lifetime of the present Lieutenant General of the Army, after which such grade shall also cease."[67]

Sheridan's four-star rank was approved on 1 June 1888. On 2 August he signed the preface to his memoirs, and on 5 August 1888, still the Army's commanding general, he died. Nine days later General Schofield, the senior major general, was appointed to succeed him as commanding general of the Army.

With his designation as the Army's senior officer, John McAllister Schofield continued the succession of West Point graduates in the commanding general's chair. Early in his career he had taught philosophy at his alma mater, and physics while on leave at Washington University of St. Louis. The Civil War drew him into field operations in Missouri, with command assignments at department, division, corps, and army levels in the western and southern theaters. In the postwar period he visited France on a confidential diplomatic mission concerning the French presence in Mexico, succeeded Stanton in mid-1868 as President Andrew Johnson's secretary of war, and then successively headed several of the Army's major geographical commands, coming to the senior officer post from command of the Division of the Atlantic.

Schofield differed from his immediate predecessors in both personality and philosophy. Operating from the premise that a soldier might properly crave recognition, including promotion, from "past services," he saw individual efforts to achieve "higher command, greater power, and more unrestrained authority" as evidence of "ambition inconsistent with due military subordination and good citizenship." Thus, upon Sheridan's death, although he was the senior major general of the Army, Schofield made no move to seek the office of commanding general and allowed no one to speak for him.[68]

When President Grover Cleveland selected him to be commanding general, Schofield brought into play special skills and experience. His teaching, command, and diplomatic background, coupled with upwards of ten months as secretary of war and "a more modest ambition" than that possessed by his predecessors, gave him a breadth of vision and a sensitive appreciation of the controversy concerning the relationships between the command and administration of the Army. He had no illusions about the state of things; as he wrote later, "the condition of the War Department at that time was deplorable." One of his first official acts was to send a written order to the adjutant general specifying that all orders issued by the commanding general or in his name should be shown to the secretary of war before being released. He submitted to the president a paper on the general subject of command of the Army, and used it as his guide while in office. Staff officers commented that "for the first time the [commanding] general actually does command the Army."[69]

Command relationships during Schofield's tenure ran smoothly because Schofield "regarded himself as a Chief of Staff of the President and Secretary of War, rather than a self-assertive commanding general." Schofield served as commanding general under Presidents Cleveland, Benjamin Harrison, and again Cleveland, and under one lawyer, Secretary William Crowninshield Endicott, and three businessmen, Secretaries Redfield Proctor, Stephen Benton Elkins, and Daniel Scott Lamont. He corrected a situation under which, as he saw it, "the adjutant general had in practice come very near being 'commander-in-chief'" by directing that no order, including routine ones, be issued in his name without his knowledge. He prided himself on the fact that perfect harmony was established between the War Department and Army headquarters.[70]

John Schofield served the bulk of his tour as commanding general in the rank of major general. His performance so impressed his superiors that

John M. Schofield, a former secretary of war, brought a new philosophy and a strong personality to the office of commanding general. His efficient and effective tour—next to last in the succession under the "command" format—provided some insights as to how the Army's senior officer could operate in a chief-of-staff mode. *Photographic portrait by Matthew Brady from the collections of the National Archives.*

President Cleveland took the unusual step of recommending to Congress that the temporary rank of lieutenant general be revived in Schofield's behalf as "a just and gracious act" that would permit his retirement "with rank befitting his merits." Although the proposal called forth old and somewhat familiar objections, a joint resolution was finally passed and became law on 5 February 1895. General Schofield completed his military service at three-star rank and retired on 29 September 1895. On 5 October Nelson A. Miles, the senior major general, assumed command of the United States Army.[71]

Unlike his six immediate predecessors, all West Pointers, Nelson Appleton Miles had entered military service through Massachusetts volunteer channels at the outset of the Civil War and advanced from lieutenant to brigadier general in the Army of the Potomac, serving with distinction through regimental and division levels. After the war, and a promotion to major general of volunteers in command of a corps, he served as commander of Fort Monroe, Virginia, and, for a time, acted as custodian over former Confederate President Jefferson Davis. Commissioned in the regular establishment in 1866, he served principally on the frontier during the quarter century of the Indian wars, forging a reputation as one of the Army's leading Indian campaigners. In the fall of 1895, while in command of the Department of the East at New York, he was designated commanding general of the Army and, shortly thereafter, moved to Washington.

Miles differed from Schofield in personality, method, and style, and the harmony cultivated so assiduously by Schofield fell before his successor's assault. As one perceptive historian describes it, "General Miles, coming to Washington as commanding general, energetic, conscious of his powers, and eager to do, had, like most of his predecessors, felt the hypnotic influence of ancient liturgies and tinkling bells. He found that in that hierarchy he counted as little as a Moravian bishop in the College of Cardinals. He might or might not have great plans for reform; in either case it did not matter. The adjutant-general was the real power; the arch-bureaucrat was pope."[72]

In the post–Civil War retrenchment Army strength had dropped sharply, finally hovering around 26,000 throughout most of the quarter century of the Indian wars. In his first few years in office Miles addressed the subject actively, proposing that military strength be cut loose from an automatic figure that had no particular significance, and be tied instead to population levels: "The Army should grow as the nation grows." In addition to pushing for increases in strength he suggested improvements in coast defenses and recommended the rotation of duties between staff and line.[73] In 1897 he spent several months in Europe, visiting Italy, Greece, Turkey, Russia, Austria, Germany, France, and England, observing their armies and attending several functions. The role of America's distinguished representative abroad may well have been more satisfying than the commanding general sinecure back home.

The commanding general was nothing if not the military adviser to the president, and when the battleship Maine exploded in Cuba's Havana Harbor on 15 February 1898 and the United States began preparations for a probable war with Spain, General Miles took the opportunity to express his views to the commander in chief. Having long pressed for expansion of the Army, he now found himself urging upon President William McKinley a more modest mobilization than the administration desired, because of the time required to train and equip large numbers of troops and the negative impact of the resulting diversion of officers and supplies. When war was declared, he differed strongly with Secretary of War Russell A. Alger's acquiescence in Navy contingency plans to invade Cuba and attack Havana, pointing out that a force could not be prepared before the onset of the unhealthy rainy season, and, in any case, it would be foolish to go up against prepared positions with inadequate forces. When he was ordered early in May to lead an expedition of 70,000 men against Cuba at once, and issued orders to put things in motion, he yet requested an audience with the president to point out that, because of diversions of stocks for a force dispatched to the Philippines, there was not on hand—and would not be for two months—sufficient ammunition to supply the designated force for one hour's battle. The president deferred operations to a later day.[74]

Because of a mix of politics, personalities, and problems, the War with Spain became a period of contention for the commanding general of the Army. His intervention with the president put him at odds with the secretary of war. His preference for an invasion of Puerto Rico ahead of Cuba was overridden in favor of an operation against Santiago. His appearance at the Tampa, Florida, staging area raised questions as to whether he intended to supersede the expedition commander, Major General William R. Shafter, and his wire request to the secretary of war seeking approval to accompany the expedition went unanswered and became a subject of sharp debate. His vocal criticism of the chaotic logistical situation at Tampa and of the poor quality of beef rations supplied the troops put him at loggerheads with the bureau chiefs, and a series of press interviews from the field voicing his complaints of War Department actions along a number of lines received such wide coverage that the president was forced to appoint a commission to investigate the conduct of the war. Though public opinion leaned his way, Miles was considered by some to be insubordinate and by others to be motivated by presidential ambition. His allegations eventually fell for lack of conclusive evidence, and the inquiry faded when the investigating body recommended that it would be in the best interests of the Army if the whole thing were dropped.[75]

The Army was ill-prepared to cope with the command and administrative complexities raised by the War with Spain. Sharp differences developed between the secretary of war, the commanding general, and the bureau chiefs, and antiquated procedures retarded timely and effective action. As Miles clashed with Secretary Alger and the department heads, President McKinley turned increasingly to the adjutant general, Henry C. Corbin, for advice and assistance. "Amid changing plans, conflicting orders, and clashing personalities, Corbin's calm, tact, physical endurance, and administrative efficiency held the creaking military machine on course. After the end of May [1898], General Miles spent much of his time away from Washington, [and] therefore, except for the actual direction of field operations, all the myriad details of army command fell upon Corbin. . . . Having lost confidence in both Alger and Miles, President McKinley began turning to Corbin for military advice and assistance in implementing his policies. By late June he had made Corbin his de facto chief of staff."[76]

Miles' propensity for keeping the government embroiled in front-page disputes might well have soured his superiors to a point where they would have been disposed to deny him any further advancement in his profession. Such was not the case, and when the respective and normally antipathetic supporters of the Army's commanding general and its adjutant general—themselves instinctive opponents by virtue of personality, function, and the long history of departmental dissension—joined forces to move both officials up a notch in the ladder of rank, the executive branch placed no barriers in the way. On 6 June 1900 Miles advanced to lieutenant gen-

eral and Corbin to major general, although not with a great degree of unanimity. The legislation took the form of amendments to the Military Appropriations Act of 1900, and at the time of the vote Miles' promotion was approved by 143 to 117 and Corbin's by 107 to 61.[77]

If Miles had held his own in skirmishes with President McKinley and Secretary Alger, he more than met his match in their successors, President Theodore Roosevelt and Secretary of War Elihu Root. When Miles wandered outside his official domain to comment publicly on the verdict of a court of inquiry that investigated a controversy between Admirals William T. Sampson and Winfield S. Schley concerning the conduct of naval operations at the battle of Santiago, he drew a public rebuke from Secretary Root on behalf of the administration in a letter released to the press on 21 December 1901. "You had no business in the controversy," wrote the secretary, "and no right, holding the office which you did, to express any opinion. Your conduct was in violation of the regulations . . . and of the rules of official propriety, and you are justly liable to censure which I now express." President Roosevelt followed this up with an oral reprimand at a White House reception when Miles attempted to discuss the matter with him.[78]

Only weeks later, on 17 February 1902, Miles had a further clash with his civilian superiors, this time over his proposal that he take a delegation of Cubans and Puerto Ricans to the Philippine Islands—where American forces had been fighting insurrectionists since the departure of the Spanish—and convince insurgent leaders of the benefits of American sovereignty. Secretary Root rejected the plan out of hand, pointing out that Governor William Howard Taft and the Philippine Commission, assisted by the commander on the scene, Major General Adna R. Chaffee, were fully capable of dealing with the situation. President Roosevelt personally endorsed Root's disapproval.[79]

Finding himself blocked at every turn at the seat of government, yet not easily repulsed, Miles tried once again in August to secure approval for a visit to the active theater in the Philippines. This time his request was approved; indeed, Root suggested that he take an extended trip, moving on to Japan and China, riding the Trans-Siberian

Railroad to Russia, and continuing on to Western Europe. Some plausible missions were raised: a military inspection of the Philippines, an inspection of the legation guard in Peking, an appraisal of military conditions in Manchuria, an evaluation of the military capacity of the Siberian railroad. In truth, the secretary was interested in having Miles out of the capital while he advanced a plan for the reorganization of the Army, one that would eliminate the position of commanding general and make the Army's senior officer chief of a general staff.[80]

Miles' departure from Washington failed to quiet agitations that seemed to eddy about the commanding general no matter what his location. He left behind him some discordant testimony before a congressional committee on Root's draft bill to create a general staff. On the island of Guam he urged but did not secure the release from imprisonment there of the former Filipino secretary of state. In the Philippines he reacted to reports of abuse of Filipino prisoners in American hands by issuing strict orders prohibiting coercive methods to obtain information, creating a stir back in Washington that produced some corrective action but also a secretarial admonition to leave such matters to the authorities on the scene. From the Philippines he finally cut loose on the more distant and remote legs of his global journey, leaving Secretary Root the respite he had sought from the commanding general's meddlesome ways.[81]

By the time Miles returned to Washington in the spring of 1903 he was nearing retirement age. Finally, at noon on 8 August, his sixty-fourth birthday, Nelson A. Miles left active service. Neither the president nor the secretary of war attended the ceremony, although Miles' successor as senior officer, Samuel B. M. Young, promoted to lieutenant general at ten o'clock that morning, was on hand to wish his predecessor "a long and happy retired life."[82]

Although General Miles was portrayed as "the last of the powerful military politicians" and was a troublesome figure in the departmental hierarchy, his power was seriously circumscribed by the unworkable structure at higher headquarters, while his clashes with authority were at once the result of his attempts to vivify his title

Secretary of War Elihu Root brought a brilliant mind, a lawyer's training, and broad experience in cases involving municipal government and corporate law to his administration of the War Department. He instituted the series of reforms that changed the senior officer's title and role from commanding general to chief of staff. *U.S. Army Signal Corps photograph from the collections of the National Archives.*

and vent his frustrations over his empty role. He was not unique in this regard, for Scott, Sherman, and Sheridan were also from the same mold. Yet Miles was exceptional after all, for his path crossed that of Elihu Root and the Root reforms made Miles the last of his kind.

President William McKinley was responsible for bringing Root to Washington. When asked to take the post of secretary of war, Root demurred, saying that he knew nothing about war and nothing about the Army. The president responded that he needed a lawyer to administer the colonial territories acquired in the recent War with Spain. This struck a chord in Root and he accepted. The president had chosen well. Born at Canton, New York, in 1845, Elihu Root had graduated from Hamilton College there and moved on to New York University Law School and admission to the bar. After a year with the firm of Mann and Parsons he established his own office, developing a practice around cases involving banks, railroads, wills and estates, but later specializing in cases involving municipal government and corporate law. By the close of the century he was considered to be "the acknowledged leader of the American bar."[83] Long active in local politics in New York, the cabinet post now drew him onto the national scene.

Upon entering office on 1 August 1899, Secretary Root began methodically to study the Army's organization and functions in the light of its responsibilities. He consulted with staff officers, notably General Corbin, the adjutant general, and one of Corbin's able and analytical subordinates, Lieutenant Colonel William Harding Carter. He read the published and unpublished works of the late Colonel and Brevet Major General Emory Upton on European and Asian armies and American military policy; read British military writer Spenser Wilkinson's The Brain of an Army; and digested the report of Major General Grenville M. Dodge's investigating commission on the conduct of the War Department in the War with Spain. Working from the premises that "the real object of having an Army is to provide for war" and that the government—and therefore the Army—was similar to an industrial establishment and could "profit by the lessons which the world of industry and of commerce has learned to such good effect," he began to cultivate support in Congress and around the country for a program of reform that he gradually exposed through a series of masterful annual reports.[84]

Root wasted no time in coming to grips with the Army's basic problems. He submitted his first report to the president within four months of his arrival on the scene. He saw the preparation of the Army for war—its fundamental purpose—as involving four main elements: systematic contingency planning, timely preparation of war materiel, merit selection of officers, and large-unit training. He recommended that an Army war college be established, that company-grade officers attend it if not already service school graduates, that the promotion system be modified to permit advancement for merit as well as seniority, and that promotion boards be established to provide competent and disinterested bodies "to pass judgment on the record. . . ."[85]

The secretary of war moved with deliberation on his plan to reshape the Army. Although some steps could be taken under existing law and by executive authority, others of a pivotal nature would require new legislation. The climate was not unfavorable for reform. The War with Spain had drawn the nation outward onto the world scene, posing new dimensions for military forces in national life. The Army had been made the executive agent in the administration of the new and widely scattered insular possessions acquired from Spain, and operations against insurgents in the Philippines and Boxers in China continued to absorb national attention. The glaring defects exposed by the recent war were matters of both official and public concern. Thus, while there was a certain amount of resistance to change and predictable opposition within the Army and in Congress from entrenched officials and special interests, the opportunities were there for an advocate of the caliber of Elihu Root.

Root proposed to correct the basic problem of divided authority at the top of the War Department by changing the title of the Army's senior officer from commanding general to chief of staff. The change was important, indeed essential, for "the titles denote and imply in the officers bearing them the existence of widely different kinds of authority."[86]

The officer invested with the title of commanding general had every right to expect to command, but such had not been the case. Experience had shown that it was impossible for any officer to really exercise "the powers which appear and are assumed to be conferred along with the title of 'Commanding General of the Army.'" The president was the constitutional commander of the Army and the secretary of war his direct representative charged with supervision over the expenditure of "the vast sums of money appropriated annually by Congress for the support of the Army." Because the Congress had always looked to the civilian head of the War Department to hold the purse strings, "the laws require all the great departments [Engineer, Ordnance, Quartermaster, Subsistence, etc.] which build the fortifications and furnish the arms, supplies, and munitions of war, and actually expend the money for those purposes . . . to act under the direction of the Secretary and withhold from the officer who is called 'Commanding General of the Army' all

In early 1903 the Congress passed legislation to implement reforms proposed by Secretary of War Elihu Root, including creation of the General Staff Corps. A board of officers convened in March to select forty-two officers from the Army at large for assignment to the General Staff. The board members were, *left to right*: Brigadier General William H. Carter; Major General Adna R. Chaffee; Major General Samuel B. M. Young, chairman; Major Henry A. Greene; Major General John C. Bates; Brigadier General Tasker H. Bliss; and Brigadier General Wallace F. Randolph. Of these, Young, Chaffee, Bates, and Bliss would all become chief of staff. *U.S. Army photograph.*

control over those departments." Thus Secretary Root explained the nub of the problem.

What was needed, proclaimed Secretary Root, was a chief of staff who would operate as the Army's general manager, presiding over a general staff that would assist him in the dual role of supervising current operations and planning for future contingencies. The very title of chief of staff, said Root, "denotes a duty to advise, inform, and assist a superior officer who has command, and to represent him, acting in his name and by his authority, in carrying out his policies and securing the execution of his commands." The incumbent must be "perfectly loyal" and must "hold the entire confidence of his commander." By relinquishing the idea of independent command embodied in the title of command-

ing general and by performing the functions Root visualized for a chief of staff, the secretary was convinced that the Army's senior officer could "exercise a great and commanding influence in the control of the Army, and practically manage it in all military matters." General Schofield had shown how it could be done.

Secretary Root obtained the corrective legislation he sought on 14 February 1903, when Congress passed an act to increase the efficiency of the Army. Under its provisions the General Staff Corps was established, to be composed of officers detailed from the Army at large and to rotate between the staff and line. The members of the corps were placed under the supervision of a chief of staff who, under the direction of the president and the secretary of war, was designated to supervise not only the troops of the line but also the Adjutant General's, Inspector General's, Judge Advocate General's, Quartermaster, Subsistence, Pay, Medical, and Ordnance Departments; the Corps of Engineers; and the Signal Corps. The General Staff Corps was assigned to the specific duties of preparing plans for the national defense and for mobilization in time of war, investigating and reporting upon all questions affecting the efficiency of the Army and its state of preparation for military operations, and rendering professional aid and assistance to the secretary of war and to general officers and other superior commanders.[87]

On 8 August 1903, the day of General Miles' retirement, Major General Samuel B. M. Young, elevated to three-star rank, was assigned to command the Army for one week, when the legislation creating the General Staff Corps would take effect and he would assume the duties of chief of staff. Second in seniority in the Army and a distinguished veteran of Civil War campaigns and operations growing out of the War with Spain, Young came to the senior officer post from recent consecutive duty as president of the War College Board established by Root in November 1901 to oversee officer education and then as senior member of a board formed in March 1903 to select forty-two officers for detail to the newly created General Staff Corps.[88]

General Young became the Army's first chief of staff, as scheduled, on 15 August 1903. The officers recommended for service on the General Staff had already been approved and assembled in Washington as a provisional staff to work out the operational details for the corps. The bureau chiefs and department commanders had been consulted concerning rules and procedures so that by mid-August the Army General Staff had been organized and could begin to function with a proper distribution of duties and a working body of regulations.[89]

The creation of the position of chief of staff and General Young's installation as the senior officer in the new mode established an organizational format that exists to this day. Yet all of the systemic problems were not solved in one stroke, for traditionalist opposition to rationalist reform remained. Although Secretary Root got his Army War College in November 1903, his

proposal that the Quartermaster, Subsistence, and Pay Departments be consolidated would not be effected until 1912 during Secretary Henry L. Stimson's administration.

One of the major causes of inceptive instability lay in personnel turnover. The secretary of war and the chief of staff both left office in January 1904, and the knowledgeable William H. Carter preceded Root and Young by a few days. General Corbin, who as adjutant general "had been sympathetic toward the General Staff idea and had worked hard in putting [it] across to both Congress and the Army although it meant the eclipse of the department he headed," moved out to a field assignment in April in line with the provisions of the act that created the General Staff Corps.[90]

Thus in the critical formative period of the newly adopted reforms, those who conceived and installed the long needed corrective measures were replaced by officials who were either lacking in the grasp and dedication required to advance the new order or were firmly wedded to the old way of things. When Secretary Root, as one of his final acts, consolidated several administrative agencies in order to centralize recordkeeping and free the chief of staff and the General Staff to exercise their policy and planning functions, he was the unwitting agent of unexpected ramifications that led to both a perpetuation of some of the very departmental problems he had done so much to resolve and a delay in the realization of their solution.[91]

The difficulty arose as a result of the departure of Adjutant General Corbin, the consolidation of the Adjutant General's Office and the Record and Pension Office into the Military Secretary's Office, and the designation of Fred C. Ainsworth of the Record and Pension Office as head of the new bureau. In the process Ainsworth, who proved to be adept at developing connections in Congress and at influencing legislation favorable to himself, was elevated to major general, which put him one grade above his fellow bureau heads.

Although Ainsworth's consolidation of his position and creeping accretion of power placed him automatically at odds with the other bureau chiefs, it was his rivalry with the General Staff, and consequently with his superiors, that

In the spring of 1903 thirty-one of the forty-two members of the newly formed General Staff assembled for this group photograph, taken by the E. B. Thompson News Service of Washington, D.C. Major General Samuel B. M. Young, soon to be the first chief of staff of the Army, is seated at center, with Brigadier General Tasker H. Bliss on his left. *From the Peyton C. March Papers in the custody of the Library of Congress.*

eventually would bring him down. He held his own through the tours of three chiefs of staff—Adna R. Chaffee, John C. Bates, and J. Franklin Bell—all of whom were interested in being relieved of as much administrative detail as possible, and three secretaries of war—William H. Taft, Luke E. Wright, and Jacob M. Dickinson—all of whom preferred harmony to internecine strife. The next lineal descendants in the respective chairs were of a different stripe: Major General Leonard Wood, who became chief of staff in April 1910, was a figure in the Winfield Scott tradition, able, ambitious, and forceful if not domineering; Secretary of War Henry L. Stimson, able, dedicated, high-minded, and public-spirited, a lawyer and protege of Elihu Root in the legal profession, entered office in May 1911 and set about consolidating his mentor's reforms.

Stimson had not been long in office when he was called upon to settle a dispute between Wood and Ainsworth over the assignment of officers to recruiting depots. Ainsworth, now adjutant general following restoration of the title in 1907, took it as an infringement of his prerogatives when the chief of staff informed him that the General Staff had selected a list of candidates for depot command from which he could make a choice. Ainsworth voiced his exception to this in a communication to the secretary of war; Wood then commented upon it in a memorandum to Secretary Stimson in which he pointed out, among other things, that the adjutant general was a subordinate officer of the War Department under the supervision of the chief of staff and his communication represented "an act of gross official insubordination and discourtesy" to his

The historic rivalry between the bureau chiefs and the Army's senior officer survived the Root reforms to erupt again in 1912, when Adjutant General Fred C. Ainsworth (*left*) challenged Chief of Staff Leonard Wood (*right*) over perceived intrusions upon his traditional domain. Ainsworth's written protest was so embellished with stinging criticisms, which inescapably reflected upon his superiors, that Wood passed it to Secretary of War Henry L. Stimson and President William H. Taft, who concurred in Wood's recommendation of strong disciplinary action. Realizing that he had overstepped his bounds, Ainsworth asked for and was granted immediate retirement. *U.S. Army Signal Corps photograph from the collections of the National Archives.*

superiors. The secretary sided with the chief of staff and so informed the adjutant general.[92]

The final act of the Ainsworth drama was played out over the relatively insignificant question of whether the muster roll, the soldier's record of service and biographical data, should be streamlined and consolidated with organizational returns and payrolls as an economy measure. A Presidential Commission on Efficiency and Economy had been directed to make a detailed investigation of governmental operations, and an offshoot War Department Board on Business Methods, chaired by Ainsworth, had moved the focus to military operations. The General Staff had sought suggestions and had approved a proposal that a descriptive list replace the cumbersome muster roll. General Wood asked General Ainsworth to comment on the proposal.

Ainsworth was at once opposed to any change in the format of the muster roll and con-vinced that inexperienced and unqualified individuals were tampering with official documents and intruding upon his special domain. His reply was so laced with derogatory statements against those who opposed his views—in this instance, the secretary of war and the chief of staff, among others—that General Wood laid the matter before Secretary Stimson and President Taft. With the commander in chief's concurrence, the secretary relieved the adjutant general of his duties "pending consideration of disciplinary measures to be taken. . . ." On the following day Ainsworth asked to be allowed to retire from the Army. His request was approved, and his departure marked "a turning point in the vexed history of the Army's command. Wood's success over Ainsworth, who had led the resistance to the General Staff for a decade, was a moral triumph for the General Staff and, henceforth, caused the bureau chiefs some concern.

The center of gravity of the War Department shifted from the bureaus to the General Staff. Having grasped the ascendancy, the General Staff could now move on to ensure and consolidate its leadership."[93]

Wartime expansion soon tested the General Staff system and exposed still unsettled weaknesses at the top of the Army. As the First World War progressed and it became increasingly clear that the United States eventually would become involved, it was also plain that the chief of staff's authority and seniority were yet short of absolute, despite his sovereign title and organizational eminence. A lingering lack of definition in the senior military office cried out for a Leonard Wood to establish unquestioned control over the bureaus and give substance to the civilian advisory function. Major General William W. Wotherspoon's six-month tour was hardly long enough for him to grasp the reins, and Major Generals Hugh L. Scott and Tasker H. Bliss both held office on the eve of retirement and fell short of what Secretary of War Newton D. Baker desired in a wartime chief of staff. It was not until Major General Peyton C. March took office in the spring of 1918 that Baker felt he had the man for the job.[94]

Peyton Conway March had graduated from Lafayette College at Easton, Pennsylvania, and the United States Military Academy. Routine garrison duties and a tour at the artillery school at Fort Monroe, Virginia, brought him to the battlefields of the War with Spain and the Philippine Insurrection, where he served with distinction. He was a provincial governor and commissary general of prisoners in the Philippines before returning to the United States to become one of the first officers posted to the new General Staff; that duty included assignment as an observer with the First Japanese Army in the Russo-Japanese War. After America's entry into the World War, he moved to France as chief of artillery of the American Expeditionary Forces, later receiving his promotion to major general. In March 1918 Secretary Baker called him home to be acting chief of staff, and in May, promoted to the temporary rank of full general, March became chief of staff.

America's entry into the war, the expansion of the military to a magnitude required in world conflict, and the dispatch overseas of major expeditionary forces had introduced a new element of competition—if not rivalry—into the uniformed leadership of the Army, namely, the precedence of the chief of staff vis-a-vis that of a substantially autonomous senior field commander. With secretarial sanction, General March opened General Order Number 18 of 21 August 1918, on the subject of reorganization of the General Staff, with a broad statement of the chief of staff's authority over the whole Army, including General John J. Pershing and the American Expeditionary Forces:

The Chief of the General Staff is the immediate adviser of the Secretary of War on all matters relating to the Military Establishment, and is charged by the Secretary of War with the planning, development, and execution of the Army program. The Chief of Staff by law (act of May 12, 1917) takes rank and precedence over all officers of the Army, and by virtue of that position and by authority of and in the name of the Secretary of War, he issues such orders as will insure that the policies of the War Department are harmoniously executed by the several corps, bureaus, and other agencies of the Military Establishment, and that the Army program is carried out speedily and efficiently.[95]

Even with this clear-cut expression of authority it was in the very nature of the war's evolution that, as the commander of a major overseas expeditionary force that finally numbered two million men, Pershing required and was granted broad discretionary powers in the conduct of the war in the operational theater. Paradoxically but inevitably, this brought him into opposition to March, who, under the secretary of war and the president, had to deal with military affairs and national interests on the broadest of planes at the seat of government. It would have been strange indeed if two strong-willed and able officers in positions of ultimate power and with different perspectives and missions had not found themselves at variance on some matters of policy, method, or decision, even with unquestioned unanimity on higher goals. Pershing and March differed, for example, on the number of divisions the United States should send to France by June 1919; Pershing wanted a hundred, while March's study of the subject indicated that eighty—the maximum number that could be organized,

Peyton C. March proved to be the thoroughly accomplished chief of staff that Secretary of War Newton D. Baker had wanted, shown here presenting March with an award for his outstanding service in the demanding position. *U.S. Army Signal Corps photograph from the collections of the National Archives.*

shipped, and sustained in theater—was adequate for the war's needs. On the subject of selection of twenty-five officers for promotion to brigadier general, Pershing objected when eight nominations were allocated for stateside selection as against seventeen in Europe. March cabled him that the Expeditionary Forces were only a part of the American Army and Secretary Baker intended to make promotions "from the entire Army."[96]

General Pershing had his opportunity to see things from the Washington headquarters horizon when, on 1 July 1921, he succeeded General March as chief of staff. A West Point graduate, his career had included frontier service in the closing years of the Indian wars, combat service in the War with Spain and the Philippine Insurrection, tours as professor of military science at the University of Nebraska and instructor in tactics

at West Point, assignment to the General Staff in Washington, and designation as military attaché to Japan during the Russo-Japanese War. His reports on that conflict and his earlier diplomatic-military achievements in the Philippines earned him President Theodore Roosevelt's nomination for promotion from captain to brigadier general over eight hundred sixty-two senior-ranking officers. He led American troops in the Mexican Punitive Expedition before assignment to command the American Expeditionary Forces.[97]

General Pershing entered the senior military office at a moment when the Congress had passed the National Defense Act of 1920, legislation that would form the basic charter of the military establishment until 1947 and the Army until 1950. The act defined the senior officers role thus:

The Chief of Staff shall preside over the War Department General Staff and, under the direction of the President or of the Secretary of War under the direction of the President, shall cause to be made, by the War Department General Staff, the necessary plans for recruiting, organizing, supplying, equipping, mobilizing, training, and demobilizing the Army of the United States and for the use of the military forces for national defense. He shall transmit to the Secretary of War the plans and recommendations prepared for that purpose by the War Department General Staff and advise him in regard thereto; upon approval of such plans or recommendations by the Secretary of War, he shall act as the agent of the Secretary of War in carrying the same into effect.[98]

Although General Pershing brought great personal prestige to the office and was enthusiastic over the promise for Army progress embodied in the National Defense Act of 1920, he became chief of staff at a moment when postwar military retrenchment was in progress and an impetus to economy in government was in the ascendant. On the plus side, the new act rejected the theory of an expansible Army in favor of a three-component Army of the United States in which regular and reserve elements could be prepared in peacetime for their wartime roles. Offices were established in the departmental headquarters for chiefs of the combat arms, placing them on a level with the service bureaus. A Finance Department, Chemical Warfare Service, and Air Service were created, and a single promotion list replaced separate branch lists. Yet much of the promise went unfulfilled when appropriations and personnel were curtailed. Army strength fluctuated annually between 133,000 and 149,000 in the period from 1922 to 1936, when it finally began to climb toward a World War II peak of almost 8.2 million. Expenditures followed similar trends, ranging within annual limits of $357 and $458 million until 1936 and the start of an ascent to a World War II zenith of $50 billion in 1945.[99]

Thus the Army in the period between the World Wars felt the effects of a postwar retrenchment, of the wishful thinking engendered by a "war-to-end-all-wars" philosophy, of peacetime relaxation, of worldwide depression. General Pershing and his immediate successors—Major General John L. Hines and Generals Charles P. Summerall (first beneficiary of a 1929 legislative act elevating the chief of staff to four stars while in office), Douglas MacArthur, and Malin Craig—guided the Army through these attenuated times. Craig's efforts during the advent of World War II were to prove invaluable, although they were largely overlooked at the time because they were not attended by crisis, and when the emergency erupted, the spotlight focused automatically upon his successor.

General Pershing brought into the chief of staff's office his aide, one of the American Expeditionary Forces' outstanding officers, Colonel George C. Marshall, and from 1921 to 1924 Marshall had the opportunity to observe and be a part of the inner workings of the Office of the Chief of Staff, excellent preparation for his own assignment, fifteen years later, as the Army's senior officer.

Unlike Generals Pershing, Hines, Summerall, MacArthur, and Craig, all of whom were products of the United States Military Academy, George Catlett Marshall had graduated from the Virginia Military Institute. Commissioned in infantry in February 1902, he served twice in the Philippines and held the usual rotation in stateside troop, staff, and school assignments—the latter as both student and instructor—before assignment to the American Expeditionary Forces as assistant chief of staff for operations of the First Army; in that capacity he executed a notable piece of staff work in connection with the shift of half a million American troops and their guns from the St. Mihiel to the Argonne front. After leaving Pershing's staff in 1924, he spent three years in China, taught briefly at the Army War College, and served as assistant commandant of the Infantry School at Fort Benning, Georgia. Following a mix of teaching, troop, and command assignments, he returned to Washington as assistant chief of staff, acting chief, and, finally, on 1 September 1939 with the rank of general, chief of staff.

The Japanese attack on Pearl Harbor and United States involvement in global war kept General Marshall in his post for six years. The size, scope, and intensity of the conflict challenged the Army's headquarters organization and leadership. World War II differed so radically from World War I that planning based upon experience derived from the earlier conflict had to be modified constantly to meet the new circumstances. General Marshall became in fact the chief strategy and operations adviser to the president, and carried out his departmental managerial role by delegating administrative responsibility to a deputy chief of staff at headquarters and to three major field commands: Army Ground Forces, Army Air Forces, and Army Service Forces. Selecting his own principal deputies and subordinates, decentralizing administrative responsibility, and using the Operations Division of the General Staff as an operating headquarters, the chief of staff, fully supported by Secretary Stimson and President Roosevelt, became the center of military authority in the War Department and the personification of the apical rank bestowed upon him in December 1944—General of the Army.[100]

At the interservice level General Marshall became the Army member of a joint committee of senior Army, Navy, and Army Air Forces officers, established to ensure coordination and cooperation between the United States armed forces and to represent American views before a similar British joint service committee. The American Joint Chiefs of Staff acquired increasing authority as the war progressed, and joined their British counterparts on the interallied Combined Chiefs of Staff—the professional military chiefs of both countries directly responsible to the American

During World War II the Army's senior civilian and senior officer—Henry L. Stimson (*left*) and George C. Marshall (*right*)—forged a close working relationship based on their dedication, cooperation, and mutual trust and respect, as illustrated by the special tribute the secretary of war accorded the chief of staff at a V–E ceremony: "Seldom can a man put aside such a thing as being the commanding general [U.S. and Allied commander in Europe] of the greatest field army in our history. This decision was made by you for wholly unselfish reasons. But you have made your position as Chief of Staff a greater one. I have never seen a task of such magnitude performed by man." *U.S. Army photographs.*

president and British prime minister for planning and overseeing the grand strategy of the coalition under the heads of state. General Marshall's influential role in this joint-combined picture represented the beginnings of the Army chief of staff's participation in the operation of the Joint Chiefs of Staff under a principle of unified command in the conduct of war, and, as noted above, a principal adviser, in company with his fellow service chiefs, to the president of the United States.

In November 1945 General of the Army Dwight D. Eisenhower, fresh from operational command over victorious Allied forces in a major theater of war, succeeded General Marshall as chief of staff. His views on the shape of things, expressed through the workings of study groups, formalized in Presidential Executive Order 9722 of 13 May 1946 and War Department Circular 138 of 14 May 1946, and characterized as the

Eisenhower reorganization, abolished the Army Service Forces and service commands, provided greater autonomy for the Army Air Forces, brought research and development into staff prominence, and emphasized the principle of decentralization. Unlike former occasions when the General Staff and the technical services had been at odds over how the department should be organized and run, those elements now joined in a common opposition to the Army Service Forces that led to its abolishment and the return to the bureau chiefs of their customary control over service activities. The General Staff was instructed to "plan, direct, coordinate, and supervise," and in general to "assist the Chief of Staff in getting things done." This was in line with General Eisenhower's view that teamwork, cooperation, and persuasion were better than tight executive control as a management philosophy.

George Washington (*left*), Ulysses S. Grant (*center*), and Dwight D. Eisenhower (*right*)—three of the country's most distinguished soldiers—served as the Army's senior officer at evenly spaced periods in American history. Their martial accomplishments thrust them onto the national political scene, and each served two terms as president of the United States. Several others who held the top uniformed position also became party standard-bearers or aspirants to the highest office in the land. *Washington portrait by William Dunlap from the United States Capitol Collection; Grant photographic portrait by Matthew Brady from the collections of the National Archives; and Eisenhower photographic portrait by Fabian Bachrach from the U.S. Army.*

Had General Eisenhower preferred to exercise tight executive control, Circular 138 provided the necessary authority:

The Chief of Staff is the principal military adviser to the President and to the Secretary of War on the conduct of war and the principal military adviser and executive to the Secretary of War on the activities of the Military Establishment. The Chief of Staff has command of all components of the Army of the United States . . . and is responsible to the Secretary of War for their use in war and plans and preparations for their readiness for war.[101]

The global nature of the Second World War, with its worldwide deployments, combined operations, and clear demonstration that warfare had become three-dimensional, could not help but draw attention to the subject of unification of the armed forces. The Marshall reorganization had worked so well for the Army that he proposed extending its features to a unified defense establishment. As early as April 1944, and again in October 1945, Army-Marshall proposals were aired before the Congress, and in December 1945 President Harry S. Truman sent an administration version to the Hill. Finally, after wide-ranging discussion, debate, and compromise, the National Security Act of 1947, passed on 26 July, became law. It provided for a civilian secretary of defense over a National Military Establishment in which the Air Force became a separate and coequal service with the Army and Navy. The War Department became the Department of the Army, and the secretary of war became the secretary of the Army. The act legalized the wartime Joint Chiefs of Staff, the body composed of the chiefs of the military services.[102]

Weaknesses that appeared in the new organizational structure were dealt with by amendment on 10 August 1949. The designation National Military Establishment was dropped in favor of a new title: Department of Defense. In another step along the road to unification, the Army, Navy, and Air Force were transformed from executive to military departments, still separately administered by their respective secretaries but under the authority, direction, and control of the secretary of defense. Under the new arrangement the service secretaries lost their cabinet status, their membership on the National Security Council, and their direct access to the president. At the same time, the position of chairman of the Joint

Chiefs of Staff was established. He would be appointed from among the Regular Army officers of the armed services, would take precedence over all other officers, and would preside, although without vote, over the committee composed of the chiefs of the uniformed services.[103]

While the National Security Act of 1947 and its 1949 amendments were being developed, the Army was studying the body of laws that governed its management and direction. Out of this review came the Army Organization Act of 1950, which clarified the function of the chief of staff as the senior officer of the Army. References to a "command" role were finally eliminated, and parallel Army regulations stated:

Command of the Army and all components thereof is exercised by the President through the Secretary of Defense and the Secretary of the Army, who directly represent him, and as the personal representatives of the President, their acts are the President's acts, and their directions and orders are the President's directions and orders.[104]

Thus the last half of the 1940s saw substantial organizational and managerial change within the Department of the Army. Bridging World War II and the Korean War and embracing the tenures of Generals Marshall, Eisenhower, Omar N. Bradley, and J. Lawton Collins, it was a period of transition when hidebound tradition, resistance to change, wartime lessons, peacetime inertia, advancing technology, and distant threat all influenced the course of military affairs.

One of the 1949 amendments to the National Security Act brought an Army chief of staff, General Omar Nelson Bradley, into the inaugural chairmanship of the Joint Chiefs of Staff, and the Army Organization Act of 1950 brought long-awaited and long-needed clarification and stability to the chief of staff's fluctuating role as the senior officer. The Army chief of staff now performed a dual role: executive manager of the department under the secretary of the Army, and military adviser to the secretary of defense and the president of the United States as a member of the Joint Chiefs of Staff. In giving substance to the advisory function, General Collins as Army chief of staff became a military adviser to his predecessor thrice-removed when General

Marshall was appointed secretary of defense. In an unusual footnote to Army history Generals Collins, Bradley, and Marshall, in their respective concurrent roles as Army chief of staff, chairman of the joint chiefs of staff, and secretary of defense, had the unpleasant but unavoidable duty of deliberating upon and concurring in President Truman's relief in 1951 of their distant predecessor as Army chief of staff, General Douglas MacArthur, then commander of American and United Nations forces in the Far East with field responsibility for the prosecution of the Korean War. In his official capacity, General MacArthur had bypassed his superiors in Washington to express personal views that were at odds with governmental positions.

Post–World War II retrenchment and a false sense of security engendered by possession of the atomic bomb had left the United States unprepared for a peripheral conventional war in Korea, and American units suffered serious reverses in 1950 before adequate forces could be readied and fielded in the theater. The nuclear deterrent failed to dissuade the North Koreans from attacking South Korea and the Chinese Communists from entering the fray when American and Allied forces advanced toward the Manchurian border. Despite this convincing evidence, and even as the Russians were fielding nuclear weapons, the United States enunciated a policy of massive retaliation as its basic doctrine. Two successive chiefs of staff—Generals Matthew B. Ridgway and Maxwell D. Taylor—spoke out against dependence upon nuclear weapons and concomitant deficiencies in the strength and capabilities of conventional forces, and both considered the policy such a threat to national security that, upon retirement, they expressed their open concern to the American people.[105]

In succeeding General Taylor in July 1959, General Lyman L. Lemnitzer followed in General Bradley's footsteps when his service as chief of staff was cut short by his designation as chairman of the Joint Chiefs of Staff. While he was the Army's senior officer he had stressed the need for increased appropriations and modernization; he found these positions susceptible to service-wide application at the Joint Chiefs level. The Defense Reorganization Act of 1958, it might be noted, authorized the uniformed

The National Security Act of 1947 legalized the wartime Joint Chiefs of Staff, and one of the 1949 amendments created the position of chairman. The incumbent Army chief of staff, General Omar N. Bradley, became the first chairman. He is seen here with his hand on the world globe, flanked by the service chiefs, *left to right*: General J. Lawton Collins, U.S. Army; Admiral Louis E. Denfeld, U.S. Navy; and General Hoyt S. Vandenberg, U.S. Air Force. The Marine Corps commandant later became a member. *Department of Defense photograph.*

chiefs of the military services to delegate duties to their vice chiefs in order to free themselves to devote more time to their functions as members of the Joint Chiefs of Staff.

A significant historical moment for the Army and its role in conventional war came as the decade of the sixties opened with John F. Kennedy's election as president and his selection of Robert S. McNamara as secretary of defense. In his budget message of March 1961, shortly after assuming office, President Kennedy enunciated a policy of flexible military response as a concomitant of American diplomacy—one that would enable the United States to defend itself against aggression

on any force level and help deter the erosion of the free world in so-called wars of national liberation conducted by conventional means. "Any potential aggressor contemplating an attack on any part of the free world with any kind of weapons, conventional or nuclear, must know that our response will be suitable, selective, swift, and effective."

Communist challenges in Berlin in 1961 and Cuba in 1962, along with ongoing commitments in Europe and Asia, provided more than enough justification and impetus to strengthen and modernize the armed forces. Secretary McNamara seconded President Kennedy in the belief that the armed forces must be prepared to respond to military chal-

Generals Matthew B. Ridgway (*left*) and Maxwell D. Taylor (*right*), successive chiefs of staff in the post-Korean and pre-Vietnam period, took issue with the government's massive retaliation doctrine and concomitant inattention to conventional capabilities. Both retired in the 1950s to write and speak out on this and other problems of national security. *U.S. Army photographs*.

lenges on any level and anywhere in the world, and he set out to achieve that capability. A key part of the McNamara reform process was the Army's Project 80, the most detailed study of its organization and management since World War I. Out of the appraisal came a major reorganization that erased some long-standing controversy and restructured the staff and command along more modern lines. The Army Staff became primarily responsible for planning and policy; the field commands, for implementing staff decisions. To organize the Army along functional lines and to centralize personnel, training, research, and development while integrating supply operations, most of the technical services were abolished, or reduced to special staff status, and their command functions, along with most of the Army Staff operating functions, redistributed among the U.S. Continental Army Command and two new functional commands—the U.S. Army Materiel Command and the U.S. Army Combat Developments Command. The entire process rep-

resented an evolutionary spurt in which rationalism gained ascendance over traditionalism.[106]

In light of the managerial and budgetary complexities of the McNamara reforms, it was fitting that the Army's part in the study and installation of revised organization and procedures was carried out under General George Henry Decker's direction as chief of staff. General Decker, a graduate of Lafayette College with a degree in economics, brought to the senior officer's position a rounded career in troop, school, and staff assignments with a focus on logistics and financial functions that culminated in the concordant assignments of comptroller of the Army and vice chief of staff preliminary to his selection as chief of staff.

For his part, Secretary McNamara became involved in one of those moments in history in which events and people coincide. He entered office in 1961; at this time the role of the United States in Vietnam was limited to advice and support. When he left office in 1968, an immense logistical base

Robert S. McNamara entered office in 1961 as President John F. Kennedy's secretary of defense. During his seven years in office he worked to strengthen and modernize the armed forces, with the United States involvement in the Vietnam conflict offering him the opportunity to introduce and test new management practices and techniques. The Army's part in the process, involving a major reorganization under Project 80, cleared up some long-standing controversies and resulted in most of the technical services being abolished and their functions realigned among major functional commands. The McNamara reforms represented a considerable advance in a long transition from traditionalism to rationalism in the Army's organization and operation. *Photographic portrait by Oscar Porter from the U.S. Army.*

and global lines of communications had been established, a force appropriate to the measured scale of the war had been fielded, and American and North Vietnamese negotiators were meeting in Paris in an attempt to find mutually acceptable grounds for reducing or ending the conflict. An unwanted and unpopular war had nevertheless created a set of circumstances that made it possible for the secretary of defense to bring to bear a new management philosophy and then test and install the practices and procedures to make it work.

The Army's part in the period is evident in some statistics that provide an order of magni-

tude. In 1961 the budget was about $10 billion, strength was around 870,000, and the active force had fifteen divisions and five separate brigades. By 1968 the budget had edged above $25 billion, strength was 1.5 million, and the active force had nineteen divisions and fourteen separate brigades.

Secretary McNamara's contribution was not unlike that of Secretary Root's in earlier times. He was credited by one knowledgeable observer with "having rebuilt the whole armed services, for the first time in its history giving the military establishment a coherent, flexible strategy, a rational weapons policy, and an effective cooperation among the services. He vastly increased the effectiveness of the military establishment, and while this [was] a different kind of achievement from that of [James V.] Forrestal and Elihu Root, who brought the defense establishment into tune with political needs, it may well rank as high."[107]

Experiences in the distant theater of Southeast Asia influenced the thinking of the subsequent senior officers. The Vietnam conflict was in its more active phases when Generals Earle G. Wheeler, Harold K. Johnson, William C. Westmoreland, and Creighton W. Abrams, Jr., were consecutive chiefs of staff, with General Bruce Palmer, Jr.,[108] filling this position for more than three months until Abrams' confirmation. As chairman of the Joint Chiefs of Staff, Generals Taylor, Lemnitzer, and Wheeler had overall direction of the war, and, prefacing their assignments as chief of staff, Generals Westmoreland, Abrams, and Fred C. Weyand experienced it successively as deputy commander and then commander of American forces in the operational theater. Thereafter, Generals Bernard W. Rogers, Edward C. Meyer, John A. Wickham, Jr., Carl E. Vuono, Gordon R. Sullivan, Dennis J. Reimer, and Eric K. Shinseki fought in it as unit officers at company, battalion, brigade, or division level. During the turbulence of the last years of the war General Peter J. Schoomaker served at the platoon and company level with units in Germany.

In recent years the rate of change for the Army itself has increased. As a result of their respective operational experiences, the post-Vietnam Army chiefs of staff have been resolute on the need for maintaining a trained and ready force, while at the

In 1970 the incumbent chief of staff, General William C. Westmoreland, hosted a luncheon at the Pentagon in honor of six of his predecessors: *at center*, General Maxwell D. Taylor and, *left to right*, Generals George H. Decker, Harold K. Johnson, Earle G. Wheeler, Lyman L. Lemnitzer, and J. Lawton Collins. *U.S. Army photograph.*

same time keenly aware that the nation will call on the Army at a moment's notice to perform tasks ranging from domestic disaster relief to overseas wars.[109] The last two years of General Vuono's tenure were marked by three great victories in which the Army played a key role: the end of the Cold War, the freeing of Panama, and the repulse of Iraqi aggression in Kuwait. His successor, General Sullivan, faced the test of maintaining a trained and ready force in the post–Cold War period as a major drawdown in American military forces commenced. General Reimer continued his predecessor's efforts to maintain readiness while the Army completed its drawdown, and his successor, General Shinseki, directed a major transformation of the Army's operational forces.

After taking office, Secretary of Defense Donald H. Rumsfeld gave his full support to overhauling military strategy and fundamentally transforming the nation's forces. Just as Secretary

McNamara's reforms were interrupted by the Vietnam conflict in the 1960s, Rumsfeld's efforts were also challenged by the 11 September 2001 terrorist attacks in America and the subsequent Global War on Terrorism. Despite having to contend with the strains of combat and subsequent stability operations in Afghanistan, Iraq, and elsewhere, Army transformation proceeded under Shinseki and his successor, General Schoomaker. With a renewed commitment to shape its forces, the Army has continued to reorganize while not only conducting major combat and reconstruction operations in Afghanistan and Iraq but also providing operational forces for other contingency missions.

The position and office of the senior officer of the Army has evolved considerably since 1775, when the Continental Congress elected George Washington as general and commander in chief of the Army of the United Colonies. Today the chief

General Peter J. Schoomaker was sworn in as chief of staff on 1 August 2003, shown here with Acting Secretary of the Army Les Brownlee extending his congratulations and with Mrs. Cynthia A. "Cindy" Schoomaker proudly looking on while holding the bible used during the ceremony. *U.S. Army photograph.*

of staff—as the principal officer of the Army—is appointed by the president, with the advice and consent of the Senate. He serves at the pleasure of the president for a period of four years and performs his duties under the direction of the secretary of the Army. He presides over the Army Staff, sends its plans and recommendations to the secretary, advises concerning them, and acts as the secretary's agent in carrying them out. He exercises general supervision over the Army's organizations and personnel, and is a member of the Joint Chiefs of Staff and the Armed Forces Policy Council.[110]

The last decade of the twentieth century and the first years of the twenty-first have experienced significant geopolitical turmoil, which has dramatically affected power and security relationships throughout the world. Perhaps the most important change has been the relative dispersal of power to regional centers. Because of long-simmering ethnic, religious, territorial, and economic disputes, often violent in nature, the calamity of failed states has resulted in new challenges for the international community. In particular, the emergence of transnational groups—such as the al Qaeda, with decentralized leadership that is harder to identify and disrupt—now looms as the dominant threat to peace. In this more unpredictable world the Army faces a new strategic situation that calls for less reliance on forward-deployed forces and presents a wider range of potential opponents. Although its own history illustrates that in postwar periods its operational abilities decline, as demonstrated during the 1990s after Desert Shield/Desert Storm, the Army's indisputable resiliency and adaptability in times of crises—

such as in Somalia, the Balkans, Afghanistan, and Iraq—are a testament to the resourcefulness and flexibility of its Soldiers.

Now the Army is undergoing its largest organizational transformation since the 1950s while concurrently fighting the Global War on Terrorism. But just as their predecessors did, today's senior leaders are responding by pooling their broad-based experiences to ensure that the Army continues to fight and win this nation's wars. Their challenge is to achieve these goals while continuing to grow the seed-corn of future leaders who will lead the Army of the twenty-first century. Throughout its history the United States Army has been the principal means of protecting our national values. The Army's paramount task is to maintain this proud tradition in the midst of rapid change.

Notes to Introduction

1. Worthington Chauncy Ford, ed., *Journals of the Continental Congress, 1774–1789*, 34 vols. (Washington, D.C.: Government Printing Office, 1904–37), 2:89–92. The battles of Lexington and Concord had occurred three months before Washington's appointment, and the battle of Bunker (Breed's) Hill took place on the day Washington received from the assembled Congress his commission as commander in chief. The "army near Boston" included militia elements from Massachusetts, New Hampshire, Rhode Island, and Connecticut.

2. For a summary of the military background of the American colonists and of colonial participation in British operations against the French in North America, see Maurice Matloff, ed., *American Military History*, Army Historical Series, rev. ed. (Washington, D.C.: Office of the Chief of Military History, United States Army, 1973), ch. 2.

3. The story of Washington's youth and early military experience, and of his part in the momentous events that brought him to command of the Army and center stage on the national scene, is detailed in Douglas Southall Freeman, *George Washington: A Biography,* 7 vols. (New York: Scribner, 1948–57), vols. 1–2, *Young Washington* (1948), and vol. 3, *Planter and Patriot* (1951).

4. Ford, *Journals,* 2:93–94, 97–99, 111–23, 220–21. The actions appointing heads of the technical services mark the establishment of the Adjutant General's Department, the Quartermaster Department, the Pay Department, and the Corps of Engineers. Further resolutions addressing hospital, legal, and religious matters marked the establishment of the Medical Department, the Judge Advocate General's Department, and the Corps of Chaplains.

5. George Washington, *The Writings of George Washington . . . , 1745–1799,* ed. John C. Fitzpatrick, 39 vols. (Washington, D.C.: Government Printing Office, 1931–44), 3:309.

6. Matloff, ed., *American Military History,* pp. 46–50.

7. Ford, *Journals,* 5:434–35. John Adams was one of several legislators who served on and chaired the Board of War and Ordnance in its early configurations. Horatio Gates was the first president of the Board of War.

8. Ibid., 2:96.

9. Ibid., 2:101. Washington's Council of War was composed of his principal subordinate commanders.

10. For a history of the development and early operation of the war office, see Harry M. Ward, *The Department of War, 1781–1795* (Pittsburgh: Univ. of Pittsburgh Press, 1962). Benjamin Lincoln of Massachusetts served in Revolutionary War operations in the North in 1776–1777 and was wounded at Saratoga. Later, as commander in the South, he was forced to surrender Charleston, South Carolina. Exchanged, he participated in the Yorktown campaign. He was a member of the Constitutional Convention, was lieutenant governor of Massachusetts and collector of the port of Boston, and served on several commissions that negotiated treaties with the Indians.

11. Ford, *Journals*, 19:126–27.

12. Ward, *Department of War*, pp. 17–19 and 33–34.

13. Matloff, ed., *American Military History,* pp. 99–101.

14. Ibid., p. 104; Ward, *Department of War,* p. 42.

15. Russell F. Weigley, *History of the United States Army,* (New York: Macmillan, 1967), p. 82.

16. Ward, *Department of War,* p. 56.

17. Ibid., p. 82.

18. Matloff, ed., *American Military History,* traces these early operations on the Indian frontier.

19. Weigley, *History of U.S. Army,* pp. 91–93.

20. James Thomas Flexner, Washington: *The Indispensable Man* (Boston: Little, Brown, 1974), pp. 372–79.

21. Ibid., p. 372.

22. Matloff, ed., *American Military History,* p. 116; John C. Miller, *Alexander Hamilton: Portrait in Paradox* (New York: Harper, 1959), pp. 507–08. Miller quotes Hamilton as being "certain that the military career in this country offers too few inducements and it is equally certain my present Station in the Army

cannot very long continue under the plan which seems to govern" (p. 508).

23. For a concise biography of Wilkinson, see *Dictionary of American Biography,* s.v. "Wilkinson, James" by I.J.C. (Isaac Joslin Cox). Wilkinson's principal biographers offer convincing evidence of his seditious conduct in dealings with Spanish officials. His place in history has been fixed in the titular characterizations and supporting substance of their major biographies. James Ripley Jacobs judges him as "a tarnished warrior," Royal Ornan Shreve sees him as a "finished scoundrel," and Thomas Robson Hay and Morris Robert Werner rate him caustically as an "admirable trumpeter." See also the Bibliography of Senior Officers.

24. It was only natural for government officials to look to Revolutionary War veterans in emergencies. Yet, by the time the War of 1812 opened, the country had been at peace for about three decades and the officer corps had had little opportunity to acquire direct experience. Only sixty-five graduates of the United States Military Academy were in service after the school's first decade of operation, and they were junior officers. The nation sustained some painful reverses as the war progressed, and the soon-to-be secretary of war, William H. Crawford, writing from Paris and his station as Minister to France, urged that efforts be made to "rid the army of old women and blockheads, at least on the general staff" (Matloff, ed., *American Military History,* p. 150).

25. Weigley, *History of U.S. Army,* pp. 135–37.

26. Ibid., pp. 137–38.

27. Oliver Lyman Spaulding, *The United States Army in War and Peace* (New York: Putnam, 1937), p. 153.

28. In the War Department Special Order of 28 February 1828 announcing Brown's death and eulogizing him, Secretary Barbour referred to the late commanding general's "gentleness of disposition" and "courtesy of deportment," and noted that "the disease which abridged his days, and has terminated his career at a period scarcely beyond the meridian of manhood, undoubtedly originated in the hardships of his campaigns on the Canadian frontier, and in that glorious wound which, though desperate, could not remove him from the field of battle, till it was won."

29. For a general discussion of brevet rank and its application to the senior officers of this period, see Lieutenant Colonel Frederick Bernays Wiener, "Mex Rank Through the Ages," *Infantry Journal,* September 1943, pp. 26–28.

30. Ibid.; see also part 2 of Colonel Wiener's five-part article, "Three Stars and Up," *Infantry Journal,* July 1945, p. 33.

31. Army Regulations, 1834, pp. 115–16.

32. Ibid., 1835, pp. 119–20.

33. Letter, Adjutant General to Secretary of War, 24 Jan 1829. The differing approaches that Generals Brown and Macomb brought to the office of commanding general are evidenced in a further comment of the adjutant general: "It has remained for the present General in Chief [Macomb] . . . to claim jurisdiction in some of the enumerated duties [of the adjutant general] . . . which, during the command of the lamented General Brown, were practically acknowledged at the War Office to pertain to the Adjutant General" (Letter, Adjutant General to Secretary of War, 10 Dec 1829). Copies in Cater File, Center of Military History.

34. Ibid., 10 Dec 1829.

35. Charles Winslow Elliott, *Winfield Scott: The Soldier and the Man* (New York: Macmillan, 1937), pp. 438–46.

36. General Order no. 49, War Department, 31 Aug 1848.

37. General Order no. 27, War Department, 10 May 1849.

38. Elliott, *Winfield Scott,* ch. 46; Weigley, *History of U.S. Army,* pp. 192–95.

39. Wiener, "Three Stars and Up," p. 34; General Order no. 2, War Department, 12 Mar 1855.

40. Matloff, ed., *American Military History,* pp. 204–05, 209, 220; Weigley, History of U.S. Army, pp. 246–47.

41. Matloff, ed., *American Military History,* p. 220.

42. Weigley, *History of U.S. Army,* pp. 248–49; see also sketch of Halleck in *Dictionary of American Biography,* s.v. "Halleck, Henry Wager" by W.A.G. (William Addleman Ganoe).

43. Wiener, "Three Stars and Up," p. 34.

44. Ibid., pp. 34–35; General Order no. 87, War Department, 3 Mar 1864.

45. General Order no. 98, War Department, 12 Mar 1864.

46. Ibid.

47. Matloff, ed., *American Military History,* p. 264; Wiener, "Three Stars and Up," pp. 34–35; George W. Cullum, *Biographical Register of the Officers and Graduates of the United States Military Academy,* 3d ed., 3 vols. (Boston: Houghton, Mifflin, 1891), 2:170–72.

48. Matloff, ed., *American Military History,* pp. 283–85.

49. Weigley, *History of U.S. Army,* pp. 258–60. For a detailed account of the play of political forces in the Johnson-Stanton controversy, see Benjamin P. Thomas and Harold M. Hyman, Stanton: *The Life and Times of Lincoln's Secretary of War* (New York: Knopf, 1962).

50. General Order no. 11, War Department, 8 Mar

1869. The order repeats instructions of 5 March 1869. The Army carries Sherman's effective date of assumption of command as 8 March.

51. Ibid.

52. General Order no. 28, War Department, 27 Mar 1869.

53. William T. Sherman, *Memoirs of Gen. William T. Sherman*, 4th ed., 2 vols. (New York: Webster, 1892), 2:444. For a general background on the department heads, see William Gardner Bell, *Secretaries of War and Secretaries of the Army: Portraits and Biographical Sketches*, rev. ed. (Washington, D.C.: Center of Military History, United States Army, 2003).

54. Lloyd Lewis, *Sherman: Fighting Prophet* (New York: Harcourt, Brace, 1932), pp. 609–13; Cullum, *Biographical Register*, 2:29. Rear Admiral James Alden, commander of the European squadron, sailing on Navy business, invited Sherman to visit Europe. Cullum accounts for the ten-month visit with the phrase "on professional duty in Europe," whereas Lewis identifies it more properly as private travel. Sherman visited Spain, Italy, Turkey, Egypt, Russia, Germany, France, Switzerland, and the British Isles.

55. Lurton D. Ingersoll, *A History of the War Department of the United States With Biographical Sketches of the Secretaries* (Washington, D.C.: Mohun, 1880), pp. 566–71; Lewis, Sherman, p. 622.

56. General Order no. 28, War Department, 6 Apr 1876; Sherman, *Memoirs,* 2:455.

57. Lewis, *Sherman,* pp. 628–29.

58. Army Regulations, 1881, art. 15, p. 20.

59. Matloff, ed., *American Military History,* p. 291.

60. John M. Schofield, *Forty-six Years in the Army* (New York: Century, 1897), pp. 471–72.

61. Ibid., pp. 472–73. Permanently assigned to their departments, the bureau chiefs were often criticized as being outside the Army. Several of them spent years, almost careers, as staff heads—notably Montgomery C. Meigs (quartermaster general from 1861 to 1882) and Joseph K. Barnes (surgeon general from 1866 to 1882).

62. U.S. War Department, *Annual Reports* (Washington, D.C., 1823–1947), *Report of the Secretary of War,* 1885, 1:64–65 and 130.

63. General Order no. 92, War Department, 22 Jul 1870, sec. 6.

64. General Order no. 2, War Department, 12 Mar 1855.

65. General Order no. 87, War Department, 3 Mar 1864.

66. General Order no. 52, War Department, 26 Jul 1866.

67. General Order no. 39, War Department, 9 Jun 1888.

68. Schofield, *Forty-six Years in the Army,* pp. 480–81.

69. Ibid., pp. 467–83.

70. Wiener, "Three Stars and Up," p. 37; Schofield, *Forty-six Years in the Army,* pp. 422–23. "It is only in this country," wrote Schofield, "where the chief of state has generally no military training, and his war minister the same, that a chief of staff of the army is supposed to be unnecessary" (p. 410).

71. Wiener, "Three Stars and Up," p. 37.

72. Hermann Hagedorn, *Leonard Wood: A Biography,* 2 vols. (New York: Harper, 1931), 1:140–41.

73. General Miles' sentiments are expressed in his annual report to the secretary of war, published in the *Report of the Secretary of War, 1895–1897.*

74. Edward Ranson, "Nelson A. Miles as Commanding General," *Military Affairs,* 29, no. 4 (Winter 1965–66): 183–85.

75. Ibid., pp. 183–90. General Miles had serious reservations as to whether General Shafter, who was sixty and weighed 300 pounds, was physically able to withstand the tropical conditions in the theater of war. Hugh L. Scott, a future chief of staff but then a captain on duty in Washington and in a position to observe and understand the workings of government, wrote later that he was convinced "that the President and [Adjutant] General [Henry C.] Corbin were only playing with General Miles and did not intend to let him go [to Cuba] at all, probably on account of his political tendencies. They did not propose that he should go and come back a successful general. . . ." (Scott, *Some Memories of a Soldier* [New York: Century, 1928], p. 221).

76. Graham A. Cosmas, *An Army for Empire: The United States Army in the Spanish-American War* (Columbia: Univ. of Missouri Press, 1971), p. 146.

77. Wiener, "Three Stars and Up," September 1945, pp. 38–39; General Order no. 79, War Department, 6 Jun 1900; General Order no. 81, War Department, 11 Jun 1900.

78. Philip C. Jessup, *Elihu Root,* 2 vols. (New York: Dodd, Mead, 1938), 1:247–48.

79. Virginia Weisal Johnson, The *Unregimented General: A Biography of Nelson A. Miles* (Boston: Houghton Mifflin, 1962), pp. 354–55.

80. Ibid., p. 355.

81. Ranson, "Miles as Commanding General," pp. 196–98.

82. Johnson, *Unregimented General,* pp. 355–59; Jessup, *Elihu Root,* 1:251.

83. Jessup, Elihu Root, 1:pt. 3, covers Root's service as secretary of war. The evaluation of Root's standing in the legal profession appears in Jessup's summary sketch of Root in the *Dictionary of American*

Biography, supp. 2, s.v. "Root, Elihu."

84. *Report of the Secretary of War, 1899,* 1:44–45.

85. Ibid.

86. This and the following two paragraphs are based upon the *Report of the Secretary of War, 1902,* 1:42–49.

87. General Order no. 15, War Department, 18 Feb 1903. General Order no. 120, issued on 14 August 1903, reproduced a set of Army regulations that specified in some detail the composition, duties, and relationships between the chief of staff, General Staff Corps, War Department General Staff, and General Staff serving with troops.

88. That President Roosevelt and Secretary Root looked forward with anticipation to the departure of General Miles, and his aggravations, is evident in the series of executive actions related to the elevation of General Young. On 2 July 1903 Secretary Root sent a memorandum to the adjutant general requesting that, by direction of the president, he prepare General Young's commission to be lieutenant general as of 8 August. On the fifth of that month the acting assistant adjutant general sent a letter to General Young, stating that the secretary of war had directed that he (Young) immediately forward his letter of acceptance, which the general did the following day. But no executive action was taken until the Congress returned in the fall, when on 11 November the president forwarded the Young nomination to the Senate. Senate confirmation came on the sixteenth, and the president signed the formal commission the following day.

89. *Report of the Secretary of War, 1903,* 1:3–5.

90. Otto L. Nelson, Jr., *National Security and the General Staff* (Washington, D.C.: Infantry Journal Press, 1946), pp. 82–85.

91. For a history of the organization and administration of the Department of the Army during the era of America's rise to global power, see James E. Hewes, Jr., *From Root to McNamara: Army Organization and Administration, 1900–1963,* Special Studies (Washington, D.C.: Center of Military History, United States Army, 1975).

92. Nelson, *National Security,* pp. 138–51.

93. Weigley, *History of U.S. Army,* pp. 332–33.

94. Frederick Palmer, *Newton D. Baker: America at War,* 2 vols. (New York: Dodd, Mead, 1931), 1:143 and 2:157–58; Weigley, *History of U.S. Army,* p. 379.

95. General Order no. 80, War Department, 26 Aug 1918.

96. Peyton C. March, *The Nation at War* (Garden City, N.Y.: Doubleday, Doran, 1932), pp. 251–54 and 264–66.

97. See ibid., pp. 266–69. March attributed some of his problems in dealing with Pershing to the latter's accelerated promotion "by the impulsive Theodore Roosevelt." The "inability to function in teamwork with his legal and authorized superiors" and to work with men like Generals George W. Goethals, Leonard Wood, William L. Sibert, and Tasker H. Bliss was, according to March, a direct result of Pershing's advancement from captain to brigadier general, thereby denying him the training and experience that career progression through the grades of major, lieutenant colonel, and colonel would have given him. In the process, March believed, Pershing had lost "the very foundation of a complete knowledge of the art of war and the command of men."

98. National Defense Act of 1920, p. 10. The 1920 act represented a substantial modification of the basic National Defense Act of 1916.

99. Bulletin no. 25, War Department, 9 Jun 1920.

100. Hewes, *From Root to McNamara,* chs. 2–3. For a history of the Office of the Chief of Staff in the two decades between the World Wars, and of the nation's unreadiness and the efforts of General Marshall and his staff to prepare it, see Mark Skinner Watson, *Chief of Staff: Prewar Plans and Preparations,* United States Army in World War II (Washington, D.C.: Historical Division, Department of the Army, 1950).

101. Hewes, *From Root to McNamara,* ch. 4; Ray S. Cline, *Washington Command Post: The Operations Division,* United States Army in World War II (Washington, D.C.: Office of the Chief of Military History, Department of the Army, 1951), pp. 358–60; Circular no. 138, War Department, 14 May 1946, sub: War Department Reorganization.

102. Alice C. Cole et al., eds., *The Department of Defense: Documents on Establishment and Organization, 1947–1978* (Washington, D.C.: Office of the Secretary of Defense, 1979), ch. 1. James V. Forrestal, the first secretary of defense, negotiated the critical interservice accords on roles and missions in 1948.

103. Ibid., ch. 2.

104. Hewes, *From Root to McNamara,* pp. 208–15.

105. For the substance of their positions, see Matthew B. Ridgway, *Soldier: The Memoirs of Matthew B. Ridgway* (New York: Harper, 1956), and Maxwell D. Taylor, *The Uncertain Trumpet* (New York: Harper, 1959). Another influential senior officer, Lieutenant General James M. Gavin, chief of research and development, also left the Army in 1958 for similar convictions and purposes. His views were set out in his book, *War and Peace in the Space Age* (New York: Harper, 1958).

106. For a detailed exposition of the Army's part in the McNamara reforms, see Hewes, *From Root to McNamara,* chs. 8–10.

107. Roger Hilsman, *To Move a Nation: The Politics of Foreign Policy in the Administration of*

John F. Kennedy (Garden City N.Y.: Doubleday, 1967), p. 44. Hilsman, a graduate of West Point (June 1943) and Yale University (1950), saw service in World War II with the Office of Strategic Services and in the postwar period with the Central Intelligence Agency, Library of Congress, and North Atlantic Treaty Organization. He was director of the State Department's Bureau of Intelligence and Research and assistant secretary of state for Far Eastern affairs during the McNamara secretaryship at the Defense Department.

108. General Palmer provided continuity during the Westmoreland-Abrams interregnum, and therefore is included in the list of Army chiefs of staff.

109. The participation of the Army chiefs of staff in combat operations is described in the respective biographies found later in this work.

110. The statutory provisions relating to the appointment and duties of the chief of staff of the United States Army are set out in sec. 3034, title 10, *United States Code* (1976).

Commanding Generals
1775–1903

GEORGE WASHINGTON was born in Westmoreland County, Virginia, on 22 February 1732; was educated in the home by his father and older brother; was appointed county surveyor for Culpeper, 1749, and a district adjutant general in the Virginia militia, 1752; was detailed by Governor Dinwiddie of Virginia to carry a British ultimatum to the French on the Ohio frontier, 1753; was commissioned a lieutenant colonel and led an abortive expedition against the French at Fort Duquesne, 1754; was aide to General Edward Braddock on the ill-fated Monongahela expedition, 1755; was promoted to colonel and named commander of all Virginia forces, 1755; participated as a brigadier general in the Forbes expedition that prompted French evacuation of Fort Duquesne, and British establishment of Pittsburgh, 1758; was elected to the Virginia House of Burgesses, 1758; married Martha Dandridge Custis, 1759; was a justice of Fairfax and held court in Alexandria, Virginia, 1760–1774; served as a Virginia delegate to the First and Second Continental Congresses, 1774 and 1775; was appointed general and elected by Congress to be commander in chief of the Army of the United Colonies, June 1775; assumed command of the Army in the field at Cambridge, Massachusetts, July 1775; served as commander in chief of the Army of the United Colonies (later designated the Continental Army), 15 June 1775–23 December 1783; commanded the field forces in significant Revolutionary War actions at Boston (March 1776), Trenton (December 1776), Princeton (January 1777), Brandywine (September 1777), Germantown (October 1777), Monmouth (June 1778), and Yorktown (October 1781); delivered his farewell address to his officers at Fraunces Tavern in New York City, December 1783; tendered his resignation as commander in chief, December 1783. (For details of Washington's second tour as commanding general and his later life, see page 66.)

The Artist

Charles Willson Peale (1741–1827) was born in St. Paul's Parish, Queen Anne's County, Maryland. He turned to portrait painting when circumstances forced him to abandon his early trade of saddler, and studied under John Hesselius in America and Benjamin West in England. A militia officer in the Revolution, his miniature portraits of his fellow officers became the nucleus of the Philadelphia Museum of Art's collection, and he was later instrumental in the establishment of the Pennsylvania Academy of the Fine Arts in Philadelphia. His contemporary standing portrait of General George Washington hangs in the Senate wing of the renowned building that houses the United States Congress in Washington, D.C., and is reproduced from the United States Capitol Collection.

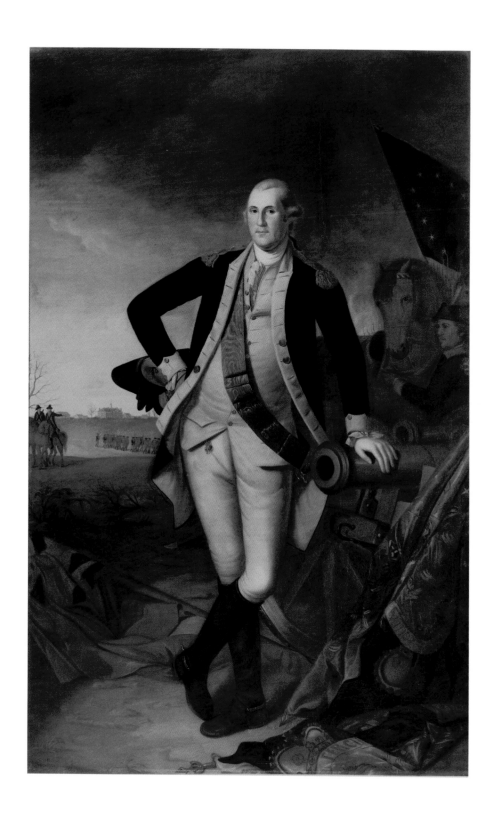

George Washington
By Charles Willson Peale
Oil on canvas, 91⅝" x 58⅜," 1779

HENRY KNOX was born in Boston, Massachusetts, on 25 July 1750; upon his father's death, left school at age twelve to work in a bookstore; joined a local military company at eighteen, was present at the Boston Massacre, 1770, and joined the Boston Grenadier Corps, 1772; married Lucy Flucker in 1774; joined the patriot cause and offered his services to General Washington, 1775; was commissioned colonel of the Continental Regiment of Artillery; led the expedition to transfer captured British guns from Fort Ticonderoga to Boston, 1776, a move that forced the British to evacuate the city; led the Delaware River crossing and participated in the battle of Trenton, 1776; was promoted to brigadier general and chief of artillery of the Continental Army, December 1776; participated in the battles of Princeton, Brandywine, and Germantown in 1777 and Monmouth in 1778; sat on the court-martial of Major John André, 1780; placed the American artillery at the Yorktown siege, 1781; commanded the West Point post, 1778–1783; organized the Society of the Cincinnati, 1783; was the senior officer of the United States Army, 23 December 1783–20 June 1784; served under the Confederation as secretary at war, 8 March 1785–11 September 1789; served under the Constitution as the first secretary of war, 12 September 1789–31 December 1794; prepared a plan for a national militia, advocated and presided over initial moves to establish a regular navy, urged and initiated the establishment of a chain of coast fortifications, and supervised Indian policy; returned to Thomaston, Maine, in 1796; engaged in lumbering, shipbuilding, stock raising, and brick manufacturing; died in Thomaston on 25 October 1806.

The Artist

Constantino Brumidi (1805–1880) was born in Rome, Italy, where he later studied art under Vincenzo Camuccini, Antonio Canova, and Bertel Thorvaldsen. He painted the portrait of Pope Pius IX and assisted in the restoration of the Raphael frescoes in the Vatican Loggia. As a captain of the Papal Guards he became involved in the political disturbances of 1848 and fled to America after a brief period of imprisonment. In Washington, D.C., to complete his naturalization, Brumidi met and was retained by Captain Montgomery C. Meigs, superintendent of the United States Capitol. The artist embarked upon a quarter of a century of work in the building, executing historical paintings, allegorical scenes, and portraits of public figures. His fresco portrait of Secretary of War Henry Knox wearing his artillery uniform adorns the President's Room of the Senate wing, and is reproduced from the United States Capitol Collection.

Henry Knox
By Constantino Brumidi
Mural medallion portrait, post-1859

JOHN DOUGHTY was born in New York City on 25 July 1754; was graduated from King's College (Columbia University) in 1770; entered military service through New Jersey state channels, January 1776; served as adjutant general of two Morris County battalions; was appointed captain-lieutenant of the Eastern Artillery Company of New Jersey, March 1776; became captain in the 2d Continental Artillery, January 1777; served as aide to Major General Philip Schuyler; was assigned to command the New York State company of artillery, March 1777; participated in the battles of Brandywine (1777), Germantown (1777), Monmouth (1778), Springfield (1780), and Yorktown (1781); was appointed brigade major of the Corps of Artillery, 1779; was appointed fort major for the West Point garrison, 1782; was transferred to the Corps of Artillery, June 1783, and promoted to brevet major in September; became the Army's ranking officer following the discharge from the Army of all but eighty men, June 1784; was the senior officer of the United States Army, 20 June–12 August 1784; superintended the construction of Fort Harmar (1785) and Fort Washington (1789) on the Ohio frontier; was designated major of the Battalion of Artillery, 1789; was dispatched by President Washington to the frontier to negotiate with the Choctaw Nation for trading post sites, 1789; repelled with serious losses an attack by Cherokee, Shawnee, and Creek Indians while leading a detachment up the Tennessee River on a negotiating mission to the Chickasaw Nation, 1790; declined a proffered appointment as lieutenant colonel of the 2d Infantry, after which he retired from the Army, March 1791; was appointed brigadier general of artillery, 2d Division, New Jersey Militia, 1793; was appointed lieutenant colonel, 2d Regiment of Artillerists and Engineers, as war with France threatened, June 1798; resigned and returned to private life on his estate at Morristown, New Jersey, to engage in agriculture and pursue literary studies, May 1800; died there on 16 September 1826.

The Artist

In 1935 Major Thomas Bennett Woodburn (1893–1980), editor and art director of *Recruiting News*, drew a sketch of Captain John Doughty for the magazine's cover for a series on the service's senior officers. Woodburn worked from a tiny engraving and brief description of Doughty in an unlocated book about the Revolution. Despite a wide search, no other likeness of Doughty has been found. Thus the Army commissioned Janet Ruth Mary Fitzgerald (1949–), a native of Lewiston, Maine, to paint a portrait after the Woodburn sketch to represent Doughty in the line of succession. Miss Fitzgerald is no stranger to the field of military art. A graduate of the Columbus (Ohio) College of Art and Design with a bachelor of fine arts, she served a five-year tour in the Army (1976–1981) as an illustrator and was awarded the Army Commendation Medal for her work. In 1979 she was selected, in Army-wide competition, to be a member of the Army Artist Team, and executed twenty works on Army engineer subjects and a dozen on women in the Army. Her portrait of Lt. Col. John Doughty is reproduced from the Army Art Collection.

John Doughty
By Janet R. M. Fitzgerald after Thomas B. Woodburn
Oil on canvas, 30" x 25," 1982

JOSIAH HARMAR was born in Philadelphia, Pennsylvania, on 10 November 1753; was educated at Robert Proud's Quaker school; was appointed a captain in the 1st Pennsylvania Battalion, October 1775; entered the Continental Army as a captain in the 3d Pennsylvania Regiment, October 1776; served as a lieutenant colonel successively in the 6th Pennsylvania (1777), 7th Pennsylvania (1780), 3d Pennsylvania (1781), and 1st Pennsylvania Regiments (1783); was brevet colonel of the 1st Pennsylvania, September–November 1783; served with General Washington's forces during the campaigns of 1778–1780, and with General Greene's division in the South, 1781–1782; carried the United States government's peace treaty ratification instruments to Paris, 1784; married Sarah Jenkins, 1784; was designated lieutenant colonel commandant of the First American Regiment, 1784; was the senior officer of the United States Army, 12 August 1784–4 March 1791; established the posts and commanded the troops on the Ohio frontier, 1784–1791; witnessed the signing of the treaty of Fort McIntosh, 1785; was brevetted brigadier general, July 1787; was present at the signing of the Wyandot and Six Nations treaties at Fort Harmar, 1789; was defeated while on a punitive expedition against the Miami Indian villages along the Maumee River, 1790; requested and was exonerated by a court of inquiry for the expedition's failure, 1791; retired from active service, 1792; served as adjutant general of Pennsylvania, 1793–1799; entered the mercantile business in Philadelphia; died in Philadelphia on 20 August 1813.

The Artist

Raphael Peale (1774–1825) was born in Annapolis, Maryland, and studied art under his celebrated father, Charles Willson Peale. By age twenty-five he had established himself as a professional painter of miniatures, working in oil and watercolor on ivory, vellum, and paper. He also painted still life subjects, several of which are in the collections of the Pennsylvania Academy of the Fine Arts in Philadelphia. His miniature of Brevet Brig. Gen. Josiah Harmar, on loan to the Department of State from the Hon. and Mrs. Robert Newbegin, is on exhibit in an inlaid Hepplewhite cabinet in the James Monroe Reception Room of the department's headquarters building in Washington, D.C. It is reproduced here through the courtesy of Ambassador and Mrs. Newbegin and the State Department's Fine Arts Committee.

Josiah Harmar
By Raphael Peale
Miniature watercolor, 3" x 2½," ca. 1790

ARTHUR ST. CLAIR was born in Thurso, Caithness County, Scotland, on 23 March 1736 (old style); attended the University of Edinburgh briefly and later studied medicine under Dr. John Hunter in London; purchased a commission as ensign in Britain's 60th Royal American Regiment and served in Canada under Generals Jeffrey Amherst and James Wolfe, 1757–1759; married Phoebe Bayard of Boston, 1760; resigned his British commission, 1762, and purchased an estate in the Ligonier Valley of Pennsylvania, 1764; commanded Fort Ligonier, 1767–1769; was appointed surveyor of the Cumberland District, 1770; was designated by Governor William Penn as agent of colonial government in his region, 1771; was a justice of Westmoreland County court; served as secretary to a congressional committee at the Treaty of Pittsburgh, 1775; was commissioned colonel in the Pennsylvania militia, 1775, and in the Continental Army, 1776, commanding the 2d Pennsylvania Battalion in abortive operations in Canada; was appointed brigadier general, 1776, and served with Washington's forces in the battles of Trenton and Princeton, 1776–1777; was promoted to major general, 1777; was assigned to command of Fort Ticonderoga in June and abandoned it in July to a British investing force; was court-martialed and exonerated of blame for failing to hold the post, 1778; was present at the battle of Yorktown and served briefly with General Nathanael Greene in the South; left military service in 1783; was a Pennsylvania delegate to the Continental Congress, 1785–1787, and president of the Congress in 1787; was governor of the Northwest Territory, 1787–1802, and administrator of Indian affairs there; was the senior officer of the United States Army, 4 March 1791–5 March 1792; led an expedition into Indian country and was disastrously defeated on the Wabash River, November 1791; resigned his commission in April 1792 and resumed the territorial governorship; was exonerated in a congressional inquiry from blame for the expedition's failure; was removed, for political reasons, as territorial governor by President Jefferson, 1802; died at his Ligonier Valley home on 31 August 1818.

The Artist

Charles Willson Peale (1741–1827) gained his initial experience in portraiture by using members of his family as subjects. As his talents expanded, he visited and developed patronage in New England, Maryland, and Virginia, as well as in London, England, finally settling in Philadelphia on the eve of active military service and the creation of his officer portrait gallery. By the close of the century he had painted many of the distinguished figures of the young nation, among them Maj. Gen. Arthur St. Clair who was completing his first military service in the Revolutionary War. The portrait is reproduced from the Independence National Historical Park Collection in Philadelphia.

Arthur St. Clair
By Charles Willson Peale
Oil on canvas, 22¼" x 19⅛," ca. 1782

ANTHONY WAYNE was born in Waynesboro, Pennsylvania, on 1 January 1745; attended his uncle Gilbert Wayne's private academy, 1761–1763; studied surveying and supervised a land settlement project in Nova Scotia, 1765; married Mary Penrose, 1766; settled on his father's estate and supervised the family tannery, assuming ownership upon his father's death, 1774; was appointed by Congress as colonel of the 4th Pennsylvania Battalion, January 1776; fought and was wounded in the attack of the British Army at Three Rivers, Quebec, June 1776; was promoted to brigadier general in the Continental Army, February 1777; commanded the Pennsylvania line under General Washington, serving with distinction at the battle of Brandywine, September 1777; requested and was cleared by a court-martial of responsibility for the defeat of his forces at the battle of Paoli; served with further distinction in the battles of Germantown (1777), Monmouth (1778), Stony Point (1779), and Yorktown (1781); was presented by Congress with a gold medal for the capture of the British garrison at Stony Point on the Hudson River; blocked the British occupation of West Point at the time of Benedict Arnold's defection, 1780; served with General Nathanael Greene in Georgia against British, Loyalist, and Indian opponents, defeating hostile Creek Indians and negotiating treaties with the Creek and Cherokee bands, 1782–1783; retired from active service as brevet major general, 1783; was a member of the Pennsylvania General Assembly, 1784–1785, and a member of the state ratifying convention on the federal Constitution, 1787; was a member of the United States Congress from Georgia, 1791–1792; was selected by President Washington to command the rehabilitated Army, 1791; was the senior officer of the United States Army, 13 April 1792–15 December 1796; defeated the northwestern Indians decisively at the Battle of Fallen Timbers, August 1794; died at Presque Isle (Erie), Pennsylvania, while en route home from frontier service, 15 December 1796.

The Artist

Peter Frederick Rothermel (1817–1895) was born in Nescopeck, Luzerne County, Pennsylvania, on 8 July 1817, supplemented his conventional schooling by studying surveying, and then opened his career as a sign painter in Philadelphia. At a friend's suggestion he studied drawing under John R. Smith, enrolled at the Pennsylvania Academy of Fine Arts in Philadelphia, and later under Bass Otis. After serving as director of the academy from 1847 to 1855, he traveled and painted in Europe, lived for two years in Rome, exhibited in Paris, and returned home in 1859. His most ambitious canvas, *The Battle of Gettysburg*, hangs in the statehouse in Harrisburg. His portrait of Brevet Maj. Gen. Anthony Wayne, completed some sixty-five years after his subject's death, may be based upon an engraving by Eugene Prud'homme. It is reproduced from the collections of the Historical Society of Pennsylvania.

Anthony Wayne
By Peter Frederick Rothermel
Oil on canvas, 30" x 25," 1861

JAMES WILKINSON was born in Calvert County, Maryland, probably in 1757; received his early education from a private tutor and later studied medicine in Philadelphia; served in Thompson's Pennsylvania rifle battalion, 1775–1776; was commissioned a captain in the Army of the United Colonies, September 1775; served in the siege of Boston and with Benedict Arnold at Montreal; was aide to General Horatio Gates in early 1776; served under General Washington in the battles of Trenton and Princeton, 1776–1777; was brevet brigadier general in the Continental Army, November 1777–March 1778, and concurrently secretary to the Board of War, January–March 1778; was forced by General Washington to resign both offices because of his part in the Conway cabal against the commander in chief; was clothier general of the Army, July 1779–March 1781, resigning as a result of irregularities in his accounts; married Ann Biddle, circa 1782; became brigadier general of Pennsylvania militia, 1782, and state assemblyman, 1783; moved to Kentucky, established trade relationships with the Spanish in New Orleans, and engaged in various intrigues; was a member of the Kentucky Convention of 1788 and advocated separation from Virginia; led a force of Kentucky volunteers against Indians north of the Ohio River, March 1791; returned to federal military service as lieutenant colonel commandant of the 2d Infantry, October 1791; was promoted to brigadier general and served on the frontier under General Anthony Wayne, commanding the right wing in the Battle of Fallen Timbers, August 1794; was the senior officer of the United States Army, 15 December 1796–13 July 1798. (For details of Wilkinson's second tour as commanding general and his later life, see page 70.)

The Artist

Charles Willson Peale (1741–1827) was only twenty-three when the agitation associated with the Stamp Act prompted him to join the Sons of Freedom. Although this lost him the support of the Loyalists who were backing him in his trade as saddler, forcing him to abandon that occupation, it proved to be a providential development, for it turned him to the field of art. His portrait of Brig. Gen. James Wilkinson reposes in the Independence National Historical Park Collection in Philadelphia, part of an invaluable element by this one artist that embraces contemporary portraits of Presidents George Washington, John Adams, and Thomas Jefferson; Revolutionary soldiers Horatio Gates, Henry Knox, Henry Dearborn, and Nathanael Greene; foreign comrades-in-arms Marquis de Marie Lafayette, Baron Johann de Kalb, Comte Jean de Rochambeau, and Friedrich Wilhelm von Steuben; and explorers Meriwether Lewis, William Clark, Zebulon Pike, and Stephen Long.

James Wilkinson
By Charles Willson Peale
Oil on canvas, 23½" x 19¼," 1797

GEORGE WASHINGTON resumed the life of a gentleman farmer at his Mount Vernon estate in Virginia following his resignation as commander in chief of the Army, December 1783; made an exploratory trip to the western frontier, 1784; served as president of the Constitutional Convention, 1787; served as the first president of the United States, 1789–1797; returned to private life at Mount Vernon, 1797; was appointed by President John Adams to be lieutenant general and commander in chief of all armies raised or to be raised for service in a prospective war with France, 1798; was the senior officer of the United States Army, 13 July 1798–14 December 1799; participated in the planning for a Provisional Army to meet any emergency that might arise, but did not take the field; died at his Mount Vernon home on 14 December 1799; was appointed posthumously to the grade of General of the Armies of the United States by congressional joint resolution of 19 January 1976, approved by President Gerald R. Ford on 11 October 1976, and formalized in Department of the Army Order Number 31–3 of 13 March 1978 with an effective appointment date of 4 July 1776. (For details of General Washington's early life, see page 52.)

The Artist

James Peale (1749–1831) was born in Chestertown, Maryland, and learned the techniques of painting from his brother, Charles Willson Peale. After Revolutionary War service with Maryland units he moved to Philadelphia. He became adept at painting miniatures on ivory, and George and Martha Washington were among his prominent subjects. Peale painted landscape detail as a background in many of his portraits. In executing this half-length figure with sword, he copied Washington's head from his brother Charles' life portrait of the general. His portrait of Commanding General George Washington is reproduced from the Independence National Historical Park Collection in Philadelphia.

George Washington
By James Peale after Charles Willson Peale
Oil on canvas, 36½" x 27¾," ca. 1787–1790

ALEXANDER HAMILTON was born on the island of Nevis in the British West Indies on 11 January 1757; received some preliminary education from his mother, from a clergyman, and at Francis Barber's grammar school in New Jersey; attended King's College (Columbia University) in New York, 1773–1776, and wrote articles and pamphlets espousing the colonists' cause; was appointed a captain in the Army of the United Colonies, March 1776; was secretary and aide-de-camp to General Washington with the rank of lieutenant colonel, 1777–1781; served with the commander in chief in the operations at Long Island, Harlem Heights, White Plains, Trenton, and Princeton, and commanded a regiment under Lafayette at Yorktown, 1776–1781; married Elizabeth Schuyler, 1780; was admitted to the New York bar and entered the practice of law; was a New York delegate to the Continental Congress, 1782–1783, to the Annapolis Convention, 1786, to the New York legislature, 1787, and to the Constitutional Convention at Philadelphia, 1787; was a signer of the Constitution, 1787, and coauthor with James Madison and John Jay of *The Federalist Papers*, 1787–1788; again sat in the Continental Congress, 1788; was secretary of the Treasury, 1789–1795; established the Bank of the United States and the United States Mint; placed his influence behind Thomas Jefferson to help break a tie with Aaron Burr for the presidency; was appointed major general and inspector general of the United States Army in anticipation of war with France, July 1798, and served as second in command to George Washington, 1798–1799; was the senior officer of the United States Army, 14 December 1799–15 June 1800; supervised the preparation of new drill regulations and discharged the unneeded Provisional Army; practiced law in New York City, 1795–1804; was a founder of the *New York Evening Post* and the Bank of New York; helped block Aaron Burr from the New York governorship; was mortally wounded in a duel with Burr at Weehawken Heights, New Jersey, 11 July 1804; died of his wound in New York City on 12 July 1804.

The Artist

P. T. Weaver is a shadowy figure who receives only incidental, incomplete, and conflicting mention in art reference works. Identified as being either English or Irish and as having the other first names of John, Joseph, William J., and William I., Weaver appears to have worked in New York City; in Salem, Massachusetts; in Halifax, Nova Scotia; and in Charleston, South Carolina. His portrait of Brig. Gen. Alexander Hamilton, which attracted attention as a faithful likeness, is the connecting link along the artist's shifting trail. It is reproduced from the collections of the Museum of the City of New York.

Alexander Hamilton
By P. T. Weaver
Oil on wood panel, 9" x 7," ca. 1799

JAMES WILKINSON was transferred to the southern frontier in 1798 and was designated to treat with the regional Indian tribes; was again the senior officer of the United States Army, 15 June 1800–27 January 1812; with Governor William C. C. Claiborne, shared the honor of taking possession of the Louisiana Purchase on behalf of the United States, 1803; was appointed governor of Louisiana Territory, 1805; was the subject of a congressional inquiry prompted by his continuing private ventures and intrigues, and was cleared by a court-martial ordered by President Madison in 1811; married his second wife, Celestine Laveau, 1810; was commissioned a major general in the War of 1812 and assigned to the St. Lawrence River sector, 1813; was relieved from active service but cleared by a military inquiry for the failure of the Montreal campaign; published his memoirs, 1816; visited Mexico in pursuit of a Texas land grant, 1821; died in Mexico City on 28 December 1825. (For details of General Wilkinson's early life, see page 64.)

The Artist

John Wesley Jarvis (1780–1840), painter, engraver, and sculptor, was born at South Shields near Newcastle-on-Tyne, England. His parents immigrated to the United States and settled in Philadelphia, and as he came of age he was apprenticed to Edward Savage, an engraver, and learned drawing and painting from his more advanced coworkers in Savage's shop. He began painting portraits while in his early twenties and established a studio in New York City, where Henry Inman and John Quidor studied and Thomas Sully was his assistant for a brief period. By the time paralysis struck him in 1834, Jarvis had become one of the leading portrait painters of the day. This Jarvis-attributed portrait of Maj. Gen. James Wilkinson hangs in The Filson Club in Louisville, Kentucky.

James Wilkinson
Attributed to John Wesley Jarvis
Oil on canvas, 29¼" x 24¼," date unknown

HENRY DEARBORN was born in Hampton, New Hampshire, on 23 February 1751; studied medicine under Dr. Hall Jackson at Portsmouth; married Mary Bartlett, 1771; entered practice as a physician in 1772; was elected captain of a military company; participated in the battle of Bunker (Breed's) Hill, served under Benedict Arnold in the Quebec expedition and was captured, 1775; was paroled in 1776 and exchanged in 1777; was appointed major of the 3d New Hampshire Regiment; participated in operations at Ticonderoga and Freeman's Farm with the 1st New Hampshire Regiment, 1777; spent the winter of 1777–1778 at Valley Forge; took part in the battle of Monmouth, 1778; was engaged in the operations against the Six Nations, 1779; married his second wife, Dorcas Marble, 1780; joined Washington's staff as deputy quartermaster general; commanded the 1st New Hampshire at the battle of Yorktown, 1781; returned to private life in Maine, 1783; was appointed brigadier, then major general of militia; was appointed United States marshal for the District of Maine (part of Massachusetts until 1820), 1790; served in the United States House of Representatives for the same congressional district, 1793–1797; served as secretary of war, 5 March 1801–7 March 1809; helped plan the removal of the Indians beyond the Mississippi; was appointed collector of the port of Boston, 1809; was the senior officer of the United States Army, 27 January 1812–15 June 1815; was ineffective in command of the northeastern theater in the War of 1812; captured York (Toronto) and Fort George, 1813; was transferred to command in New York City, 1813, and married his third wife, Sarah Bowdoin; was nominated and withdrawn for the post of secretary of war, 1815; served as minister to Portugal, 1822–1824; died at Roxbury, Massachusetts, on 6 June 1829.

The Artist

Walter M. Brackett (1823–1919), the younger brother of sculptor Edward A. Brackett, was born in Unity, Maine. He spent most of his professional career in Boston, Massachusetts, exhibiting his work at the Boston Athenaeum, the Apollo Association, and the National Academy of Design. He was one of the artists engaged by Secretary of War William W. Belknap in the early 1870s to execute portraits of the line of succession of the secretaries, and he painted the portraits of Timothy Pickering, Samuel Dexter, William Eustis, and Henry Dearborn, all prominent residents of his native state. His portrait of Maj. Gen. Henry Dearborn serves the dual purpose of representing an Army official who was both the senior officer and senior civilian, and is reproduced from the Army Art Collection.

Henry Dearborn
By Walter M. Brackett
Oil on canvas, 29½" x 24½," 1873

JACOB JENNINGS BROWN was born in Bucks County, Pennsylvania, on 9 May 1775; was raised by Quaker parents on the family farm; was reported by one anonymous biographer to have "pursued learning with zeal and perseverance and acquired it with facility"; supervised a school at Crosswicks, New Jersey, 1793–1796; engaged in surveying on the Ohio frontier, 1796–1798; taught briefly in New York City; was briefly military secretary to Major General Alexander Hamilton; purchased wilderness shorelands on Lake Ontario in northern New York, 1799; founded the village of Brownville and became a successful farmer; married Pamelia Williams, 1802; was elected to the state legislature and served also as a county judge; was appointed colonel of militia, 1809, brigadier general, 1811, and major general, 1812; was appointed major general of New York Volunteers and assigned to command the Oswego–Lake St. Francis sector; participated in an action at Ogdensburg, New York, 1812, and repulsed the British at Sackett's Harbor, 1813; was appointed brigadier general in the Regular Army, July 1813; participated in the abortive Wilkinson expedition against Montreal but emerged with his reputation unimpaired; was appointed major general and assigned to command of the Niagara frontier, January 1814; defeated the British in the battles of Chippewa and Lundy's Lane, suffering severe wounds in the latter action, July 1814; received the thanks of Congress for his battlefield achievements and was presented by that body with a gold medal, November 1814; was the senior officer of the United States Army, 15 June 1815–24 February 1828; by act of Congress, assumed the formal title of commanding general of the Army, June 1821; recommended pay incentives to encourage reenlistments, pay increases for noncommissioned officers, and periodic centralized unit training to avert deterioration in widely scattered and fragmented elements; died while in office at Washington, D.C., on 24 February 1828.

The Artist

John Wesley Jarvis (1780–1840) spent the first five years of his life in his native England in the care of a maternal relative, John Wesley, the founder of Methodism, after whom he was named. His parents immigrated to United States, where he later completed an apprenticeship with Edward Savage in Philadelphia and New York City. His interests turned to engraving and then portrait painting, first opening a studio with Joseph Wood and later operating one independently. At the height of his career he made regular winter trips to the South to paint clients in Baltimore, Washington, D.C., Richmond, Charleston, and New Orleans. His full-length portraits of military figures of the War of 1812 hang in New York's City Hall. His portrait of Maj. Gen. Jacob J. Brown is reproduced from the collections of the Corcoran Gallery of Art in Washington, D.C.

Jacob Jennings Brown
By John Wesley Jarvis
Oil on canvas, 42½" x 35," ca. 1815

ALEXANDER MACOMB was born in British-held Detroit on 3 April 1782; moved with his parents to New York City and received a classical education at a Newark (New Jersey) academy; enrolled at age sixteen in a New York militia company; at Alexander Hamilton's recommendation during the emergency with France, was commissioned a cornet in the Regular Army, January 1799, and promoted to second lieutenant in March; was honorably discharged, June 1800; was commissioned a second lieutenant, 2d Infantry, February 1801, and served as secretary to a commission that treated with the Indians of the Southeast; was commissioned a first lieutenant in the Corps of Engineers, established in 1802 at West Point to constitute a military academy, and was thus one of the first officers to receive formal training there; married a cousin, Catharine Macomb, 1803; was promoted to captain, June 1805, major, February 1808, and lieutenant colonel, July 1810, in the Corps of Engineers; was chief engineer in charge of coastal fortifications in the Carolinas and Georgia, 1807–1812; was acting adjutant general of the Army, April–July 1812; was appointed colonel, 3d Artillery, July 1812, and transferred to the field; commanded American troops at Sackett's Harbor and participated in the capture of Fort George and in General James Wilkinson's St. Lawrence campaign, 1813; was promoted to brigadier general, January 1814, and assigned to the Lake Champlain area; repulsed a superior British force at Plattsburg, New York, September 1814, for which he received a brevet major generalcy; as a token of thanks, was awarded a gold medal by Congress, November 1814; was a member of a board on Army reorganization, then commanded the Third Military District at New York and the Fifth at Detroit; became chief of engineers with the rank of colonel, June 1821; married his second wife, Harriet Balch Wilson, 1826; was promoted to major general, May 1828; was commanding general of the United States Army, 29 May 1828–25 June 1841; espoused the position that the commanding general should have active command of the whole Army including the staff bureaus, under the loose supervision of the secretary of war; recommended a doubling of Army strength to hold the Indians in check, increases in enlisted pay to discourage desertion, augmentation of officers in the service branches to free line officers for field duty, relief for widows and orphans of Regular Army officer victims of wounds and disease, and a system of officer retirement and replacement; died while in office at Washington, D.C., on 25 June 1841.

The Artist

Thomas Sully (1783–1872) was born in England and came to America with his family when he was ten. He received his early art instruction from an older brother and a brother-in-law, both of artistic talent, and after a formative period in Richmond and Norfolk, Virginia, he moved to New York City to enter the mainstream of his career as a portraitist. He met and received valuable guidance from Gilbert Stuart in Boston and Benjamin West in London, and his introduction to Sir Thomas Lawrence opened the way to commissions for portraits of a number of important people. He established his home base in Philadelphia, where he painted the Marquis de Lafayette among others, and reached the pinnacle of his career on a second trip to England to paint Queen Victoria. His portrait of Maj. Gen. Alexander Macomb is reproduced from the collections of the West Point Museum, United States Military Academy.

Alexander Macomb
By Thomas Sully
Oil on canvas, 30" x 25," 1829

WINFIELD SCOTT was born on the family estate near Petersburg, Virginia, on 13 June 1786; attended William and Mary College briefly and studied law in the office of David Robinson; enlisted in Petersburg's cavalry troop, 1807, and became a captain in the regular service, May 1808; received a one-year suspension for open criticism of General James Wilkinson, 1810; served in New Orleans on General Wade Hampton's staff, 1811–1812; was promoted to lieutenant colonel, July 1812, and colonel, March 1813; served on the Niagara front in the War of 1812, was captured and paroled, then participated in actions at Fort George, where he was wounded, and at Uphold's Creek; was promoted to brigadier general, March 1814; as a brigade commander, was largely instrumental in American successes in the battles of Chippewa and Lundy's Lane (where he was seriously wounded); for his valor, was brevetted major general, July 1814; supervised the preparation of the Army's first standard drill regulations and headed a postwar officer retention selection board, 1815; visited Europe to study French military methods, 1815–1816; held regional command in the Division of the North, 1816; married Maria D. Mayo, 1817; was president of the Board of Tactics, 1815, 1821, 1824, and 1826; commanded the Eastern Department, 1825; his resignation at being passed over for Army command refused, 1828; again visited Europe, then resumed command of the Eastern Department, 1829; his field command of the Black Hawk War forces forestalled by cholera among his reinforcing troops, 1832; was an effective presidential emissary to South Carolina during nullification troubles; commanded the field forces in the Second Seminole and Creek Wars, 1836; was cleared by a court of inquiry on his handling of both operations; assumed command of the Eastern Division, 1837; was dispatched to maintain order on the Canadian border, where American patriots were aiding Canadian rebels seeking an end to British rule; supervised removal of the Cherokees to the trans-Mississippi region, 1838; negotiated a peaceful resolution to the boundary dispute between Maine and New Brunswick, 1839; was promoted to major general, June 1841; was commanding general of the United States Army, 5 July 1841–1 November 1861; led American forces in the decisive campaign of the Mexican War from the Vera Cruz landings to the capture of Mexico City, 1847; was the unsuccessful Whig candidate for president, 1852; received the brevet of lieutenant general by special act of Congress, 1855, retroactive to the date of Vera Cruz; settled the Anglo-American dispute over San Juan Island in Puget Sound, 1859; retired from active service, November 1861; died in West Point, New York, on 29 May 1866.

The Artist

Giuseppina Vannutelli (1874–1948), portrait and genre painter, was born in Rome, Italy, where she studied art under the tutelage of her accomplished father, Scipione Vannutelli (1834–1894). In 1897 she won an award in a competition of original works launched by the Académie St. Luc, and in 1900 she entered a major work, *Mater Purissima*, in the Espositzione Alinari. Her portrait of Brevet Lt. Gen. Winfield Scott, which bears her signature and the inscription *Roma*, is reproduced from the Army Art Collection.

Winfield Scott
By Giuseppina Vannutelli
Oil on canvas, 25¼" x 20¼," date unknown

GEORGE BRINTON MCCLELLAN was born in Philadelphia, Pennsylvania, on 3 December 1826; attended preparatory schools and left the University of Pennsylvania to accept an appointment to the United States Military Academy, graduating in 1846; served with distinction as an engineer officer under Generals Zachary Taylor and Winfield Scott in the Mexican War, 1847, receiving brevets to first lieutenant in August and captain in September; was assistant instructor in practical military engineering at West Point, 1848–1851; was assistant engineer for the construction of Fort Delaware; participated in the Marcy expedition to explore the sources of the Red River, Texas, 1852; was chief engineer of the Department of Texas, 1852; conducted a survey for the projected Northern Pacific Railroad over the Cascade Mountains; was promoted to captain, March 1855, and assigned to the new 1st Cavalry Regiment; visited Europe to study foreign military systems and observe Crimean War operations, 1855–1856; designed and secured adoption of the McClellan saddle; resigned from the Army to become chief engineer (1857–1858) and vice president (1858–1860) of the Illinois Central Railroad; married Mary Ellen Marcy, 1860; was president of the Ohio and Mississippi Railroad, 1860–1861; was appointed major general of Ohio Volunteers, April 1861; was appointed major general in the Regular Army and commander of the Department of the Ohio, May 1861; cleared Confederate troops from western Virginia; successively commanded the Division, Department, and Army of the Potomac, July–November 1861; was commanding general of the Army, 1 November 1861–11 March 1862; was relieved of overall command to lead the Army of the Potomac in the Peninsular Campaign, including the siege of Yorktown, the battle of Fair Oaks, and the Seven Days' Battles, 1862; commanded the Washington defenses, September 1862; commanded the Army of the Potomac in the Maryland operations at South Mountain and Antietam and was placed on inactive status by President Lincoln for his failure to pursue Lee after Antietam, 1862–1864; resigned his commission to run unsuccessfully against Lincoln for the Presidency, 1864; spent three years in Europe; declined the presidency of two colleges and appointment as comptroller of New York City; was chief engineer of New York City's Department of Docks, 1870–1872; was governor of New Jersey, 1878–1881; was on the Board of Governors of the National Home for Disabled Soldiers, 1881–1885; died in Orange, New Jersey, on 29 October 1885.

The Artist

Alexander Lawrie (1828–1917) was born in New York City, New York. He pursued his art training at the National Academy of Design in New York City and then went abroad to study under Emanuel Leutze in Düsseldorf, Francois Picot in Paris, and Greek and Italian painters in Florence. He later opened a studio in Philadelphia to exhibit his portraits, landscapes, and genre subjects; served in Pennsylvania volunteer units in the Civil War; and then returned to New York, participating annually in the National Academy's exhibitions. His portrait of Maj. Gen. George B. McClellan was probably painted in this highly productive period of his career. It is reproduced from the collections of the West Point Museum, United States Military Academy.

George Brinton McClellan
By Alexander Lawrie
Oil on canvas, 34" x 32," date unknown

HENRY WAGER HALLECK was born in Westernville, Oneida County, New York, on 16 January 1815; was educated at Hudson Academy, received the bachelor of arts degree from Union College, and graduated from the United States Military Academy in 1839; was commissioned in engineers and assigned to work on New York harbor fortifications; visited Europe and wrote a report on French fortifications that was published by the Congress as an official document, 1844; delivered a series of twelve lectures before the Lowell Institute of Boston, published in 1846 under the title *Elements of Military Art and Science*; while en route by sea to Mexican War service in California, translated Henri Jomini's *Vie politique et militaire de Napoléon*, 1846; participated in military operations in Mexico and Lower California and held staff positions, including that of secretary of state of California, in the military government under Generals Richard B. Mason and Bennet Riley, 1847–1849; was brevetted captain for gallant conduct and meritorious service, May 1847; was aide to General Riley, 1850, and a member of an engineer board for Pacific Coast fortifications, 1853–1854; resigned from the Army to pursue private interests, August 1854; married Elizabeth Hamilton, 1855; entered the practice of law as head of the firm of Halleck, Peachy and Billings, 1853–1854; was president of the Pacific and Atlantic Railroad, 1855, and director of the New Almaden Quicksilver Mine, 1853–1861; was major general of California militia, 1860–1861; published treatises on mining and international law; was reappointed major general in the Regular Army, August 1861; commanded the Department of the Missouri, 1861–1862, and the Department of the Mississippi, 1862; commanded the Union forces in the Corinth operations; was commanding general of the United States Army, 23 July 1862–9 March 1864; was an influential champion of discipline; published his Jomini translation in four volumes; was reassigned as chief of staff of the Army, 12 March 1864–19 April 1865; commanded the Division of the James, April–July 1865; commanded the Division of the Pacific, 1865–1869; commanded the Division of the South, 1869–1872; died at his headquarters in Louisville, Kentucky, on 9 January 1872.

The Artist

Jacob H. Lazarus (1822–1891) was born in New York City, New York. He later studied portraiture under Henry Inman and, after establishing his own studio, painted a number of eminent figures of his time. His portrait of Inman was presented to the Metropolitan Museum of Art, where his widow and daughter sponsored and supported a scholarship bearing his name and awarded annually to the most proficient male pupil in the painting class at the museum's art school. An associate member of the National Academy of Design, Lazarus also painted miniature portraits and was represented in this medium in the academy's centennial exhibition in 1925. His portrait of Maj. Gen. Henry W. Halleck is reproduced from the collections of the West Point Museum, United States Military Academy.

Henry Wager Halleck
By Jacob H. Lazarus
Oil on canvas, 34¾" x 28⅞," date unknown

ULYSSES SIMPSON GRANT was born at Point Pleasant, Ohio, on 27 April 1822; was educated at local schools; attended the United States Military Academy, 1839–1843, and was commissioned in infantry; served with the 4th Infantry on the frontier and in the occupation of Texas, 1843–1846; served under Generals Zachary Taylor and Winfield Scott in the Mexican War and was brevetted first lieutenant and captain for gallant conduct at Molino del Rey and Chapultepec, 1846–1848; married Julia Dent, 1848; was promoted to first lieutenant, September 1847, and served as quartermaster, 4th Infantry at various posts; was promoted to captain while on frontier duty in the Northwest, August 1853; resigned from the Army, July 1854; was generally unsuccessful at farming, real estate, and clerical activities, 1854–1861; was appointed colonel of the 21st Illinois Volunteer Infantry, June 1861, then brigadier general of volunteers, August 1861; commanded the field forces in the battles of Forts Henry and Donelson and at Shiloh, 1862; was promoted to major general of volunteers, February 1862; commanded the District of West Tennessee and then the Department of Tennessee, 1862–1863; defeated the Confederate forces at Vicksburg, July 1863, to bring the Mississippi River under Union control; was appointed major general in the Regular Army, July 1863; received the thanks of Congress and a gold medal, December 1863; commanded the Division of the Mississippi, 1863–1864, and defeated the Confederates at Chattanooga in November 1863; was promoted to lieutenant general, March 1864; was commanding general of the United States Army, 9 March 1864–4 March 1869; commanded the Union armies in the final battles in Virginia, 1864–1865; received the unconditional surrender of General Lee at Appomattox Court House, April 1865; presided over the Army's participation in Reconstruction, railroad construction, and Indian affairs; was promoted to general, July 1866; was secretary of war ad interim, 12 August 1867–13 January 1868; was the Republican candidate for president, 1868; was president of the United States, 4 March 1869–3 March 1877; toured Europe with his family, 1877–1879, then engaged in several unsuccessful business ventures; was reappointed general and placed on the retired list, March 1885; died in Mount McGregor, New York, on 23 July 1885.

The Artist

Daniel Huntington (1816–1906) was born in New York City, New York. He developed an interest in art while attending Hamilton College at Utica, where the young portraitist Charles Loring Elliott encouraged Huntington's artistic bent. He went on to study under Samuel F. B. Morse and Henry Inman in New York City and then pursued his studies in Europe, notably in Rome, in the late 1830s and into the 1840s, finally achieving a reputation as a leading portrait, historical, and landscape painter. He was elected a national academician and was twice president of the National Academy of Design. He received commissions from the Army to paint the portraits of a number of departmental secretaries and chiefs of staff. His portrait of General Ulysses S. Grant is reproduced from the Army Art Collection.

Ulysses Simpson Grant
By Daniel Huntington
Oil on canvas, 30¼" x 25¼," 1875

WILLIAM TECUMSEH SHERMAN was born at Lancaster, Ohio, on 8 February 1820; upon his father's death, was adopted into the family of Thomas Ewing, 1829; was educated in a local academy, then attended the United States Military Academy, 1836–1840; was commissioned a second lieutenant, July 1840, and posted to the 3d Cavalry in Florida; was promoted to first lieutenant, November 1841, and served at various southern stations; served in California during the Mexican War as adjutant and aide to Generals Stephen W. Kearny, Persifor F. Smith, and Richard B. Mason, 1847–1850; married Ellen Ewing, 1850; was appointed captain, September 1850, and assigned to commissary duty in St. Louis and New Orleans, 1850–1853; resigned his commission, September 1853; engaged unsuccessfully in banking and law, 1853–1859; was superintendent of a military college at Alexandria, Louisiana, 1859–1861; was reappointed in the Regular Army as colonel, 13th Infantry, May 1861; was appointed brigadier general of volunteers, May 1861, and commanded a brigade at Bull Run in July; served in Missouri and Kentucky and commanded the Department of the Cumberland and the District of Paducah, 1861–1862; was appointed major general of volunteers, May 1862; commanded a division in the Tennessee-Mississippi campaigns and was wounded at Shiloh, April 1862; commanded the District of Memphis and the Vicksburg expedition, 1862; commanded the XV Corps in the Vicksburg operations to its surrender and was appointed brigadier general in the Regular Army, July 1863; commanded the Army of the Tennessee in the Chattanooga-Knoxville operations, 1863–1864; commanded the Division of the Mississippi, 1864–1865, leading Union forces in the invasion of Georgia; was promoted to major general, August 1864; commanded the Armies of the Ohio, Tennessee, and Georgia in the final operations in the South, receiving the surrender of Confederate forces there, April 1865; was promoted to lieutenant general while in command of the Division of the Mississippi, July 1866; was on a special mission to Mexico, November–December 1866; commanded the Division of the Missouri, 1866–1869; was promoted to general, March 1869; was commanding general of the United States Army, 8 March 1869–1 November 1883; was acting secretary of war, 6 September–25 October 1869; sought to establish senior officer control over bureau heads, pressed for Army control over Indian affairs, urged consolidation of troops at strategic locations, and established a school for infantry and cavalry; retired from active service, February 1884; died in New York City on 14 February 1891.

The Artist

Daniel Huntington (1816–1906) painted the portraits of presidents and generals, writers and artists, Astors and Vanderbilts during seventy productive years as a working artist. About a thousand of his twelve hundred known works are portraits; of these, fifteen are of secretaries of war and two of secretaries ad interim who also were incumbent commanding generals—Ulysses S. Grant and William T. Sherman. Army records indicate that Huntington painted Grant and Sherman from life at a fee of $300 per portrait. His portrait of General William T. Sherman came into Army holdings in 1875, and is reproduced from the Army Art Collection.

William Tecumseh Sherman
By Daniel Huntington
Oil on canvas, 29½" x 24½," 1875

PHILIP HENRY SHERIDAN was born in Albany, New York, on 6 March 1831; received a rudimentary education in a village school when his family moved to Somerset, Ohio; graduated from the United States Military Academy, July 1853; served as a brevet second lieutenant, 1st Infantry, on the Texas frontier and as a second lieutenant, 4th Infantry, on the northwestern frontier, 1854–1861; was promoted to first lieutenant, March 1861, then captain, 13th Infantry, May 1861; was quartermaster of the Army of Southwest Missouri and General Henry W. Halleck's headquarters, 1861–1862; was appointed colonel, 2d Michigan Volunteer Cavalry, and commanded a brigade in Mississippi operations, May–July 1862; for his performance in the battle of Boonville, was promoted to brigadier general of volunteers; commanded a division in operations in Kentucky and Tennessee, including the battles of Perryville and Stones River, 1862; was promoted to major general of volunteers, December 1862; commanded a division in the battles of Chickamauga and Chattanooga, 1863; commanded the Army of the Potomac's Cavalry Corps in the battles of the Wilderness, Todd's Tavern, Yellow Tavern, and Trevilian Station, 1864; commanded the Army of the Shenandoah and the Middle Military Division, 1864–1865; was promoted to brigadier general (September) and major general (November) in the Regular Army, 1864; was cavalry field commander in final Civil War operations in Virginia, including Five Forks and Appomattox Station; commanded the Divisions of the Southwest and of the Gulf, 1865, the Department of the Gulf, 1866–1867, and the Fifth Military District, 1867, with Reconstruction responsibilities; commanded the Department of the Missouri, 1867–1869, and conducted successful winter operations against Central Plains tribes; was promoted to lieutenant general, March 1869; commanded the Division of the Missouri, 1869–1883, with military responsibility for the heart of the trans-Mississippi West; visited the German armies in the field, 1870–1871; married Irene Rucker, 1875; was commanding general of the United States Army, 1 November 1883–5 August 1888; urged congressional action to support the National Guard, pointed to the defenseless condition of the coasts to seaborne attack, made recommendations for a solution to the Indian problem, and sought a resolution of the problem of senior officer authority; was promoted to general, June 1888; died in Nonquitt, Massachusetts, on 5 August 1888.

The Artist

William F. Cogswell (1819–1903) was born in Sandusky, New York, and worked in a color factory in Buffalo before moving to New York City to take up a career as a professional artist and see his work exhibited at the National Academy of Design and the American Art Union. In 1849, the year of the gold rush, he explored California and then returned to New York to continue his career. His work includes the portraits of Abraham Lincoln and Ulysses S. Grant, which hang respectively in the Smithsonian's National Museum of American Art and in the Senate wing of the United States Capitol. His portrait of Commanding General Philip H. Sheridan, given by the latter as a gift to his valued aide and friend, Colonel Schuyler Crosby, and initially hung in the Readiness Region 3 headquarters at Fort George G. Meade, Maryland, is reproduced from the Army Art Collection.

Philip Henry Sheridan
By William F. Cogswell
Oil on canvas, 44⅜" x 32½," date unknown

JOHN MCALLISTER SCHOFIELD was born in Gerry, New York, on 29 September 1831; was educated in the public schools, then graduated from the United States Military Academy, 1853; was commissioned in artillery and served in the South, 1854–1855; was promoted to second lieutenant, August 1853, and first lieutenant, August 1855; was assistant professor of natural and experimental philosophy at West Point, 1855–1860; married Harriet Bartlett, 1857; taught physics at Washington University of St. Louis, 1860–1861; was mustering officer for Missouri as the Civil War opened; was major, 1st Missouri Volunteer Infantry, and captain, 1st Artillery, in Missouri operations; was appointed brigadier general of volunteers and Missouri militia, November 1861, and major general of volunteers, November 1862; successively commanded the Missouri militia, 1861–1862, the Army of the Frontier, 1862–1863, the 3d Division of XIV Corps, 1863, the Department of the Missouri, 1863–1864, and the Department of the Ohio, 1864–1865; commanded the Army of the Ohio in the invasion of Georgia, including the battles of Kenesaw Mountain and Atlanta, 1864; commanded the XXIII Corps in Alabama-Tennessee operations, including the battles of Franklin and Nashville, 1864; was appointed brigadier general in the Regular Army, November 1864; commanded the Department of North Carolina, 1865; was brevetted major general, March 1865; served as a confidential diplomatic emissary to France concerning withdrawal of French troops from Mexico, 1865–1866; commanded the Department of the Potomac, 1867; served as secretary of war, 1 June 1868–13 March 1869; was appointed major general, March 1869; commanded the Department of the Missouri, 1869–1870; commanded the Division of the Pacific, 1870–1876; served on a special mission to the Hawaiian Islands to assess their military value, 1872–1873; was superintendent of the United States Military Academy, 1876–1881; successively commanded the Divisions of the Pacific (1882–1883), the Missouri (1883–1886), and the Atlantic (1886–1888); married his second wife, Georgia Kilbourne, 1891; was commanding general of the United States Army, 14 August 1888–29 September 1895; was instrumental in clarifying lines of authority and achieving harmony between staff and line, espoused increases in pay for noncommissioned officers, advanced a plan to reduce desertions, initiated efficiency reports on officers, and recommended that incompetent officers be denied promotion; was promoted to lieutenant general, February 1895; retired from active service, September 1895; died in St. Augustine, Florida, on 4 March 1906.

The Artist

Stephen William Shaw (1817–1900) was born in Windsor, Vermont. At thirty-one he journeyed to California by way of New Orleans and Panama to settle in San Francisco, where he pursued a career as a portrait painter. He became the official artist to the Masonic order there, painting a large number of Masons and other Western notables. He also participated in the expedition that discovered Humboldt (now Kayo) Bay in New Guinea. He painted Maj. Gen. John McA. Schofield from life in 1874. The Schofield portrait, commissioned as one of the series on departmental secretaries, is reproduced from the Army Art Collection.

John McAllister Schofield
By Stephen William Shaw
Oil on canvas, 30" x 25," 1874

NELSON APPLETON MILES was born on the family farm near Westminster, Massachusetts, on 8 August 1839; attended local schools and received rudimentary military instruction from a former French officer; recruited a company of volunteers and received a commission as captain, September 1861; served on General Oliver O. Howard's staff and was wounded at the battle of Fair Oaks; was promoted to lieutenant colonel, 61st New York Volunteer Infantry, for gallantry in action, May 1862; replaced his seriously wounded commander at the battle of Antietam and was promoted to colonel, September 1862; was again wounded in the battle of Fredericksburg, 1862; was again wounded at the battle of Chancellorsville, 1863, where his gallant conduct later was recognized with the brevet of brigadier general (1867) and the Medal of Honor (1892); received the thanks of Congress for his conduct in the battles of the Wilderness and Spotsylvania, suffered slight wounds at the battle of Petersburg, and was appointed brigadier general of volunteers, May 1864; received his promotion to major general of volunteers, October 1865; commanded the District of Fort Monroe with supervision over Confederate President Jefferson Davis confined there; was appointed colonel in the regular establishment, July 1866; commanded the District of North Carolina during Reconstruction, 1866–1867; married General Sherman's niece, Mary Hoyt Sherman, 1868; served in the frontier Indian wars, participating importantly in operations against Central Plains tribes, 1869–1874, and Northern Plains tribes, 1874–1880; commanded the Department of the Columbia, 1880–1884; commanded the Department of the Missouri, 1885–1886; commanded the Department of Arizona, 1886–1887, bringing the Apache Wars to a close; commanded the Division of the Pacific, 1888–1889; commanded the Division of the Missouri, 1889–1894, with overall responsibility for operations at Wounded Knee and in the Pullman Strike; was commanding general of the United States Army, 5 October 1895–8 August 1903; represented the United States at the Queen Victoria Jubilee Celebration, was an observer of Turco-Grecian War operations, and attended the maneuvers of the Russian, German, and French armies, 1897, observed operations in Cuba and conducted the campaign in Puerto Rico in the War with Spain, 1898; was advanced to three-star rank under the provisions of a 6 June 1900 act that specified the senior major general of the line commanding the Army shall have the rank, pay and allowances of a lieutenant general; was promoted to permanent lieutenant general, February 1901; visited the Philippines, the Far East, and Europe, 1902; retired from active service, August 1903; was the author of three books published in 1896, 1897, and 1911; died in Washington, D.C., on 15 May 1925.

The Artist

Caroline Thurber (1864–1950) was born in Oberlin, Ohio, and was reared and educated in Philadelphia. She studied in Italy, Germany, and England, and received some of her art training in Paris under Jean Paul Laurens and Benjamin Constant. Around the turn of the century she exhibited at the Royal Academy in London and the Paris Salon. Although her early subjects were children, she turned later to portraits of prominent individuals in the professions that include Supreme Court justices of several states, Governor Lucius Garvin of Rhode Island, and President Elizabeth Storrs Meade of Mount Holyoke College. Her portrait of Lt. Gen. Nelson A. Miles hangs in the United States Army Military History Institute at Carlisle Barracks, Pennsylvania.

Nelson Appleton Miles
By Caroline Thurber
Oil on canvas, 58" x 40," 1903

Chiefs of Staff

1903–2005

SAMUEL BALDWIN MARKS YOUNG was born in Pittsburgh, Pennsylvania, on 9 January 1840; attended Jefferson College at Canonsburg, Pennsylvania; enlisted as a private in Company K, 12th Pennsylvania Infantry, April 1861; was commissioned a captain in the 4th Pennsylvania Cavalry, September 1861; married Margaret McFadden, 1861; served in the Civil War with the Army of the Potomac, receiving promotions in the volunteers to major (1862), lieutenant colonel and colonel (1864), and brevet brigadier general (1865); entered the regular establishment as a second lieutenant, 12th Infantry, May 1866; was promoted to captain and transferred to the 8th Cavalry, July 1866; served on the frontier in operations against southwestern Indian tribes, 1866–1879, receiving in 1867 three retroactive brevet ranks for gallantry and meritorious service in earlier actions at Sulphur Springs (major), Amelia Springs (lieutenant colonel), and Sayler's Creek (colonel); served on the organizing faculty of the School of Application for Infantry and Cavalry at Fort Leavenworth, 1882; was promoted to major, 3rd Cavalry, April 1883, to lieutenant colonel, 4th Cavalry, August 1892, and to colonel, 3d Cavalry, June 1897; was appointed brigadier general (May 1898) and major general (July 1898) of volunteers; commanded a brigade in the Santiago campaign in the War with Spain, 1898; was a brigade commander in the Philippine Insurrection, 1899–1901, led the advance forces in the final operations in northern Luzon, and was military governor of that district; was promoted to brigadier general in the regular establishment, January 1900, and advanced to major general, February 1901; commanded the Department of California, 1901–1902; was appointed president of the War College Board, November 1901; was first president of the Army War College, July 1902; was appointed a member of the General Staff Selection Board; March 1903, and of an Army and Navy board for cooperation between the services, 1903; was promoted to lieutenant general, August 1903, and commanded the Army for one week; was the first chief of staff of the United States Army, 15 August 1903–8 January 1904; supervised the initial implementation of the General Staff concept and recommended establishment of a general service corps to relieve combat personnel of technical service functions; retired from active service, January 1904; was president of a board that reviewed the circumstances and findings in the Brownsville Affair; died in Helena, Montana, on 1 December 1924.

The Artist

Marion Potter Sharpe (1924–) was born in Albany, New York. She attended Russell Sage College in Troy, New York; studied at the Art Students League in New York City; and established studios in Kennebunkport, Maine, Charleston, South Carolina, and Middleburg, Virginia, before moving her operations to Slingerlands, New York, during the winter and to Nantucket, Massachusetts, during the summer. In addition to painting, she taught at the Portland School of Fine Arts and the Albany Institute of History and Art, as well as was artist-in-residence at her alma mater. She has won a number of awards for her work, which has appeared in national shows at several locations. Her portrait of Lt. Gen. Samuel B. M. Young holds the anchor position in the Chiefs of Staff Portrait Gallery at the Pentagon, Washington, D.C, and is reproduced from the Army Art Collection.

Samuel Baldwin Marks Young
By Marion Potter Sharpe
Oil on canvas, 40" x 34," 1974

ADNA ROMANZA CHAFFEE was born at Orwell, Ohio, on 14 April 1842; enlisted in the 6th Cavalry, July 1861; was promoted to sergeant and participated in the Peninsular and Antietam Campaigns, 1862; was advanced to first sergeant of Company K, September 1862; was commissioned a second lieutenant by direction of the secretary of war, May 1863; continued his Civil War service in the 6th Cavalry; was twice wounded and received the brevet of captain for gallant and meritorious service in action at Dinwiddie Court House, Virginia; was promoted to first lieutenant, February 1865, and captain, October 1867; married Kate Haynie Reynolds, 1868 (deceased 1869); served in the Indian wars against Central Plains and southwestern tribes, 1867–1894; was brevetted major for action at Paint Creek, Texas (1868), and lieutenant colonel for actions at Red River, Texas (1874), and Big Dry Wash, Arizona (1882); married his second wife, Annie Frances Rockwell, 1875; was promoted to major and posted to the 9th Cavalry, July 1888; was instructor in tactics at the Infantry and Cavalry School, Fort Leavenworth, 1894–1896; was promoted to lieutenant colonel and transferred to the 3d Cavalry June 1897; was commandant of the Cavalry School, Fort Riley, 1897–1898; as the War with Spain opened, was promoted to brigadier general (May 1898) and major general (July 1898) of volunteers, and was reappointed to both grades after procedural lapse, April 1899 and July 1900, respectively; commanded a brigade in the Santiago campaign and served as chief of staff to the military governor of Cuba, 1898–1900; was promoted to colonel, 8th Cavalry, in the regular establishment, May 1899; commanded the American contingent in the multinational relief force sent to China during the Boxer uprising, 1900–1901; was promoted to major general in the permanent establishment, February 1901; commanded the Department of the Philippines and served as military governor, July 1901–October 1902; commanded the Department of the East, 1902–1903; was promoted to lieutenant general, January 1904; was chief of staff of the United States Army, 9 January 1904–14 January 1906; established territorial divisions to supervise field departments, emphasized the need for canteen services to forestall disciplinary problems, sought increases in officer strength to counteract diversions from troop duty, and pressed for increases in quarters allowances; served on an Army and Navy board for cooperation between the services; retired from active service, February 1906; was president of the Board of Public Works for the city of Los Angeles; died in Los Angeles, California, on 1 November 1914.

The Artist

Cedric Baldwin Egeli (1936–) was born in Shady Side, Maryland. He attended Principia College in Illinois before enrolling for two years of study at the Corcoran School of Art in Washington, D.C. A scholarship took him to the Art Students League in New York City for three years of work under Sidney Dickerson, Frank Reilly, and Frank Mason. He was artist-in-residence at the University of Delaware in 1964–1965 before continuing his studies under his accomplished father, Bjorn Egeli, also a contributor to the Chiefs of Staff Portrait Gallery at the Pentagon, Washington, D.C. The portrait of Lt. Gen. Adna R. Chaffee was developed from a black and white photograph, and is reproduced from the Army Art Collection.

Adna Romanza Chaffee
By Cedric Baldwin Egeli
Oil on canvas, 48" x 34," 1973

JOHN COALTER BATES was born in St. Charles County, Missouri, on 26 August 1842; was educated at Washington University of St. Louis; was commissioned a first lieutenant and assigned to the 11th Infantry, May 1861; served in the 11th with the Army of the Potomac during the Civil War, including the battles of Antietam, Fredericksburg, Chancellorsville, and Gettysburg, and as aide to General George G. Meade; was promoted to captain, May 1863; received the brevet of major for faithful and meritorious service in the field, August 1864; was brevetted lieutenant colonel for gallant and meritorious service in operations resulting in the fall of Richmond and surrender of Lee's Army, April 1865; was transferred to the 20th Infantry, 1866; served on the Indian frontier from junior officer to regimental commander with extended service in both the 20th and 2d Infantry, 1866–1898; commanded a company on escort duty with the Northern Pacific Railroad survey party, 1871, and commanded the troops that captured insurgent Creek Indians during Indian Territory disturbances, 1883; was promoted to major (1882), lieutenant colonel (1886), and colonel (1892); was a member of a board that considered magazine rifles for Army use; upon the outbreak of the War with Spain, was promoted to brigadier general of volunteers, May 1898; commanded the American base at Siboney and participated in the assault on El Caney; was promoted to major general of volunteers, July 1898, and commanded the 3d Division, V Corps, in the closing stages of the Santiago campaign; commanded the Department of Santa Clara, 1899; was transferred to the Philippines, directed affairs in the Jolo-Mindanao districts and negotiated a treaty on American sovereignty with the Sultan of Sulu, 1899; was reappointed to major general of volunteers, 1900; commanded the 1st Division, VIII Corps, conducted operations against insurgents in southern Luzon, and then commanded that department, 1900–1901; was commissioned a brigadier general in the Regular Army, February 1901, and promoted to major general, July 1902; commanded a provisional division in maneuvers at Fort Riley, 1902; commanded the Departments of the Missouri and the Lakes, 1901–1904; commanded the Northern Division, 1904–1905; was chief of staff of the United States Army, 15 January–13 April 1906; was promoted to lieutenant general, February 1906; retired from active service, April 1906; died in San Diego, California, 4 February 1919.

The Artist

Cedric Baldwin Egeli (1936–), portrait painter, art teacher, and founder of the Maryland Society of Portrait Painters, is represented in the collections of the state of Maryland with portraits of John Hanson, Lord Sterling, Judy Agnew, and Blair Lee. Among his portraits of prominent military figures are those of Admiral Arleigh Burke and General Arthur G. Trudeau in the collection of the American Defense Preparedness Association in Arlington, Virginia. He was elected as an "Exceptional Member" of the American Portrait Society, and his widely acclaimed work has appeared in many exhibitions and won him numerous prizes—the National Portrait Competition's Best in the Show Award (1979), the Corcoran's Prix de Rome Award, the American Artists Professional League's Gold Medal, and the Anne Arundel County Cultural Arts Foundation's Annie Award for Visual Arts (2001). His portrait of Lt. Gen. John C. Bates was developed from a black and white photograph, and is reproduced from the Army Art Collection.

John Coalter Bates
By Cedric Baldwin Egeli
Oil on canvas, 36" x 30," 1974

JAMES FRANKLIN BELL was born near Shelbyville, Kentucky, on 9 January 1856; was educated at local schools and graduated from the United States Military Academy, 1878; was commissioned a second lieutenant, 9th Cavalry, June 1878; transferred to the 7th Cavalry, Fort Lincoln, August 1878; married Sarah Buford, 1881; served with the military escort for Northern Pacific Railroad construction crews, 1882; was engaged in troop training and escort duty, Fort Buford, 1882–1886; was professor of military science and tactics at Southern Illinois University, 1886–1899; while there studied law and was admitted to the bar; was promoted to first lieutenant, December 1890, and served as adjutant of the 7th Cavalry, 1891–1894; was concurrently secretary of the Cavalry and Light Artillery School, Fort Riley, 1893–1894; was aide to the commander of the Department of California, 1894–1897; was on garrison duty, Fort Apache, 1897–1898; was appointed judge advocate, Department of the Columbia, 1898; was assigned to General Wesley Merritt's Philippines expedition as major of volunteers and engineer officer, May 1898; was appointed chief of military information, Department of the Pacific, and dispatched to Manila to gather information, June 1898; participated in military operations against insurrectionists; was promoted to captain, 7th Cavalry, March 1899, and major of volunteers and assistant adjutant general, April 1899; was acting judge advocate and mustering officer, 2d Division, VIII Corps; was appointed colonel, 36th Volunteer Infantry, July 1899, earning the Medal of Honor for gallantry in action near Porac, Luzon, in September; was appointed brigadier general of volunteers, December 1899; commanded the 4th Brigade, 2d Division, Department of the Pacific, January 1900; was provost marshal of Manila, 1900–1901; was promoted to brigadier general in the regular establishment, February 1901; commanded the First District, Department of Luzon, 1901, and 3d Brigade in field operations, 1901–1902; was commandant of the Army service schools, Fort Leavenworth, 1902–1906; was promoted to major general, January 1907; was chief of staff of the United States Army, 14 April 1906–21 April 1910; prepared and secured progressive passage of elements of a long-range legislative program calling for increases in strength, pay, technical services, and reserve forces; installed and commanded the Army of Cuban Pacification; presided over the development of Army aviation and relief efforts in the San Francisco earthquake; commanded the Department of the Philippines, 1911–1914, the 2d Division (Tactical), 1914–1915, the Western Department, 1915–1917, and the Eastern Department, 1917; commanded Camp Upton and the 77th Division and visited the theater of war in France, 1917–1918; resumed command of the Eastern Department, 1918–1919; died in New York City on 8 January 1919.

The Artist

Adrian Lamb (1901–1988) was born in New York City, where in the mid-1920s he studied at the Art Students League under Frank Vincent DuMond and George Bridgman. After attending the Académie Julien in Paris in 1929, he went on to travel and work in England, France, Spain, Germany, Italy, Greece, and Mexico as he developed his talent as a portrait painter. He painted many prominent subjects, including David Rockefeller, John J. McCloy, Joseph P. Kennedy, and Bernard Baruch. He executed the Gordon Gray portrait for the Secretarial Portrait Gallery at the Pentagon, Washington, D.C., and his paintings of other public figures hang in the United States Capitol, the Supreme Court, the Department of State, and the National Gallery of Art. His portrait of Maj. Gen. J. Franklin Bell is reproduced from the Army Art Collection.

James Franklin Bell
By Adrian Lamb
Oil on canvas, 36½" x 30," 1973

LEONARD WOOD was born in Winchester, New Hampshire, on 9 October 1860; was educated in local schools and at Pierce Academy in Middleboro, Massachusetts; attended Harvard Medical School and received his doctor of medicine degree via internship at Boston City Hospital, 1884; received an interim appointment as contract surgeon with the Army, 1885; received an appointment as assistant surgeon in the regular establishment and served in Arizona as a medical and provisional troop officer in the final Apache operations, 1886; was later awarded the Medal of Honor for distinguished conduct in the Geronimo campaign; served as staff surgeon at department headquarters in Los Angeles and in the field in Arizona, 1887–1889; married Laura Condit Smith, 1890; was promoted to captain, January 1891; was assigned to Army headquarters in Washington, D.C., as assistant attending surgeon, 1895, with responsibility for the care of senior government officials including the president; was appointed colonel of the 1st Volunteer Cavalry (Roosevelt's "Rough Riders"), May 1898, and led it in the Cuban operations at Las Guasimas and San Juan Hill, June 1898; for his gallant services, was promoted to brigadier general (July 1898) and major general (December 1898) of volunteers; was successively military governor of the city of Santiago, Santiago Province, and Cuba, 1898–1902, receiving reappointments to brigadier general (April 1899) and major general (December 1899) of volunteers; was promoted to brigadier general in the regular service, February 1901, and major general in August 1903; was transferred to the Philippines and served as governor of Moro Province, 1903–1906; commanded the Philippine Division, 1906–1908; commanded the Department of the East, 1908–1910; served as special ambassador to Argentina for its centennial celebration, 1910; was chief of staff of the United States Army, 22 April 1910–20 April 1914; was a leading advocate of national preparedness, initiated the Plattsburg (New York) officer training camps, streamlined Army staff and administrative procedures, and pressed for increases in officer strength; commanded the Department of the East, 1914–1917; organized the new Southern Department, 1917; commanded the 89th Division and Camp Funston, 1917; visited Europe to observe allied operations, 1917–1918; trained the 10th Division at Camp Funston, 1918; was an unsuccessful candidate for the Republican nomination for president, 1920; commanded the Central Division (Sixth Corps Area), 1919–1921; served on a special mission to the Philippines, 1921; retired from active service, October 1921; was governor general of the Philippines, 1921–1927; died in Boston, Massachusetts, on 7 August 1927.

The Artist

Charles J. Fox is the pseudonym of Leo Fox, a New York City entrepreneur who for many years commissioned portraits of leading figures in government, business, society, and the professions. The portraits, signed C. J. Fox, were painted for the most part by New York artist Irving Resnikoff (1897–1988) during a forty-year association with Fox. Mr. Resnikoff was born in Russia and studied art at the Imperial Art Academy in St. Petersburg. He left his native land after the revolution and came to the United States in 1923 to settle in New York City and embark upon a career as a portraitist. In fulfillment of C. J. Fox commissions Resnikoff also painted the portraits of Secretaries of the Army Wilber M. Brucker, Elvis J. Stahr, Jr., and Stephen Ailes. His portrait of Maj. Gen. Leonard Wood is reproduced from the Army Art Collection.

Leonard Wood
By Irving Resnikoff [signed C. J. Fox]
Oil on canvas, 40¼" x 30¼," 1974

WILLIAM WALLACE WOTHERSPOON was born in Washington, D.C., on 16 November 1850; was educated in private schools; served aboard ship as a mate in the United States Navy, 1870–1873; was commissioned a second lieutenant and assigned to the 12th Infantry, October 1873; served in the West during the Indian wars as a troop officer and quartermaster, 1874–1881; served with the 12th in northern New York, 1881–1887; married Mary C. Adams, 1887; was on sick leave 1888–1889; superintended the enlargement of the Soldiers' Home in Washington, 1889–1890; served at Fort Sully and at Mount Vernon Barracks, where he trained a company of Apache prisoners, 1890–1894; was promoted to captain, 1893; was aide to General Oliver O. Howard, commander of the Department of the East, 1894; was professor of military science and tactics at Rhode Island College, 1894–1898; was on recruiting duty at Fort McPherson and organized the 3d Battalion, 12th Infantry, 1898; served in the Philippines against insurgents and as collector of customs at Iloilo, 1899–1901; was promoted to major and transferred to the 30th Infantry, 1901; commanded the 2d Battalion, 6th Infantry, at Fort Leavenworth and then taught at the General Staff College, 1902–1904; was promoted to lieutenant colonel and assigned to the 14th Infantry, 1904; was transferred to the 19th Infantry and graduated from the Army War College, 1905; was director of the Army War College, 1904–1906; was chief of staff of the Army of Cuban Pacification, 1906–1907; was acting president of the Army War College and chief of the Third Division, General Staff, 1907; was promoted to brigadier general, October 1907; was president of the Army War College, 1907–1909 and 1910–1912, and largely instrumental in transforming it from an adjunct of the General Staff to an autonomous educational institution; was assistant to the chief of staff, 1901–1910 and 1912–1914; was promoted to major general, May 1912, serving as commander of the Department of the Gulf until September; was chief of staff of the United States Army 21 April–15 November 1914; called attention to shortages of officers and noncommissioned officers for Army missions, emphasized the need to reevaluate coast defenses to meet heavier-gunned battleships, saw establishment of an aviation section in the Signal Corps and the completion of the Panama Canal; retired from active service, November 1914; served as superintendent of public works for the state of New York, 1915–1920; died in Washington, D.C., on 21 October 1921.

The Artist

Thomas W. Orlando (1931–) received a bachelor of arts from City College of New York in 1954 and then pursued advanced studies at the Art Students League, the National Academy of Design, the Cape School of Art, and the Brooklyn Museum. During a two-year tour in the United States Navy (1956–1957) he directed a number of art projects for the Office of Public Information. He later joined the faculty of the Pratt Institute on Manhattan, where he taught advanced drawing and painting until his retirement in 1994. During his career his work was featured in one-man shows at the Berkshire Museum, Newsweek Gallery 10, and a number of private galleries, as well as represented in group shows at the Allied Artists of America, the National Art Club, the Salmagundi Club, the Pratt Institute Gallery, and others. His portrait of Maj. Gen. William W. Wotherspoon was developed from photographs, and is reproduced from the Army Art Collection.

William Wallace Wotherspoon
By Thomas W. Orlando
Oil on canvas, 46" x 32," 1974

HUGH LENOX SCOTT was born at Danville, Kentucky, on 22 September 1853; graduated from the United States Military Academy, 1876; was commissioned a second lieutenant and assigned to the 9th Cavalry, June 1876, assuming that month a vacancy in the 7th Cavalry created by Little Bighorn battle casualties; was stationed at various posts in Dakota Territory and participated in the Nez Percé campaign, 1877; was promoted to first lieutenant, June 1878, and engaged in scouting and constructing telegraph lines, 1879–1882; married Mary Merrill, 1880; studied and became an authority on the language, customs, and history of the Plains Indians; served on an exploring expedition with the Geological Survey, 1884; was on recruiting service, 1886–1888; was on duty at Fort Sill and scouting in the Central Plains, 1889; served in the Sioux outbreak of 1890, being involved in actions at Porcupine, Wounded Knee, and White Clay Creeks; organized and commanded Troop L (composed of Kiowa, Comanche, and Apache Indians), 7th Cavalry, Fort Sill, 1892–1897; was promoted to captain, 1895; was in charge of Geronimo's band of Chiricahua prisoners of war, 1894–1897; was assigned to the Adjutant General's Department to work on the Indian sign language, 1897–1898; was promoted to major of volunteers and assigned as assistant adjutant general, I Corps, 1898–1899; became lieutenant colonel of volunteers and assistant adjutant general on the staff of the military governor of Cuba, 1899–1900; was military governor of Sulu Archipelago, Philippines, and commander of the Jolo military post, 1903–1906; was wounded in action at Crater Lake while campaigning against the Moros, November 1903; was superintendent of the United States Military Academy, 1906–1910; served in the Office of the Chief of Staff, 1911; dealt with problems of various Indian tribes, 1908–1915; was promoted to lieutenant colonel (March) and colonel (August), 1911; commanded the 3d Cavalry, 1912, and the 2d Cavalry Brigade, 1913–1914, on the Mexican border; was assistant chief of staff of the United States Army, 1914; was promoted to brigadier general, March 1913, and major general, April 1915; was chief of staff of the United States Army, 16 November 1914–21 September 1917; supervised the concentration of troops on the Mexican border preliminary to the Punitive Expedition; laid the foundations for mobilizing, training, and equipping the Army for World War I; espoused conscription over a volunteer system for the Army; was a member of the Root commission to Russia, 1917; retired from active duty, September 1917, but was recalled to inspect the battlefront in Europe; commanded the 78th Division and Camp Dix, 1918; retired permanently from the Army, May 1919; was a member of the Board of Indian Commissioners, 1919–1920; died in Washington, D.C., on 30 April 1934.

The Artist

Robert Oliver Skemp (1910–1984), portraitist and muralist, studied at the Art Students League under Thomas Hart Benton, Frank Vincent DuMond, and Robert Laurent; at the Grand Central Art School under Harry Ballinger and Pruett Carter; and at the George Luks and Charles Baskerville studios. He enlarged upon this background with study in France and Spain. During his career he received a number of awards for his work, which is represented in numerous collections. He painted the portraits of many prominent personalities, including J. Paul Getty of Getty Oil Corporation, Chief Executive Officer Walter B. Wriston of Citicorp, and Chief Executive Officer Donald T. Regan of Merrill Lynch & Company. His portrait of Maj. Gen. Hugh L. Scott is reproduced from the Army Art Collection.

Hugh Lenox Scott
By Robert Oliver Skemp
Oil on canvas, 36" x 30," 1973

TASKER HOWARD BLISS was born in Lewisburg, Pennsylvania, on 31 December 1853; graduated from the United States Military Academy, 1875; was commissioned second lieutenant and assigned to the 1st Artillery, June 1875; performed routine garrison duties in Georgia and New York, 1875–1876; was assistant professor of French and assistant instructor of artillery tactics at West Point, 1876–1880; was promoted to first lieutenant, July 1880; was again on garrison duty in Connecticut and California, 1880–1882; married Eleanore E. Anderson, 1882; was adjutant of the Artillery School at Fort Monroe, 1884–1885, recorder of the Board on Interior Waterways, 1884, and instructor at the Naval War College, 1885–1888; was aide to the commanding general of the Army and concurrently inspector of artillery and small arms target practice, 1888–1895; was promoted to captain and staff subsistence (commissary) officer, 1892; was on special duty in the Office of the Secretary of War, 1895–1897; was military attache to Spain, 1897–1898; was promoted to major and staff commissary officer, 1898; was promoted to lieutenant colonel of volunteers and chief commissary officer, May 1898; was chief of staff of the 1st Division, I Corps, in the Puerto Rican campaign, 1898, collector of customs for the port of Havana and island of Cuba, 1898–1899, and president of the commission to revise the Cuban tariff, 1901; was promoted to brigadier general of volunteers, 1901; was a member of the War College Board, 1902; was promoted to brigadier general in the Regular Army, July 1902; served as chief of the Third Division, General Staff, and as president of the Army War College, August 1903–June 1905; was successively commander of the Departments of Luzon and Mindanao, governor of Moro Province, and commander of the Philippine Division, 1905–1909; returned to the General Staff and again headed the Army War College, 1909–1910; served successively as commander of the Departments of California, 1910–1911, the East, 1911–1913, and the South, 1913–1915; was assistant chief of staff of the United States Army, February 1915–September 1916; was promoted to major general, November 1915, and to temporary general, October 1917; was chief of staff of the United States Army, 22 September 1917–18 May 1918; visited Europe twice to observe conditions at the front and serve as the War Departments representative with the American section of the Supreme War Council at Versailles, his reports contributing to the formulation of policy and the prosecution of the war; was a delegate to the Paris Peace Conference, 1918–1919; was governor of the Soldiers' Home in Washington, D.C., 1920–1927; retired from active service, June 1930; was advanced to general on the retired list by act of Congress, June 1930; died in Washington, D.C., on 9 November 1930.

The Artist

Frank Ingoglia (1907–1998) was born in Brooklyn, New York. He began as an active artist from the early age of nine, when he won the Wanamaker Award in a citywide contest for school children. He graduated from the Fawcett School of Applied Arts and then attended the Art Students League in New York City, where he studied under George Bridgman, Alvin Kleinfeld, and Kinon Nickolaides before entering upon a career in design and illustration. In 1950 he turned to portraiture, studying with Jerry Farnsworth, Robert Phillips, Wallace Bassford, and Sam Oppenheim. During his career his illustrations appeared in national newspapers and magazines, and his paintings were widely exhibited and collected. His portrait of General Tasker H. Bliss is reproduced from the Army Art Collection.

Tasker Howard Bliss
By Frank Ingoglia
Oil on canvas, 40" x 32," 1973

PEYTON CONWAY MARCH was born in Easton, Pennsylvania, on 27 December 1864; attended Lafayette College, 1880–1884, and graduated from the United States Military Academy, 1888; was commissioned an additional second lieutenant and assigned to the 3d Artillery, June 1888, advancing to second lieutenant in November; performed routine garrison duties in Washington, D.C., and California, 1888–1896; married Josephine Smith Cunningham, 1891 (deceased 1904); was promoted to first lieutenant and assigned to the 5th Artillery, 1894; attended the Artillery School, Fort Monroe, 1896–1898; organized and was designated captain of the Astor Battery, 1898; commanded it in the Philippines campaign and in the capture of Manila, 1898–1899; was aide to General Arthur MacArthur, 1899; was promoted to major, 33d Volunteer Infantry, July 1899, and participated in numerous operations of the Philippine Insurrection; was promoted to temporary lieutenant colonel, 1900; was a provincial governor and commissary of prisoners, 1900–1901; was reverted to regular captaincy in artillery, 1901, and commanded the 19th Battery, Field Artillery, at Fort Riley, to 1903; was a member of the new War Department General Staff, 1903–1907, and a military observer to the Japanese Army during the Russo-Japanese War, 1904; was promoted to major, January 1907, and served on the Artillery Board; commanded the 1st Battalion, 6th Field Artillery, 1907–1911; was detailed to the Adjutant General's Department and served successively as adjutant of Fort Riley, the Department of the Missouri, the Central Department, the 2d Division, and at department headquarters in Washington, D.C., 1911–1916; was promoted to colonel, July 1916, and commanded the 8th Field Artillery on the Mexican border, 1916–1917; was promoted to brigadier general, June 1917, and placed in command of the 1st Field Artillery Brigade, 1st Division, American Expeditionary Forces; was promoted to major general in the National Army, August 1917, and commanded the first Army and nondivisional artillery, American Expeditionary Forces, June 1917; was promoted to major general in the regular establishment, September 1917; was again assigned to the General Staff and was acting chief of staff, March–May 1918; was promoted to temporary general, May 1918; was chief of staff of the United States Army, 19 May 1918–30 June 1921; established the primacy of the chief of staff in the Army hierarchy; presided over the buildup of American forces in World War I; centralized control over supply; created an Air Service, Tank Corps, and Chemical Warfare Service; and supervised the demobilization at war's end; retired as a major general, November 1921, and was advanced to general on the retired list, June 1930; married Cora V. McEntee, 1923; died in Washington, D.C., on 13 April 1955.

The Artist

Nicodemus David Hufford (1915–1986) was born in Columbus, Ohio. In the 1930s he studied his chosen profession at the Art Institute of Chicago, the Chicago School of Professional Art, and the American Academy of Art in Chicago, and in the early 1940s he served an apprenticeship under two top illustrators, Haddon Sundblom and Harry Anderson. During his career he painted the portraits of a number of leading American families, including the Rockefellers, du Ponts, and Dukes, and his paintings hang in many homes in the United States and abroad. His portrait of General Peyton C. March was developed from photographs, and is reproduced from the Army Art Collection

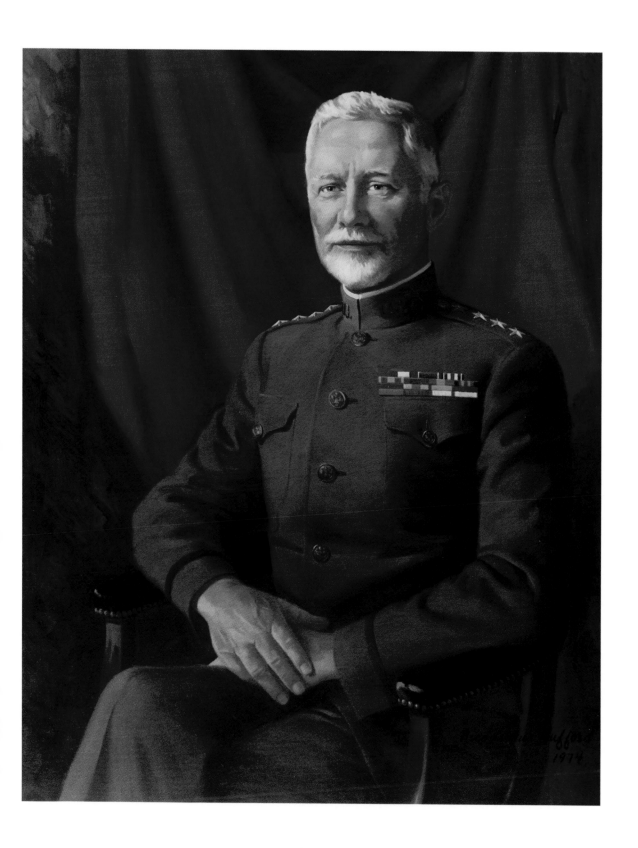

Peyton Conway March
By Nicodemus David Hufford
Oil on canvas, 40" x 32," 1974

JOHN JOSEPH PERSHING was born near Laclede, Missouri, on 13 September 1860; attended the State Normal School, then graduated from the United States Military Academy, 1886; was commissioned a second lieutenant and assigned to the 6th Cavalry, July 1886; performed garrison and field duties in the Southwest and Northern Plains, 1886–1890, and participated in the Wounded Knee campaign; was professor of military science and tactics at University of Nebraska, 1891–1895, studying law concurrently and receiving his degree, 1893; was promoted to first lieutenant and assigned to the 10th Cavalry, October 1892; served in Montana, 1895–1896; after a brief tour at Army headquarters, was assistant instructor in tactics at West Point, 1897–1898; served with the 10th in Cuba, including operations at San Juan Hill; was promoted to major of volunteers, detailed in ordnance, and assigned to Army headquarters and the Office of the Assistant Secretary of War, 1898–1899, where he organized a Bureau of Insular Affairs; was reverted to a regular captaincy, June 1901, and assigned successively to the 1st and 10th Cavalry; served in the Philippines as a departmental adjutant general and engineer officer, collector of customs, and cavalry squadron commander, participating in actions against Moros, 1899–1903; served on the War Department General Staff, 1903–1904, and as assistant chief of staff of the Southwestern Division, 1904; attended the Army War College, 1904–1905; married Frances Warren, 1905; was military attaché to Japan and an observer of the Russo-Japanese War, 1905–1906; at President Roosevelt's nomination, was promoted to brigadier general over 862 senior-ranking officers, September 1906; commanded the Department of California, 1906, and Fort McKinley, 1907–1908; was assigned to the Office of the Chief of Staff, 1908–1909; was governor of Moro Province and commander, Department of Mindanao, 1909–1913; commanded the 8th Infantry Brigade at the Presidio of San Francisco, 1914–1916, where in 1915 he lost his wife and three daughters in a fire; led the Mexican Punitive Expedition, 1916–1917, receiving promotion to major general during the campaign; was promoted to general, October 1917; commanded the American Expeditionary Forces in France in World War I, 1917–1919; was advanced to General of the Armies, September 1919; moved his headquarters to Washington, prepared a report on the war, and made an extended tour of military inspection, 1919–1921; was chief of staff of the United States Army, 1 July 1921–13 September 1924; established the War Plans Board; pressed for national preparedness, a strong Army, increased efficiency and economy, officer schooling, and a well-regulated militia; retired from active service, September 1924; was chairman of the American Battle Monuments Commission, 1923–1948, and headed the Tacna-Arica Boundary Commission, 1925–1926; died in Washington, D.C., on 15 July 1948.

The Artist

Richard Leopold Seyffert (1915–1979), son of the renowned portraitist Leopold Seyffert, was born in Philadelphia, received his formal schooling in Switzerland, and then studied with Leon Kroll and Gifford Beal at the National Academy of Design in New York City. He continued his studies in Italy before embarking upon his professional career in Chicago at the end of the 1930s. During World War II he served in the Navy as a photographer's mate and then spent three postwar years in Peru painting prominent personalities in the diplomatic and social worlds. Later, established in New York City, he continued painting such notable figures as W. K. Kellogg, Edward R. Murrow, Fannie Hurst, W. H. Auden, and Richard Rogers. His portrait of General John J. Pershing is reproduced from the Army Art Collection.

John Joseph Pershing
By Richard Leopold Seyffert
Oil on canvas, 36" x 30," 1975

JOHN LEONARD HINES was born in White Sulphur Springs, West Virginia, on 21 May 1868; graduated from the United States Military Academy, 1891; was commissioned a second lieutenant and assigned to the 2d Infantry, June 1891; performed troop and staff duties on the frontier in Nebraska and Montana, 1891–1898; was promoted to first lieutenant, April 1898; was acting quartermaster of the 2d Infantry in the Cuban expedition and participated in action at San Juan Hill; married Harriet Schofield Wherry, 1898; served with his regiment in the United States and returned to Cuba for quartermaster and civil affairs duty, 1899–1900; served against the Moros in the Philippine Insurrection, 1900–1901; was promoted to captain and assigned to the 23d Infantry, December 1900; was post and organizational quartermaster at various locations in the United States, the Philippines, and Japan, 1901–1912; was promoted to major, 6th Infantry, May 1912; was adjutant general of the Western Department, 1913, and detailed in that service, 1914; was adjutant of the 8th Infantry Brigade and the El Paso District, 1914–1916; was adjutant of the Mexican Punitive Expedition, 1916–1917; was assistant adjutant of the Eastern Department, 1917; was promoted to lieutenant colonel and designated adjutant general, May 1917; was assistant to the adjutant general of the American Expeditionary Forces, May–October 1917; was promoted to colonel, 16th Infantry, October 1917, and attached to French First Army at the front, 1917–1918; was promoted to brigadier general in the National Army, April 1918, and commanded the 1st Infantry Brigade, 1st Division, in the Montdidier, Marne, and Saizerais operations, May–August 1918; was promoted to major general in the National Army, August 1918, and commanded the 4th Division and then V Corps in final World War I operations, and the III Corps in the occupation of the Rhineland, 1918–1919; was promoted to brigadier general in the Regular Army, November 1918; commanded the 4th, 5th, and 2d Divisions in postwar training, 1919–1921; received a recess appointment as major general in the Regular Army, July 1920; confirmed as permanent major general, March 1921; commanded the Eighth Corps Area, 1921–1922; was deputy chief of staff of the United States Army, December 1922–September 1924; was chief of staff of the United States Army, 14 September 1924–20 November 1926; stressed the need for balance in funding and personnel for all parts of the permanent establishment, pointed up the effects of strength deficiencies upon Army capability to meet the provisions of the National Defense Act of 1920, and urged action on housing and promotions to promote personnel retention; commanded the Ninth Corps Area, 1926–1930, and the Philippine Department, 1930–1932; retired from active service, May 1932; died in Washington, D.C., on 13 October 1968, aged 100 years.

The Artist

Joyce Ballantyne Brand (1918–) was born in Norfolk, Nebraska. After attending the University of Nebraska, she completed her art education at the American Academy of Art in Chicago and at the Art Students League in New York City. She worked as an illustrator for the outdoor magazine *Sports Afield* for over twenty years, and also as a pinup artist in the 1940s. Throughout her career she specialized in commercial art for such major corporations as Ovaltine, Coca Cola, Pepsi, and General Motors, to name a few; two of her most famous images were the Coppertone Girl and the Pampers Baby. Highly respected for creating realistic images that capture the persona of her subjects, she received many commissions to paint the portraits of prominent TV personalities, including Jonathan Winters, Durward Kirby, and Commander Whitehead, as well as other luminaries in the fields of business and the professions. Her portrait of Maj. Gen. John J. Hines was developed from photographs, and is reproduced from the Army Art Collection.

John Leonard Hines
By Joyce Ballantyne Brand
Oil on canvas, 72" x 36," 1974

CHARLES PELOT SUMMERALL was born in Blunts Ferry, Florida, on 4 March 1867; graduated from the United States Military Academy, 1892; was commissioned a second lieutenant and assigned to the 1st Infantry, June 1892; transferred to the 5th Artillery, March 1893; performed garrison duty in California, 1893–1895; served at Fort Hamilton, 1895–1898; was assigned to the Department of the Gulf as aide to the commander and as an engineer officer, 1898–1899; was promoted to first lieutenant, March 1899; participated with his unit in the Philippine Insurrection, 1899–1900; was a member of the China Relief Expedition, 1900–1901, and participated in the attack on Peking; was promoted to captain and assigned to the 106th Coast Artillery Company, July 1901; married Laura Mordecai, August 1901; served at Forts Walla Walla and Lawton, commanding the latter post, 1901–1902; was on duty at Camp Skagway and commanded and was in charge of preliminary work at Fort Seward; commanded Fort Flagler, 1902–1903; was transferred to the 3d Field Artillery Battery with duty at Camp Thomas and Fort Myer, 1903–1905; was senior instructor of artillery tactics at West Point, 1905–1911; was promoted to major, March 1911; commanded the field artillery of the Maneuver Division, San Antonio, Texas; commanded the summer camps of instruction for Army and National Guard artillery, 1912–1914; was assistant chief of the Militia Bureau and in charge of National Guard artillery, 1915–1917; was engaged in purchasing artillery ranges and was a member of the Ordnance Board, 1915–1916, the commission to investigate the manufacture of munitions, 1916, the Board of Ordnance and Fortification, 1917, and the military mission to British and French armies, 1917; was promoted to lieutenant colonel, 1916, colonel, 1917, and brigadier general in the National Army, August 1917; commanded the 67th Field Artillery Brigade and the 1st Field Artillery Brigade in operations in France, 1917; was promoted to major general in the National Army and successively commanded his brigade, the 1st Division, and the V Corps in the Cantigny, Soissons, St. Mihiel, and Meuse-Argonne operations, 1918; commanded the IX and IV Corps and served on the American Peace Commission, 1919; commanded the 1st Division, 1919–1921, receiving promotions in the Regular Army to brigadier general (February 1919) and major general (April 1920); commanded the Hawaiian Department, 1921–1924, and Eighth and Second Corps Areas, 1924–1926; was chief of staff of the United States Army, 21 November 1926–20 November 1930, with promotion to general in February 1929; directed the formation of a mechanized force and recommended an integrated mobile force of tank, artillery, engineer, and quartermaster elements; retired from active service, March 1931; was president of The Citadel, in Charleston, South Carolina, 1931–1953; died in Washington, D.C., on 14 May 1955.

The Artist

Ray Edward Goodbred (1929–) was born in Brooklyn, New York. His studied art in New York City, first at the Art Students League under Robert Brackman and then at the National Academy of Design under Ogden Pleissner. After moving to Charleston, South Carolina, he opened a studio and specialized in portraits, figures, and still life. He also taught at the Gibes Museum's Hastie School of Art in Charleston, and in 1975 he was invited to teach at the Art Students League of New York. During his career he received numerous awards for his work, which has been widely exhibited and collected. He painted the portraits of many prominent individuals in the fields of business and the professions, as well as three of The Citadel's presidents—Army General Mark W. Clark, Army Maj. Gen. James W. Duckett, and Air Force Lt. Gen. Claudius E. Watts III. His portrait of General Charles P. Summerall is reproduced from the Army Art Collection.

Charles Pelot Summerall
By Ray Edward Goodbred
Oil on canvas, 36" x 30," 1974

DOUGLAS MACARTHUR was born in Little Rock, Arkansas, on 26 January 1880; graduated from the United States Military Academy, 1903; was commissioned a second lieutenant of engineers and served in the Philippines, 1903–1904; was promoted to first lieutenant, April 1904; was an engineer officer and aide to the commander of the Pacific Division, 1904–1906; served with the 2d Engineer Battalion, attended the Engineer School, and was aide to President Theodore Roosevelt, 1906–1908; was troop commander, adjutant, and Army service schools instructor, Fort Leavenworth, 1908–1912; was promoted to captain, February 1911; was on the General Staff, 1913–1917; took part in the Vera Cruz Expedition; was promoted to major, December 1915, and colonel, August 1917; was chief of staff of the 42d Division in France, 1917–1918; was promoted to brigadier general in the National Army, June 1918, took part in Marne operations, and commanded the 84th Infantry Brigade in the St. Mihiel and Meuse-Argonne offensives; commanded the 42d Division in the Sedan offensive, 1918; served with the Army of Occupation, 1918–1919; was superintendent of the United States Military Academy, 1919–1922; became a brigadier general in the Regular Army, January 1920; married Louise Cromwell Brooks, 1922 (divorced 1929); was promoted to major general, January 1925; successively commanded the District of Manila, 1922–1923, the Fourth and Third Corps Areas, 1925–1928, and the Ninth Corps Area, 1930; was promoted to temporary general, November 1930; was chief of staff of the United States Army, 21 November 1930–1 October 1935; stressed Army deficiencies in personnel and materiel, presided over development of plans for industrial mobilization and manpower procurement, established an Air Force headquarters, administered Army control over the Civilian Conservation Corps, and supervised eviction of "bonus marchers" from Washington; resumed his permanent rank of major general and became military adviser to the government of the Philippines, 1935–1941; married Jean Marie Faircloth, 1937; retired from active service, December 1937, but continued as adviser to the Philippine government; was recalled to active duty as lieutenant general and named commander, United States Army Forces in the Far East, July 1941; was promoted to temporary general, December 1941; led American forces in Pacific campaigns as Supreme Allied Commander, 1941–1945; was promoted to temporary General of the Army December 1944; received the Medal of Honor for Philippine defense preparations and operations; was appointed Supreme Allied Commander, Japan, 1945; rank as General of the Army made permanent, April 1946; was designated commander in chief, Far East Command, 1947; upon the North Korean invasion of South Korea, was designated commander, United Nations Command in the Far East, July 1950; was relieved of his command by President Truman, April 1951; died in Washington, D.C., on 5 April 1964.

The Artist

Robert Oliver Skemp (1910–1984) was born in Scottdale, Pennsylvania. He taught private art classes at Gary, Indiana, in the mid-1930s and was an instructor at the Chicago School of Professional Art in the mid-1940s, during which time he pursued his primary professional occupation of portraitist and muralist. In addition to his portraits of prominent figures in business and the professions, he illustrated war bond publications during World War II; executed murals for the Mormon Church and for the world's fairs at New York and Osaka, Japan; and, as a fellow of the American Society of Marine Artists, painted nineteenth-century clipper ships and other marine subjects. His portrait of General Douglas MacArthur is reproduced from the Army Art Collection.

Douglas MacArthur
By Robert Oliver Skemp
Oil on canvas, 44" x 32," 1973

MALIN CRAIG was born in St. Joseph, Missouri, on 5 August 1875; graduated from the United States Military Academy, 1898; was commissioned a second lieutenant and assigned to the 4th Infantry, April 1898; served with the 6th Cavalry in the Santiago campaign in Cuba, 1898; was transferred to the 4th Cavalry and served in Wyoming and Oklahoma, 1898–1900; participated in the China Relief Expedition, 1900–1902; was promoted to first lieutenant and assigned to the 6th Cavalry, February 1901; married Genevieve Woodruff, April 1901; attended the Infantry and Cavalry School (1903–1904) and Staff College (1904–1905), Fort Leavenworth; was promoted to captain and assigned to the 10th Cavalry, May 1904, and the 1st Cavalry, 1905; was regimental quartermaster, Fort Clark, 1906–1909, then adjutant in the Philippines, 1909; was at the Army War College as student, 1909–1910, and instructor, 1910–1911; was a member of the General Staff and chief of staff of the Maneuver Division, 1911; was assistant to the chief of staff of the Western Department, 1911–1912; served with the 1st Cavalry in the West, 1912–1916; was instructor at the Army service schools, Fort Leavenworth, 1916–1917; served in the Adjutant General's Department and was detailed to the General Staff Corps, 1917; was promoted to major of cavalry, May 1917; was promoted to lieutenant colonel of field artillery and appointed chief of staff of the 41st Division, August 1917; served with the American Expeditionary Forces in France in that position and as chief of staff of I Corps, participating in the Toul, Marne, St. Mihiel, and Meuse-Argonne operations; was promoted to colonel (February) and brigadier general (June) in the National Army, 1918; was chief of staff of the Army of Occupation in Germany, 1918–1919; reverted to basic rank of major and was director of the Army War College, 1919–1920; was promoted to colonel of cavalry and assigned as commander, District of Arizona, 1920–1921; was promoted to brigadier general in the Regular Army, April 1921; served as commandant of the Cavalry School, Fort Riley, 1921–1923; commanded the Coast Artillery District of Manila, 1923–1924; was promoted to major general and assigned as chief of cavalry, 1924–1926; was assistant chief of staff, G–3, of the Army, 1926–1927, then commanded the Fourth Corps Area, 1927, the Panama Canal Division, 1927–1928, the Panama Canal Department, 1928–1930, and the Ninth Corps Area, 1930–1935; was commandant of the Army War College, 1935; was promoted to general, October 1935; was chief of staff of the United States Army, 2 October 1935–31 August 1939; pointed out to Congress the Army's lack of preparedness in manpower and materiel, stressed the essentiality of lead time in military preparedness, focused attention on Army planning, and, within governmental constraints, prepared the Army for World War II; retired from active service, August 1939; was recalled to head the secretary of war's Personnel Board, September 1941; died in Washington, D.C., on 25 July 1945.

The Artist

Frank Ingoglia (1907–1998), designer, illustrator, and portraitist, used his diverse talents in a number of military-related artistic endeavors. During World War II he designed the instruction manual for the Sperry Gyroscope Corporation and worked on Army and Navy recruiting publicity materials among other armed services undertakings, receiving a citation for meritorious service from the National War Fund. From 1926 to 1938 he was a member of the New York Athletic Club's fencing team and competed against cadets of the military and naval academies. After turning from design and illustration to portraiture, he painted the portraits of members of some of America's leading business families and also other distinguished personalities. His portrait of General Malin Craig is reproduced from the Army Art Collection.

Malin Craig
By Frank Ingoglia
Oil on canvas, 42" x 34½," 1973

GEORGE CATLETT MARSHALL was born in Uniontown, Pennsylvania, on 31 December 1880; graduated from Virginia Military Institute, 1901; married Elizabeth Carter Cole, 1902 (deceased 1927); was commissioned a second lieutenant, February 1902, and served with the 30th Infantry in the Philippines, 1902–1903, and at Fort Reno, 1903–1906; was promoted to first lieutenant, March 1907; graduated from the Infantry and Cavalry School (1907) and was a student (1908) and instructor (1908–1910) at the Staff College, Fort Leavenworth; was inspector-instructor of the Massachusetts National Guard, 1911–1912, and then served with the 4th Infantry at Forts Logan H. Roots and Crocket, and the 13th Infantry in the Philippines, 1913–1916; was promoted to captain, July 1917, and then to temporary major, August 1917, lieutenant colonel, January 1918, and colonel, August 1918; served with the American Expeditionary Forces in France as operations officer of the 1st Division and the First Army, and chief of staff of the VIII Corps, 1917–1918, participating in the Cantigny, Aisne-Marne, St. Mihiel, and Meuse-Argonne operations; was aide to General John J. Pershing, 1919–1924; was promoted to permanent major, July 1920, and lieutenant colonel, August 1923; commanded the 15th Infantry in China, 1924–1927; was instructor at the Army War College, 1927, and assistant commandant of the Infantry School, Fort Benning, 1927–1932; married Katherine Boyce Tupper Brown, 1930; was promoted to colonel and placed in command of the 8th Infantry at Fort Screven, September 1933; was senior instructor of the Illinois National Guard, 1933–1936; was promoted to brigadier general, October 1936, and was commander of the 5th Infantry Brigade, 1936–1938; was head of the War Plans Division, General Staff, 1938; was deputy chief of staff, 1938–1939, and acting chief, July–September 1939; was promoted to major general and immediately full general, September 1939; was chief of staff of the United States Army, 1 September 1939–18 November 1945; centralized the professional leadership of the Army in the chief of staff's office; exercised control over mobilization, staff planning, industrial conversion, and personnel requirements; streamlined administration and tactical organization; mastered grand strategy and was the principal American military architect of Allied victory; was promoted to temporary grade of General of the Army, December 1944 (made permanent retroactively in April 1946); was special representative of the president to China, 1945–1947; retired from active service, February 1947; was secretary of state, 21 January 1947–21 January 1949; was the architect of the Marshall Plan to aid European nations, April 1948; was restored to the active list, March 1949; was president of the American Red Cross, 1949–1950; was secretary of defense, 12 September 1950–12 September 1951; received the Nobel Peace Prize for the Marshall Plan, 1953; was chairman of the American Battle Monuments Commission, 1949–1959; died in Washington, D.C., on 16 October 1959.

The Artist

John Edward Bannon (1933–) was born in Baltimore, Maryland. He received a bachelor of fine arts from the Maryland Institute of Art and a master of fine arts from the University of Pennsylvania. Initially as a student and later as an associate, he studied with M. Jacques Maroger, former technical director of the laboratories of The Louvre and president of the Society of Restorers of France, and in the course of his career mastered a variety of media, including oil, pastel, pen, sculpture, and lithography. His vibrant portraits, still lifes, and landscapes are housed in many public and private collections. A member of the Oil Painters of America, he has won the Henry Walters Award and numerous others. He has painted the portraits of many prominent figures, including Pope John XXIII, Senator Charles M. Mathias, Judge Edward A. Beard, and conductor Reginald Stewart. His portrait of General of the Army George C. Marshall is reproduced from the Army Art Collection.

George Catlett Marshall
By John Edward Bannon
Oil on canvas, 40¼" x 36," 1974

DWIGHT DAVID EISENHOWER was born in Denison, Texas, on 14 October 1890; graduated from the United States Military Academy, 1915; was commissioned a second lieutenant and served with the 19th Infantry, 1915–1917; married Mamie Geneva Doud, 1916; was promoted to first lieutenant, July 1916, and to captain, May 1917; served successively with the 57th Infantry and as instructor in officer courses at Forts Oglethorpe and Leavenworth, 1917–1918; commanded the Tank Corps at Camp Colt and served with it at several posts, 1918–1919; was promoted to temporary major (June) and lieutenant colonel (October), 1918; commanded the Heavy Tank Brigade at Camp Meade, 1919–1920; reverted to grade of captain (June) and advanced to major (July), 1920; graduated from the Infantry Tank School at Camp Meade, 1921, and commanded the 301st Tank Battalion, 1921–1922; was executive officer at Camp Gaillard, Panama Canal Zone, 1922–1924; again reverted to grade of captain, November 1922, and was again promoted to major, August 1924; graduated from the Command and General Staff School at Fort Leavenworth, 1926, and the Army War College, 1928; served in the Office of the Assistant Secretary of War and attended the Army Industrial College, 1929–1933; served in the Office of the Chief of Staff as aide to General Douglas MacArthur, 1933–1935; was a military adviser to the Philippine government under MacArthur, 1935–1939; was promoted to lieutenant colonel, July 1936; was executive officer of the 15th Infantry at Fort Ord, and successively chief of staff of the 3d Division, IX Corps, and Third Army, 1940–1942; received temporary promotions to colonel (March 1941), brigadier general (September 1941), major general (March 1942), and lieutenant general (July 1942); was chief of the War Plans Division and assistant chief of staff of the Operations Division, 1942; was designated commanding general, European Theater of Operations, June 1942; commanded American forces in North African landings and was designated commander in chief for Allied operations in North Africa, Sicily, and Italy, 1942–1943; was promoted to temporary general, February 1943, temporary General of the Army, December 1944, and permanent General of the Army, April 1946, with rank from December 1944; was Supreme Commander of the Allied Expeditionary Forces in Western European operations that led to Nazi Germany's defeat, 1944–1945; was military governor of the United States Occupation Zone of Germany, 1945; was chief of staff of the United States Army, 19 November 1945–7 February 1948; presided over postwar demobilization, spoke out against excessive reduction of the armed forces, supported unification of the services, stressed the importance of research and development, and carried out a reorganization of the Army that decentralized functions; retired from active service to become president of Columbia University, 1948–1950; was recalled to active duty to be Supreme Allied Commander, North Atlantic Treaty Organization, 1950–1952; was president of the United States, 20 January 1953–20 January 1961; was reappointed General of the Army, March 1961; died in Washington, D.C., on 28 March 1969.

The Artist

Nicodemus David Hufford (1915–1986) was no stranger to the military subject area, for he served in the Army during World War II and spent two years in the art section at Fort Knox, Kentucky, applying his special talents to the field of training literature. To fulfill a commission by the Army, he painted Dwight Eisenhower's portrait some four years after the death of the former chief of staff and thirty-fourth president of the United States, drawing inspiration from photographs. His portrait of General of the Army Dwight D. Eisenhower is reproduced from the Army Art Collection.

Dwight David Eisenhower
By Nicodemus David Hufford
Oil on canvas, 38" x 30," 1973

OMAR NELSON BRADLEY was born in Clark, Missouri, on 12 February 1893; graduated from the United States Military Academy, 1915, was commissioned a second lieutenant, and assigned to the 14th Infantry, June 1915; married Mary Quayle, 1916 (deceased 1965); performed troop duty in the West, 1915–1919; was promoted to first lieutenant, July 1916, to captain, May 1917, and to temporary major, June 1918; was on Reserve Officer Training Corps duty in Minnesota and South Dakota, 1919–1920; was instructor in mathematics at West Point, 1920–1924; reverted to grade of captain, 1920 and 1922, and was returned to major, 1922 and 1924; graduated from the advanced course at the Infantry School, Fort Benning, 1925; served in Hawaii with both the 19th and 27th Infantry, 1925–1927, and was in charge of National Guard and Reserve affairs for the Hawaiian Islands, 1927–1928; graduated from the Command and General Staff School, Fort Leavenworth, 1929; was instructor in tactics and weapons at the Infantry School, 1929–1933; graduated from the Army War College, 1934; was instructor in tactics and plans and training officer at the United States Military Academy, 1934–1938; was promoted to lieutenant colonel, June 1936; was chief of the Operations Branch, G–1, War Department headquarters, 1938–1940; was assistant secretary of the General Staff, 1940–1941; was promoted to temporary brigadier general, February 1941; was commandant of the Infantry School and set up the Infantry Officer Candidate Program, 1941–1942; was promoted to the temporary ranks of major general, February 1942, and lieutenant general, June 1943; successively commanded the 82d and 28th Infantry Divisions, 1942–1943; was personal representative in the field for the commander of the North African Theater of Operations, 1943; commanded II Corps in operations against Axis forces in North Africa and Sicily, 1943; was promoted to permanent ranks of brigadier general, September 1943, and major general, September 1944; commanded the First Army and the 12th Army Group in the invasion and final campaigns of Western Europe, 1944–1945; was promoted to temporary general, March 1945, a rank and date made permanent in January 1949; was administrator of veterans affairs, 1945–1947; was chief of staff of the United States Army, 7 February 1948–16 August 1949; responded to the National Security Act of 1947 by initiating a study of Army organization that led to appointment of a vice chief of staff and two deputies and to consolidation of technical services under the director of logistics, administrative services under the director of personnel and administration, and financial and management functions under the comptroller of the Army; was the first chairman of the Joint Chiefs of Staff, 16 August 1949–16 August 1953; was promoted to General of the Army, September 1950; was first chairman of the Military Staff Committee of the North Atlantic Treaty Organization, 1949–1950; married Esther Dora Buhler, 1966; while attending an Army Association meeting in New York City, died on 8 April 1981.

The Artist

Clarence Lamont MacNelly (1920–1986) came to art and portraiture in middle life after successful careers in several other lines of endeavor. A graduate of Rutgers University with a degree in economics, he saw World War II service as a Navy officer and then became a senior executive and creative director of a Madison Avenue advertising agency, as well as a magazine publisher. He was in his forties when he turned to art and the study of portraiture under Austrian-born Frederic Taubes—instructor at Cooper Union School, lecturer at the Art Students League, and author of numerous works on art subjects. Taubes considered MacNelly a born portrait painter. The portrait of General Omar Bradley is reproduced from the Army Art Collection.

Omar Nelson Bradley
By Clarence Lamont MacNelly
Oil on canvas, 38¼" x 28¼," 1972

JOSEPH LAWTON COLLINS was born in New Orleans, Louisiana, on 1 May 1896; graduated from the United States Military Academy, 1917; was commissioned a second lieutenant and assigned to the 22d Infantry, April 1917; was promoted to first lieutenant, May 1917, and temporary captain, August 1917; attended the Infantry School of Arms, Fort Sill and served with his regiment at various locations, 1917–1919; was promoted to captain, June 1918, and to temporary major, September 1918; commanded the 3d Battalion, 22d Infantry, in France, 1919, and was assistant chief of staff, G–3, of American Forces in Germany, 1920–1921; married Gladys Easterbrook, 1921; reverted to captain, 1920; was instructor in the department of chemistry at West Point, 1921–1925; graduated from the company officer course at the Infantry School, Fort Benning, 1926, and from the advanced course at the Field Artillery School, Fort Sill, 1927; was an instructor in weapons and tactics at the Infantry School, 1927–1931; was promoted to major, August 1932; was executive officer of the 23d Brigade, Manila, and assistant chief of staff, G–2, Philippine Division, 1933–1934; graduated from the Army Industrial College, 1937, and the Army War College, 1938; was an instructor at the Army War College, 1938–1940; was promoted to lieutenant colonel, June 1940; was chief of staff of the VII Corps, 1941; was promoted to the temporary ranks of colonel, January 1941, brigadier general, February 1942, and major general, May 1942; was chief of staff of the Hawaiian Department, 1941–1942, and commanding general of the 25th Infantry Division on Oahu and in operations against the Japanese on Guadalcanal, 1942–1943; commanded VII Corps in the Normandy invasion and in Western European campaigns until German surrender, 1944–1945; was promoted to temporary lieutenant general (April) and permanent brigadier general (June), 1945; was deputy commanding general and chief of staff of Army Ground Forces, August–December 1945; was director of information (later chief of public information) of the Army, 1945–1947; was deputy (later vice) chief of staff of the United States Army, 1947–1949; was promoted to temporary general and permanent major general, January 1948; was chief of staff of the United States Army, 16 August 1949–15 August 1953; was the Army's senior officer throughout the Korean War, directed the Army's operation of the railroads, brought the first Special Forces group into the order of battle, and was closely associated with the development of the Army's contribution to the newly established North Atlantic Treaty Organization; was representative of the United States to the Military Staff Committee and the Standing Group of NATO, 1953–1954; was special representative of the United States in Vietnam with ambassadorial rank, 1954–1955; returned to his NATO assignment; retired from active service, March 1956; died in Washington, D.C., on 12 September 1987.

The Artist

Lloyd Bowers Embrey (1913–1979) was born in Washington, D.C. He studied there at the Corcoran School of Art in his younger years, was granted a scholarship at the Phillips Gallery, and then completed his specialized education with a degree in fine arts from Yale University. He dedicated his efforts to the field of portraiture. He particularly enjoyed painting beautiful women and children, but his subjects also included prominent figures in various walks of life—from government, business, society, and the professions. His portrait of General J. Lawton Collins is reproduced from the Army Art Collection.

Joseph Lawton Collins
By Lloyd Bowers Embrey
Oil on canvas, 40" x 40," 1972

MATTHEW BUNKER RIDGWAY was born at Fort Monroe, Virginia, on 3 March 1895; graduated from the United States Military Academy, 1917; was commissioned a second lieutenant in April, a first lieutenant in May, and a temporary captain in August 1917; was a company commander and adjutant of the 3d Infantry, 1917–1918; was instructor in Spanish and athletics executive at West Point, 1918–1924; was promoted to permanent captain, 1919; graduated from the Infantry School at Fort Benning and served with the 15th Infantry in China and the 9th Infantry in Texas, 1925–1927; served on the American Electoral Commission in Nicaragua and the Bolivia-Paraguay Commission of Inquiry and Conciliation, 1927–1929; married Margaret Wilcox, 1930 (divorced 1946); served with the 33d Infantry in the Canal Zone, 1931–1932; was technical adviser to the governor general of the Philippines, 1932–1933; was promoted to major, October 1932; graduated from the Command and General Staff School, Fort Leavenworth, 1935, and the Army War College, 1937; was assistant chief of staff, G–3, of Sixth Corps Area, Second Army, and Fourth Army, 1935–1939; served in the War Plans Division of the General Staff, 1939–1942; was promoted to lieutenant colonel, July 1940, and to temporary ranks of colonel, December 1941, brigadier general, January 1942, and major general, August 1942; commanded the 82d Airborne Division in operations against Axis forces in Sicily, Italy, and France, 1942–1944, and the XVIII Airborne Corps in European operations leading to Germany's surrender, 1944–1945; was promoted to temporary lieutenant general, June 1945; commanded the Mediterranean Theater of Operations and was Deputy Supreme Allied Commander there, 1945–1946; married Mary Anthony, 1947; was representative of the United States to the United Nations Military Staff Committee and chairman of the Inter-American Defense Board, 1946–1948; was commander in chief, Caribbean Command, 1948–1949; was deputy chief of staff for administration, 1949–1950; commanded the Eighth Army against Communist forces in Korea, 1950–1951; was promoted to general, May 1951; was American and Supreme Allied Commander in the Far East, 1951–1952; was Supreme Allied Commander in Europe, 1952–1953; was chief of staff of the United States Army, 16 August 1953–30 June 1955; dealt with postwar demobilization, training of the South Korean Army, strengthening of the North Atlantic Treaty Organization, establishment of a NATO line of communications, potential crises in Indochina and Formosa, and the effects of budget cuts upon the Army's capability to carry out its mission; retired from active service, June 1955, died in Fox Chapel, Pennsylvania, on 26 July 1993.

The Artist

Clarence Lamont MacNelly (1920–1986), graduate economist, Navy officer, pilot, advertising executive, magazine publisher, jazz pianist, and portraitist, has created the likenesses of a wide variety of subjects. His images of children are especially appealing, and his Navy background led him spontaneously to the field of yachting and portraits of several prominent skippers like Robert Lyon Hamill. His portrait of one of America's great performers, Jimmy Durante, has garnered considerable critical acclaim. Art runs in the family; MacNelly's son Jeffrey won a Pulitzer Prize as cartoonist of the Richmond (Virginia) News Leader. The portrait of General Matthew B. Ridgway is reproduced from the Army Art Collection.

Matthew Bunker Ridgway
By Clarence Lamont MacNelly
Oil on canvas, 38¼" x 28¼," 1972

MAXWELL DAVENPORT TAYLOR was born in Keytesville, Missouri, on 26 August 1901; graduated from the United States Military Academy, 1922; was commissioned a second lieutenant of engineering, June 1922, and attended his branch course; served in Hawaii with the 3d Engineers, 1923–1926; married Lydia Gardner Hopper, 1925; transferred to field artillery and served with the 10th Field Artillery, 1926–1927; was promoted to first lieutenant, February 1927; studied French in Paris and was instructor in French and later Spanish at West Point, 1927–1932; graduated from the Field Artillery School, Fort Sill, 1933, and the Command and General Staff School, Fort Leavenworth, 1935; was promoted to captain, August 1935; was a student of Japanese at the American embassy in Tokyo, 1935–1939, with detached military attache duty at Peking, China, 1937; graduated from the Army War College, 1940; was promoted to permanent major, July 1940; served in the War Plans Division and on a Hemisphere defense mission to Latin American countries, 1940; commanded the 12th Field Artillery Battalion, 1940–1941; served in the Office of the Secretary of the General Staff, 1941–1942; received temporary promotions to lieutenant colonel, December 1941, colonel, February 1942, and brigadier general, December 1942; was chief of staff of the 82d Airborne Division, 1942, and then its artillery commander in operations in Sicily and Italy, 1942–1944; received temporary promotion to major general, May 1944; commanded the 101st Airborne Division in the Normandy invasion and the Western European campaigns, 1944–1945; was promoted to permanent lieutenant colonel, June 1945, and brigadier general, January 1948; was chief of staff of the United States European Command, Germany, 1949, and commander of the United States forces in Berlin, 1949–1951; was promoted to temporary lieutenant general and permanent major general, August 1951; was assistant chief of staff for operations, G–3, and deputy chief of staff for operations and administration, 1951–1953; was promoted to temporary general, June 1953; was commander of the Eighth Army in the final operations of the Korean War, 1953; initiated the Korean armed forces assistance program, 1953–1954; commanded United States Forces, Far East, and the Eighth Army, 1954–1955, and was commander in chief, United Nations Command, 1955; was chief of staff of the United States Army, 30 June 1955–30 June 1959; opposed dependence upon a massive retaliation doctrine, pushed for an increase in conventional forces to ensure a capability of flexible response, guided the transition to a "pentomic" concept, and directed Army participation in sensitive operations at Little Rock, Lebanon, Taiwan, and Berlin; retired from active service, July 1959; was recalled as chairman of the Joint Chiefs of Staff, 1962–1964; again retired; became ambassador to South Vietnam, 1964–1965; was special consultant to the president and chairman of the Foreign Intelligence Advisory Board, 1965–1969; was president of the Institute of Defense Analysis, 1966–1969; died in Washington, D.C., on 19 April 1987.

The Artist

Bjorn Peter Egeli (1900–1984) was born in Horten, Norway. He attended school there until his mid-teens, when he came to the United States. During the 1920s he studied at the Miller Art School in Brooklyn, New York, and then attended the Corcoran School of Art in Washington, D.C., where he graduated with top honors after four years of tutelage under such leading instructors as Richard Meryman, Eugen Weisz, S. Burtis Baker, and Mathilda Leisenring. Mr. Egeli's son, Cedric Baldwin Egeli, is also a contributor to the Chiefs of Staff Portrait Gallery at the Pentagon, Washington, D.C. The portrait of General Maxwell D. Taylor is reproduced from the Army Art Collection.

Maxwell Davenport Taylor
By Bjorn Peter Egeli
Oil on canvas, 47" x 33," 1972

LYMAN LOUIS LEMNITZER was born in Honesdale, Pennsylvania, on 29 August 1899; graduated from the United States Military Academy, 1920; was commissioned a second lieutenant, July 1920; attended the Coast Artillery School, Fort Monroe and then served with his battery in the United States and Philippines, 1921–1926; married Katherine Mead Tryon, 1923; was promoted to first lieutenant, June 1925; was twice instructor of natural and experimental philosophy at West Point, 1926–1930 and 1934–1935; again served as a troop and staff officer in the Philippines, 1931–1934; was promoted to captain, August 1935; was instructor in tactics at the Coast Artillery School, 1936; graduated from the Command and General Staff School, Fort Leavenworth, 1936, and the Army War College, 1940; served in the 70th Coast Artillery and the 38th Coast Artillery (Antiaircraft) Brigade, 1940–1941; was promoted to major, July 1940, and to temporary lieutenant colonel, December 1941; was a plans and operations officer on the General Staff and at Army Ground Forces Headquarters, 1941–1942; was promoted to temporary colonel and brigadier general, June 1942; commanded the 34th Coast Artillery (Antiaircraft) Brigade and was concurrently plans and operations officer at Allied Forces Headquarters in England and North Africa and deputy chief of staff of Fifth Army in North Africa, 1942–1943; was promoted to temporary major general (May) and permanent brigadier general (June), 1944; was chief of staff to the Supreme Allied Commander, Mediterranean, and United States theater commander there, 1944–1945; was senior Army member of the Joint Strategic Survey Committee, Joint Chiefs of Staff, 1945–1947; was deputy commandant of the National War College, 1947–1949; was director of the Office of Military Assistance, Office of the Secretary of Defense, 1949–1950; was promoted to permanent major general (April) and temporary lieutenant general (August), 1952; commanded the 11th Airborne Division in the United States and the 7th Infantry Division in operations in Korea, 1951–1952; was deputy chief of staff for Plans and Research, 1952–1955; was promoted to temporary general, March 1955; was commanding general of United States Forces, Far East, and the Eighth Army, 1955; was commander in chief of the Far East and United Nations Commands and governor of the Ryukyu Islands, 1955–1957; was vice chief of staff of the United States Army, 1957–1959; was chief of staff of the United States Army, 1 July 1959–30 September 1960; stressed the need to modernize the Army and pressed for adequate appropriations; was chairman of the Joint Chiefs of Staff, 1960–1962; was commanding general of United States Forces, Europe, 1962–1969; was Supreme Allied Commander, Europe, 1963–1969; retired from active service, July 1969; was a member of a panel that investigated domestic activities of the Central Intelligence Agency, 1975; died in Washington, D.C., on 12 November 1988.

The Artist

Bjorn Peter Egeli (1900–1984), Norwegian-born and American-trained portraitist, painted the likenesses of many prominent military figures, such as Army General Dwight D. Eisenhower, Army General Douglas MacArthur, and Marine General Alexander A. Vandegrift, during an active career in the national capital region. His work is represented at numerous public institutions, including the Pentagon, the United States Military Academy, the Supreme Court, the National Archives, the Maryland statehouse, Brandeis University, the Mayo Clinic, and others. His portrait of General Lyman L. Lemnitzer is reproduced from the Army Art Collection.

Lyman Louis Lemnitzer
By Bjorn Peter Egeli
Oil on canvas, 38⅛" x 32⅛," 1972

GEORGE HENRY DECKER was born in Catskill, New York, on 16 February 1902; graduated from Lafayette College, Easton, Pennsylvania, with a degree in economics, 1924; was commissioned a second lieutenant, June 1924, and served with the 26th Infantry at Plattsburg Barracks, 1924–1928; married Helen E. Inman, 1926; served with the 35th Infantry in Hawaii, 1928–1931; was promoted to first lieutenant, April 1930; graduated from the Infantry School, Fort Benning, 1932, and then served with the 29th Infantry, Fort Benning, 1932–1935, and with the 7th Infantry, Fort Vancouver, 1935–1936; was promoted to captain, August 1935; graduated from the Command and General Staff School at Fort Leavenworth, 1937; served with the 10th Infantry, Forts Thomas and McClellan, and the 9th Infantry, Fort Bragg, 1937–1940; established and commanded Headquarters Company, I Corps, Fort Jackson, and was assistant supply and logistics officer, 1940–1941; was promoted to temporary major (January), permanent major (June), and temporary lieutenant colonel (December), 1941; served on the War Department General Staff in the Office of the Assistant Chief of Staff for Supply, 1941–1942; was promoted to temporary colonel, October 1942; was deputy chief of staff of the Third Army, Fort Sam Houston, 1942–1944; served in the Southwest Pacific as deputy chief of staff (1943–1944) and chief of staff (1944–1946) of the Sixth Army; participated in operations from New Guinea to the Philippines and in the early occupation of Japan; was promoted to temporary ranks of brigadier general, August 1944, and major general, June 1945; served in Washington successively in Army Ground Forces and Army Service Forces headquarters, 1946; was deputy commander and chief of staff of United States Forces, Middle Pacific, Hawaii, 1946–1948; was promoted to the permanent ranks of lieutenant colonel, June 1947, and colonel, June 1948; commanded the 5th Infantry Division, Fort Jackson, 1948–1950; served in the Office of the Comptroller of the Army as chief of the Budget Division, 1950–1952; was promoted to temporary lieutenant general, June 1952; was comptroller of the Army, 1952–1955; was promoted to permanent brigadier general, April 1953, and major general, July 1954; commanded VII Corps at Stuttgart, Germany, 1955–1956; was promoted to temporary general, May 1956; was deputy commander in chief of the United States European Command, France, 1956–1957; was concurrently commander in chief of the United Nations Command and commander of United States Forces and Eighth Army, Korea, 1957–1959; was vice chief of staff of the Army, 1959–1960; was chief of staff of the United States Army, 1 October 1960–30 September 1962; supervised augmentations to meet a crisis in Berlin, an increase in special warfare forces, initiation of new divisional (ROAD) and forward depot concepts, and expansion of the Army to sixteen divisions; retired from active service, September 1962; died in Washington, D.C., on 6 February 1980.

The Artist

Woodi Ishmael (1914–1995) was born in Lewis County, Kentucky, and entered his profession through the Cleveland (Ohio) Institute of Arts and the Art Students League in New York City. As a painter and illustrator, he illustrated a weekly syndicated column for Associated Press Newsfeatures, called "The Power of Faith"; served as an official artist for the United States Air Force, completing several portraits of Air Force chiefs of staff; sailed as artist-in-residence on major ocean liners to deliver art lectures and demonstrations; and officiated as the only courtroom artist at the Jack Ruby trial. His portrait of General George H. Decker is reproduced from the Army Art Collection.

George Henry Decker
By Woodi Ishmael
Oil on canvas, 36" x 30," 1972

EARLE GILMORE WHEELER was born in Washington, D.C., on 13 January 1908; graduated from the United States Military Academy, 1932; was commissioned a second lieutenant and served with the 29th Infantry, Fort Benning, 1932–1936; married Frances Rogers Howell, 1932; was promoted to first lieutenant, August 1935; completed the Infantry School regular course, 1937; served with the 15th Infantry in China and at Fort Lewis, 1937–1940; was promoted to temporary captain, September 1940; taught mathematics at West Point, 1940–1941; was aide to the commander of the 36th Infantry Division, 1941; graduated from the Command and General Staff College, Fort Leavenworth, 1942; was promoted to temporary major (February), permanent captain (June), and temporary lieutenant colonel (November), 1942; was a battalion commander, 141st Infantry, 36th Infantry Division, 1942; was promoted to temporary colonel, June 1943; was assistant chief of staff for operations of the 99th Infantry Division, 1942–1944, and chief of staff of the 63d Infantry Division in the final battles in Europe, 1944–1945; was instructor in combined arms training at the Field Artillery School, Fort Sill, 1945–1946; was assistant chief of staff for supply at the Western Base Section in Paris, 1946, and deputy chief of staff for operations of the United States Constabulary in Germany, 1947–1949; after reversion to peacetime rank, was again promoted to temporary ranks of lieutenant colonel, July 1947 (made permanent July 1948), and colonel, September 1950 (made permanent October 1953); graduated from the Army War College, 1950; was a member of the Joint Intelligence Group, Office of the Joint Chiefs of Staff, 1950–1951; commanded the 351st Infantry in Italy 1951–1952, and was briefly deputy commander of Trieste United States Troops, 1952; was promoted to temporary brigadier general, November 1952; was assistant chief of staff for plans and operations at Allied Forces Southern Europe headquarters, Naples, Italy, 1952–1955; was promoted to temporary major general, December 1955; was director of plans in the Office of the Deputy Chief of Staff for Plans and Operations, 1955–1957; was assistant deputy chief of staff for military operations, 1957–1958; commanded the 2d Armored Division, Fort Hood, 1958–1959, and III Corps there, 1959–1960; was promoted to temporary ranks of lieutenant general, April 1960, and general, March 1962, and permanent ranks of brigadier general, May 1960, and major general, June 1961; was deputy commander in chief of the United States European Command, France, 1962; was chief of staff of the United States Army, 1 October 1962–2 July 1964; supervised a major reorganization of the Department of the Army, the deployment of troops in Cuban missile, school integration, and Vietnam crises, and tests of an air assault division concept and overseas reinforcement system; was chairman of the Joint Chiefs of Staff during most of the Vietnam War, 1964–1970; retired from active service, July 1970; died in Frederick, Maryland, on 18 December 1975.

The Artist

Lloyd Bowers Embrey (1913–1979), noted Washington portrait painter, exhibited widely during his career as an artist, and is represented in numerous collections in the United States and abroad. His work extended well beyond the confines of oil portraiture; his sculpture of President John F. Kennedy, for example, is displayed in New York City's Harvard Club, and his bronze bust of Nikita Khrushchev, sculpted to commemorate the visit of the Russian premier to the United States, is in the Kremlin. In the military line, he painted the Arctic landscape surrounding the Thule Air Force Base in Greenland. His portrait of General Earle G. Wheeler is reproduced from the Army Art Collection.

Earle Gilmore Wheeler
By Lloyd Bowers Embrey
Oil on canvas, 42" x 32," 1972

HAROLD KEITH JOHNSON was born in Bowesmont, North Dakota, on 22 February 1912; graduated from the United States Military Academy, 1933; was commissioned a second lieutenant and assigned to the 3d Infantry, Fort Snelling, 1933–1937; married Dorothy Rennix, 1935; was promoted to first lieutenant, June 1936; graduated from the Infantry School, Fort Benning, 1938; served in the 28th Infantry, Fort Niagara, 1938–1940; was assigned to the 57th Infantry, Philippine Scouts, at Fort McKinley, 1940; was promoted to temporary ranks of captain, September 1940, major, September 1941, and lieutenant colonel, April 1942, and permanent captain, June 1943; was a battalion commander in the defense of the Philippines, was taken prisoner when Bataan fell, survived the "Death March" and imprisonment in the Philippines, Japan, and Korea, and was liberated by the 7th Infantry Division, 1942–1945; was promoted to temporary colonel, September 1945; graduated from the Command and General Staff College, Fort Leavenworth, 1947, and was an instructor there, 1947–1949; graduated from the Armed Forces Staff College, 1950; commanded the 3d Battalion, 7th Infantry, at Fort Devens, 1950; was a battalion commander and commander of both the 5th and 8th Cavalry in Korean War operations, 1950–1951; was plans and operations officer of the I Corps, Far East Command, 1951; was a plans and operations officer in the Office of the Chief of Army Field Forces, Fort Monroe, 1951–1952; graduated from the National War College, 1953; was chief of the Joint War Plans Branch, Office of the Assistant Chief of Staff, G–3, 1954–1955; was promoted to temporary brigadier general (January) and permanent colonel (February), 1956; was executive officer in the Office of the Assistant Chief of Staff, G–3, 1955–1956; was assistant division commander of the 8th Infantry Division, 1956–1957; was chief of staff of the American Seventh Army in Germany 1957–1959, and of the Central Army Group, North Atlantic Treaty Organization, 1959–1960; was promoted to permanent brigadier general, June 1960, was commandant of the Command and General Staff College, 1960–1963; was assistant and then acting deputy chief of staff for military operations, 1963; was promoted to temporary major general, October 1959, permanent major general, April 1963, temporary lieutenant general, July 1963, and temporary general, July 1964; was deputy chief of staff for military operations, 1963–1964, was chief of staff of the United States Army, 3 July 1964–2 July 1968; supervised the Army during the major expansion and deployments occasioned by the Vietnam War, the commitment in the Dominican Republic, the fielding of an airmobile division, and the shift of the United States line of communications in Europe from France to Germany and the Benelux countries; retired from active service, July 1968; died in Washington, D.C., on 24 September 1983. Died in Charleston, South Carolina, on 18 July 2005.

The Artist

Joseph Richards Essig (1902–1975) was born in Wallingford, Pennsylvania. He pursued his art training at the Pennsylvania Museum School of Industrial Art in Philadelphia, the Metropolitan Museum of Art in New York City, the Pennsylvania Academy of the Fine Arts in Philadelphia, and the British Academy of Arts in Rome, Italy. While in the Army from 1941 to 1945, he took advantage of a period in England to study under Augustus John and then served on the Continent as a draftsman in the 655th Engineer Topographic Battalion attached to the Ninth Army. Later established in Philadelphia, he studied art with Sam Morrow Palmer, Charles H. Woodbury, Leopold Seyffert, and Ceasar Riccardi. His portrait of General Harold K. Johnson, which was painted from life, is reproduced from the Army Art Collection.

Harold Keith Johnson
By Joseph Richards Essig
Oil on canvas, 40" x 30," 1972

WILLIAM CHILDS WESTMORELAND was born in Spartanburg County, South Carolina, on 26 March 1914; graduated from the United States Military Academy, 1936; was commissioned a second lieutenant, June 1936, and served with the 18th Field Artillery, Fort Sill, 1936–1939; was promoted to first lieutenant, June 1939; was a battery officer and commander and a battalion staff officer of the 8th Field Artillery, Schofield Barracks, 1939–1941; was promoted to temporary major (February) and lieutenant colonel (September), 1942; was operations officer of the 34th Field Artillery Battalion, 9th Infantry Division, in the United States and North Africa and a battalion commander in operations in Tunisia and Sicily, 1942–1944; was executive officer of the 9th Division Artillery in Western European operations, 1944; was promoted to temporary colonel, July 1944; was chief of staff of the 9th Infantry Division in the closing operations of World War II in Germany, 1944–1945; commanded the 60th Infantry, 1945–1946; was promoted to permanent captain, June 1946; was chief of staff and later commander of the 71st Infantry Division, 1946; received airborne training at the Infantry School, 1946; commanded the 504th Parachute Infantry, 82d Airborne Division, 1946–1947; married Katherine S. Van Deusen, 1947; was chief of staff of the 82d Airborne Division, Fort Bragg, 1947–1950, receiving his promotion to permanent major in July 1948; was instructor at the Command and General Staff College, Fort Leavenworth, 1950–1951, and the Army War College, 1951–1952; commanded the 187th Airborne Regimental Combat Team in operations in Korea, 1952–1953; was promoted to temporary brigadier general, November 1952, and permanent lieutenant colonel, July 1953; was deputy assistant chief of staff, G–1, for manpower control, 1953–1955; attended the advanced management program at Harvard Business School, 1954; was secretary of the General Staff, 1955–1958; was promoted to temporary major general, December 1956; was commander of the 101st Airborne Division and Fort Campbell, 1958–1960; was superintendent of the United States Military Academy, 1960–1963; was promoted to permanent ranks of colonel, June 1961, and brigadier general, February 1963, and to temporary lieutenant general, July 1963; was commander of the Strategic Army Corps and XVIII Airborne Corps, 1963–1964; was successively deputy commander and acting commander of United States Military Assistance Command, Vietnam, 1964; was promoted to temporary general, August 1964, and permanent major general, August 1965; was commander of United States Military Assistance Command, Vietnam, and United States Army, Vietnam, at the peak of the Vietnam War, 1964–1968; was chief of staff of the United States Army, 3 July 1968–30 June 1972; supervised the Army's disengagement from Vietnam, the transition from the draft to an all-volunteer footing, and the employment of troops in a period of active civil disturbance; centered attention upon efforts to improve service life, officer professionalism, job attractiveness, and public understanding; retired from active service, July 1972; died in Charleston, South Carolina, on 18 July 2005.

The Artist

Herbert Elmer Abrams (1921–2003) was born in Greenfield, Massachusetts. He studied art at the Norwich Art School in Connecticut and the Pratt Institute in Brooklyn, New York, as well as under Frank Vincent DuMond at the Art Students League in New York City. Drafted into World War II, he trained as a pilot and, by war's end, was an advanced flying instructor for multiengine aircraft. Thereafter he pursued his career as a painter, earning critical acclaim for his work. In 1972, commissioned by the Army to depict scenes from the war in Vietnam, he executed a number of paintings of soldiers in various activities. His portrait of General William C. Westmoreland is reproduced from the Army Art Collection.

William Childs Westmoreland

By Herbert Elmer Abrams

Oil on canvas, 36" x 30," 1972

BRUCE PALMER, JR., was born in Austin, Texas, on 13 April 1913; graduated from the United States Military Academy in 1936; was commissioned a second lieutenant and served with the 8th Cavalry, Fort Bliss, 1936–1939; married Kay Sibert, 1936; was promoted to first lieutenant, June 1939, and served as regimental adjutant, June–September 1939; graduated from the Cavalry School at Fort Riley, 1940; was a troop and squadron commander of the 6th Cavalry (Mechanized), 1940–1942; was promoted to temporary ranks of captain, October 1940, and major, February 1942; served in the Operations Division of the War Department General Staff, 1942–1943; was promoted to temporary lieutenant colonel, February 1943; was chief of staff of the 6th Infantry Division in Southwest Pacific operations in World War II, 1944–1945; was promoted to temporary colonel, January 1945, and permanent captain, June 1946, and major, July 1948; commanded the 63d Infantry in the Korean occupation, 1945–1946; was chief of plans and operations of the First Army, 1947–1949; was instructor of tactics and then director of instruction at the Infantry School, Fort Benning, 1949–1951; concurrently completed the basic airborne course; graduated from the Army War College, 1952; was secretary of the general staff and chief of the Plans Division, United States Army, Europe, 1952–1954; was promoted to permanent lieutenant colonel, July 1953; was commander of the 16th Infantry, 1954–1955; served on the faculty of the Army War College, 1955–1957; was deputy secretary of the General Staff and White House liaison officer, Office of the Chief of Staff, 1957–1959; was promoted to temporary brigadier general, August 1959; was deputy commandant of the Army War College, 1959–1961; was assistant division commander of the 82d Airborne Division, Fort Bragg, 1961–1962; was promoted to permanent colonel, June 1961, and temporary major general, May 1962; was chief of staff of the Eighth Army, Korea, 1962–1963; was assistant deputy chief of staff for plans and operations, 1963–1964, and deputy chief of staff for military operations, 1964–1965; was promoted to permanent brigadier general, February 1963, and temporary lieutenant general, July 1964; was commander of Task Force 120 and United States Land Forces, Dominican Republic, May 1965; was concurrently commander of United States Forces and Army Forces and deputy commander of the Inter-American Peace Force in operations in the Dominican Republic, May 1965–January 1966; was commander of the XVIII Airborne Corps, 1965–1967; was commander of the II Field Force, Vietnam, and deputy commander of the United States Army, Vietnam, 1967–1968; was promoted to temporary general, August 1968, and served as vice chief of staff of the United States Army, 1 August 1968–30 June 1972; was acting chief of staff of the United States Army 1 July–11 October 1972; provided managerial continuity at the top of the Army during the Westmoreland-Abrams interregnum, supervised the continuing drawdown of Army forces from Vietnam and related Army-wide readjustments, and prepared major revisions in Army organizational structure; resumed duties as vice chief of staff; was commander in chief of the United States Readiness Command, 1973–1974; retired from the Army, September 1974; died in Alexandria, Virginia, on 10 October 2000.

The Artist

Herbert Elmer Abrams (1921–2003) gave televised lectures on painting, discussed art during interviews on radio, and wrote about the work of his distinguished teacher, Frank Vincent DuMond, for *American Artist*. A 1975 film, *A Different Light*, on Abrams and his art won the Keith L. Ware Annual Award for Excellence in Newspapers, Magazines, Radio, and Television, as well as the Department of Defense's Thomas Jefferson Award for outstanding achievement in promoting a fuller understanding of the mission of the armed forces. The portrait of General Bruce Palmer, Jr., is reproduced from the Army Art Collection.

Bruce Palmer, Jr.
By Herbert Elmer Abrams
Oil on canvas, 42" x 36," 1975

CREIGHTON WILLIAMS ABRAMS, JR., was born in Springfield, Massachusetts, on 15 September 1914; graduated from the United States Military Academy, 1936; married Julia Harvey, 1936; was commissioned a second lieutenant and served in the 1st Cavalry Division, 1936–1940; was promoted to first lieutenant, June 1939, and to temporary captain, September 1940; was briefly a tank company commander in the 1st Armored Division, 1941; was a battalion commander in the 37th Armored Regiment, 1942–1943; was promoted to temporary major (February) and lieutenant colonel (September), 1943; commanded the 37th Tank Battalion and Combat Command B, 4th Armored Division, in Allied operations across Europe, 1943–1945; was promoted to temporary colonel, April 1945; served on the Army General Staff, 1945, and in the War Plans section of the Army Ground Forces headquarters, 1945–1946; was director of tactics of the Armored School, Fort Knox, 1946–1948; was promoted to permanent ranks of captain, June 1946, and major, July 1948; graduated from the Command and General Staff College, Fort Leavenworth, 1949; commanded the 63d Tank Battalion, 1st Infantry Division, United States Army, Europe, 1949–1951; was again promoted to temporary colonel after postwar reversion, June 1951; commanded the 2d Armored Cavalry, United States Army, Europe, 1951–1952; graduated from the Army War College, 1953; was successively chief of staff of the I, X, and IX Corps, United States Army Forces, Far East, Korea, 1953–1954; was chief of staff of the Armor Center, Fort Knox, 1954–1956; was promoted to temporary brigadier general, February 1956; was deputy assistant chief of staff for reserve components, 1956–1959; was assistant division commander of the 3d Armored Division, 1959–1960, and deputy chief of staff for military operations, United States Army, Europe, 1960; was promoted to temporary major general, June 1960, and permanent colonel, June 1961; was commander of the 3d Armored Division, 1960–1962; was assistant deputy chief of staff and director of operations, Office of the Deputy Chief of Staff for Operations, 1962–1963; was assistant chief of staff for force development, 1963; commanded V Corps in Germany, 1963–1964; was promoted to permanent brigadier general (February) and temporary lieutenant general (August), 1963; was acting vice chief of staff and vice chief of staff of the United States Army, August 1964–April 1967; was promoted to general, September 1964, and permanent major general, August 1965; was deputy commander and then commander of United States Military Assistance Command, Vietnam, 1967–1972; was chief of staff of the United States Army, 12 October 1972–4 September 1974; supervised the Army in the closing stages of the Vietnam War, including withdrawal of American troops from the war zone, overall reductions in Army strength, elimination of the draft, transition to a volunteer status, and execution of a major reorganization; died of cancer in Washington, D.C., on 4 September 1974.

The Artist

Herbert Elmer Abrams (1921–2003) painted the portraits of many prominent personalities in the fields of government, business, and the professions, including President Jimmy Carter, Governor Thomas E. Meskill of Connecticut, Texas oilman Clint Murchison, and playwright Arthur Miller. During his career as a painter he taught art, including classes for officers at the United States Military Academy, as well as lectured on art for commercial and cable television stations. His portrait of General Creighton W. Abrams, Jr., is reproduced from the Army Art Collection.

Creighton Williams Abrams, Jr.
By Herbert Elmer Abrams
Oil on canvas, 42" x 36," 1975

FREDERICK CARLTON WEYAND was born in Arbuckle, California, on 15 September 1916; was commissioned a second lieutenant through the Reserve Officers Training Corps program at the University of California at Berkeley, 1938, where he graduated in 1939; married Arline Langhart, 1940; was called to active duty and served with the 6th Artillery, 1940–1942; was promoted to temporary first lieutenant, June 1941, and to captain in February and major in November 1942; graduated from the Command and General Staff College, Fort Leavenworth, 1942; was adjutant of the Harbor Defense Command, San Francisco, 1942–1943; served in the Office of the Chief of Intelligence, War Department General Staff, 1944; was assistant chief of staff for intelligence, China-Burma-India Theater, 1944–1945; was in the Military Intelligence Service, Washington, 1945–1946; was promoted to temporary lieutenant colonel, March 1945, and permanent captain, July 1948; was chief of staff for intelligence, United States Army Forces, Middle Pacific, 1946–1949; graduated from the Infantry School, Fort Benning, 1950; was battalion commander in the 7th Infantry and assistant chief of staff, G–3, of the 3d Infantry Division in the Korean War, 1950–1951; served on the faculty of the Infantry School, 1952–1953; attended the Armed Forces Staff College, 1953; was military assistant in the Office of the Assistant Secretary of the Army for Financial Management, 1953–1954; was military assistant and executive to the secretary of the Army, 1954–1957; was promoted to permanent major, July 1953, and temporary colonel, July 1955; graduated from the Army War College, 1958; commanded the 3d Battle Group, 6th Infantry, in Europe, 1958–1959; served in the Office of the United States Commander in Berlin, 1960; was promoted to temporary brigadier general, July 1960; was chief of staff, Communications Zone, United States Army, Europe, 1960–1961; was deputy chief and chief of legislative liaison, Department of the Army, 1961–1964; was promoted to permanent lieutenant colonel, September 1961, and to temporary major general, November 1962; was commander of the 25th Infantry Division, Hawaii, 1964–1966, and in Vietnam operations, 1966–1967; was promoted to permanent colonel, September 1966; was deputy, acting commander, and commander of II Field Force, Vietnam, 1967–1968; was chief of the Office of Reserve Components, 1968–1969; was promoted to permanent brigadier and major general and temporary lieutenant general, August 1968, and temporary general, October 1970; was military adviser at the Paris peace talks, 1969–1970; was assistant chief of staff for force development, 1970; was successively deputy commander and commander of the United States Military Assistance Command, Vietnam, 1970–1973; was commander in chief of the United States Army, Pacific, 1973; was vice chief of staff of the United States Army, 1973–1974; was chief of staff of the United States Army, 3 October 1974–31 September 1976; supervised Army moves to improve the combat-to-support troop ratio, to achieve a sixteen-division force, to enhance the effectiveness of roundout units, and to improve personnel and logistical readiness; retired from active service, October 1976.

The Artist

Bjorn Peter Egeli (1900–1984), who won several awards for portraiture, drew upon his native Norwegian connections to execute the likenesses of Crown Princess Martha, wife of future King Olav V of Norway, and of the nation's longtime ambassador to the United States, Wilhelm Munthe de Morgenstierne. Mr. Egeli's children have become accomplished artists in their own right. His son, Cedric Baldwin Egeli, is also a contributor to the Chiefs of Staff Portrait Gallery at the Pentagon, Washington, D.C. The portrait of General Frederick C. Weyand is reproduced from the Army Art Collection.

Frederick Carlton Weyand
By Bjorn Peter Egeli
Oil on canvas, 45" x 36," 1975

BERNARD WILLIAM ROGERS was born in Fairview, Kansas, on 16 July 1921; graduated from the United States Military Academy, 1943; was commissioned a second lieutenant, June 1943, and attended the basic course at the Infantry School, Fort Benning; was promoted to temporary first lieutenant, December 1943, and assigned to the 275th Infantry, 1943–1944; married Ann Ellen Jones, 1944; was instructor of economics, government, and history at West Point, 1944–1946; was promoted to temporary captain, February 1945; was aide to the High Commissioner to Austria and to the commander of the Sixth Army, 1946–1947; attended Oxford University, England, as a Rhodes scholar, 1947–1950, receiving bachelor and master of arts degrees in philosophy, politics, and economics; was aide to the chief of Army Field Forces, 1950–1951; was promoted to permanent captain, January 1949, and temporary major, July 1951; graduated from the Infantry School advanced course, 1952; commanded the 3d Battalion, 9th Infantry, in Korean operations, 1952–1953; was promoted to temporary lieutenant colonel, August 1953; was aide to the commander in chief and staff intelligence officer of the United Nations and Far East Commands, 1953–1954; graduated from the Command and General Staff College, Fort Leavenworth, 1955; commanded the 1st Battalion, 23d Infantry, 1955–1956; served in the Coordination Division, Office of the Chief of Staff, 1956–1958; was executive and senior aide to the chief of staff, 1958–1959; was promoted to permanent major (January) and temporary colonel (September), 1959; graduated from the Army War College, 1960; commanded the 1st Battle Group, 19th Infantry, 24th Infantry Division, in Europe, 1960–1961; was chief of staff of the 24th Division and chief of the Troop Operation Branch, Operations Division, United States Army, Europe, 1961–1962; was military assistant and executive officer to the chairman of the Joint Chiefs of Staffs, 1962–1966; was promoted to permanent lieutenant colonel, January 1964, temporary brigadier general, October 1966, and permanent colonel, June 1968; was assistant division commander of the 1st Infantry Division in Vietnam, 1966–1967; was commandant of cadets at West Point, 1967–1969; was commander of the 5th Infantry Division (Mechanized) and Fort Carson, 1969–1970; was promoted to temporary major general, February 1970, and permanent brigadier general, August 1971; was chief of legislative liaison, 1971–1972; was promoted to temporary lieutenant general, November 1972, and permanent major general, June 1973; was deputy chief of staff for personnel of the Army, 1972–1974; was promoted to temporary general, November 1974; was commander of the United States Army Forces Command, Fort McPherson, 1974–1976; was chief of staff of the United States Army, 1 October 1976–21 June 1979; supervised the Army's move to a 24-division all-component force, established priorities for near-term readiness, midterm modernization, and long-term sustainability, established a program to enhance the quality of life of Army personnel, and suggested a limited draft to fill the Individual Ready Reserve; was appointed Supreme Allied Commander, North Atlantic Treaty Organization, July 1979; retired from active service, June 1987.

The Artist

Robert Clark Templeton (1929–1991) was born in Red Oak, Iowa. He studied at the Kansas City Art Institute in the late 1940s; pursued private study with John Sloan; and attended the Art Students League in New York City in the early 1950s, training under Louis Bouche, Reginald Marsh, and Louis Bosa. During a tour of military service in the 1950s he designed and executed murals for the Army and was an Army staff photographer for a service newspaper in Heidelberg, Germany. He painted the portraits of many prominent individuals, including President and Mrs. Jimmy Carter, Vice President Hubert H. Humphrey, Roy Wilkins, and Stan Musial. His portrait of General Bernard W. Rogers is reproduced from the Army Art Collection.

Bernard William Rogers
By Robert Clark Templeton
Oil on canvas, 46" x 36," 1977

EDWARD CHARLES MEYER was born in St. Mary's, Pennsylvania, on 11 December 1928; graduated from the United States Military Academy, 1951; was commissioned a second lieutenant and attended the Infantry School, Fort Benning, 1951; was a platoon leader, Company C, 25th Armored Infantry Battalion, in Korean operations, 1951–1952; was promoted to first lieutenant, July 1952; was a platoon leader, company commander, and battalion staff officer, 224th Infantry, in Korean operations, 1952–1953; served in the 1st Officer Candidate Regiment, Infantry School, 1953–1954; married Carol McCunliffe, 1954; was aide to the assistant commandant, Infantry School, 1954, and instructor in operations there, 1954–1957; was promoted to temporary captain, July 1956; graduated from the infantry officers advanced and basic airborne courses, Fort Benning, 1957; was commander of Headquarters and Headquarters Company, 1st Airborne Battle Group, 501st Infantry, 1957–1958, and commander of Company D, 1958–1959; graduated from the Command and General Staff College, Fort Leavenworth, 1960; was promoted to permanent captain, February 1958, and to temporary major, October 1960; was manpower control officer, Office of the Assistant Chief of Staff, G–1, United States Army, Europe (Rear), 1960–1961; was assistant executive and aide to the chief of staff at Supreme Headquarters, Allied Powers Europe, 1961–1963; graduated from the Armed Forces Staff College, 1964; was promoted to temporary lieutenant colonel, May 1964, and permanent major, June 1965; served in the Coordination Division of the Office of the Chief of Staff, 1964–1965; was deputy commander of the 3d Brigade, 1st Cavalry Division (Airmobile), in Vietnam operations, 1965; was commander of the 2d Battalion, 5th Cavalry, in Vietnam operations, 1965–1966; graduated from the National War College, 1967; served in the Plans and Operations Division, Office of the Joint Chiefs of Staff, 1967–1969; was promoted to temporary colonel, November 1968; was commander of the 2d Brigade, 1st Cavalry Division (Airmobile), and division chief of staff in Vietnam operations, 1969–1970; was a federal executive fellow at the Brookings Institution, 1970–1971; was promoted to temporary brigadier general, August 1971, and permanent lieutenant colonel, June 1972; was assistant division commander (support) of the 82d Airborne Division, 1971–1972; was deputy commandant of the Army War College, 1972–1973; was deputy chief of staff for operations, United States Army, Europe, and Seventh Army, 1973–1974; was promoted to temporary major general, August 1973; was commanding general of the 3d Infantry Division, United States Army, Europe, 1974–1975; was assistant deputy chief and deputy chief of staff for operations and plans, United States Army, 1975–1979; was promoted to permanent colonel, March 1976, and temporary lieutenant general, October 1976, and general, June 1979; was chief of staff of the United States Army, 22 June 1979–21 June 1983; prosecuted an Army-wide modernization program with emphasis on quality over quantity, stressed the need for a long-term investment in land force materiel, and launched a unit-manning system to reduce personnel turbulence and to enhance readiness; retired from active service, June 1983.

The Artist

Everett Raymond Kinstler (1926–) began his art career drawing comic strips while still in his teens. A protégé of James Montgomery Flagg, he also studied under Frank Vincent DuMond and Sidney Dickinson at New York City's Art Students League, where he would later teach. In 1955 he made the transition from illustrator to portraitist, to become one of the foremost in his field. He is an academician of the National Academy of Design, as well as a member of a number of art societies. He has won several awards, including the Copley Medal from the Smithsonian's National Portrait Gallery. His portrait of General Edward C. Meyer is reproduced from the Army Art Collection.

Edward Charles Meyer
By Everett Raymond Kinstler
Oil on canvas, 50" x 40," 1984

JOHN ADAMS WICKHAM, JR., was born in Dobbs Ferry, New York on 25 June 1928; graduated from the United States Military Academy, 1950; was commissioned a second lieutenant and assigned to the 18th Infantry; was a troop officer in the 6th Infantry in the United States and Europe, 1950–1953; was promoted to temporary first lieutenant, December 1951; graduated from the infantry officer basic course at the Infantry School, Fort Benning, 1953; was a platoon leader and executive officer in Company L, 511th Airborne Infantry, 1953–1954; was an aide-de-camp successively in Headquarters, 37th and 10th Infantry Divisions, 1954; was promoted to temporary captain, October 1954; attended Harvard University to earn degrees in public administration and in politics, economics, and government, 1954–1956; married Ann Lindsley Prior, 1955; was instructor/assistant professor of the department of social sciences, West Point, 1956–1960; attended infantry officer advanced course at the Infantry School, Fort Benning, 1958; was promoted to temporary major, June 1959; graduated from the Command and General Staff College, Fort Leavenworth, 1961; was operations officer of the 1st Battle Group, 5th Cavalry, in Korea, 1961–1962; graduated from the Armed Forces Staff College, 1963; served in the Strategic Plans and Policy Directorate, Office of the Deputy Chief of Staff for Military Operations, 1963–1964; was promoted to temporary lieutenant colonel, July 1963; served in the Special Studies Group, Office of the Chief of Staff, 1964; was assistant executive officer and aide to the chief of staff of the United States Army, 1964–1966; graduated from the National War College, 1967; commanded the 5th Battalion, 7th Cavalry, 1st Cavalry Division (Airmobile), in Vietnam, 1967; was wounded and hospitalized at Walter Reed Medical Center, 1967–1968; was promoted to temporary colonel, August 1968; served in the Strategic Plans and Policy Division, Office of the Joint Chiefs of Staff, 1968–1969; was commander of the 1st Brigade, 3d Infantry Division, United States Army, Europe, 1969–1970; was a staff group member in the Office of the Chairman of the Joint Chiefs of Staff, 1970–1971; was deputy chief of staff for economic affairs, United States Military Assistance Command, Vietnam, 1971–1973; was promoted to temporary brigadier general, July 1972; was deputy chief and U.S. representative, Four-Party Joint Military Commission, Vietnam, 1973; was promoted to temporary major general, July 1973; was military assistant to the secretary of defense, 1973–1976; commanded the 101st Airborne Division (Air Assault), 1976–1978; was assistant deputy chief of staff for operations and plans in the Office of the Deputy Chief of Staff for Operations and Plans, 1978; was promoted to temporary lieutenant general, August 1978; was director of the Joint Staff, 1978–1979; was promoted to temporary general, July 1979; was commander in chief of the United Nations Command and commander of the United States Forces and Eighth Army, Korea, 1979–1982; was vice chief of staff of the United States Army, 1982–1983; was chief of staff of the United States Army, 23 July 1983–23 June 1987; implemented an Army concept for a new light division structure, supervised a corollary increase in force structure from sixteen to eighteen regular divisions and eight to ten reserve divisions with attendant stationing arrangements, and stressed measures to care for Army families; retired from active service, June 1987.

The Artist

Margaret Holland Sargent (1927–) was born in Hollywood, California. She received her education in art at the University of California–Los Angeles and the Art Students League in New York City, supplemented by private study with Herbert Abrams and John Sanden. Praised for outstanding achievement, especially her ability to use light and explore special relationships, she was the first woman artist certified by the American Portrait Society, and in 2001 was given the added distinction of being listed as one of twelve best portraitists in America. Her widely exhibited and collected work has won her a number of awards, including several from the Salmagundi Club and from the Painter's Club. She has painted the portraits of many prominent government leaders, celebrated personalities, and private citizens. Her portrait of General John A. Wickham, Jr., is reproduced from the Army Art Collection.

John Adams Wickham, Jr.
By Margaret Holland Sargent
Oil on canvas, 52" x 32," 1986

CARL EDWARD VUONO was born in Monongahela, Pennsylvania, on 18 October 1934; graduated from the United States Military Academy, 1957; was commissioned a second lieutenant and attended artillery officer basic course at the Artillery and Missile School, Fort Sill, 1957; served with howitzer elements, 3d Armored Cavalry, 1958–1960; was promoted to temporary and permanent first lieutenant, December 1958 and June 1960, respectively; married Patricia A. Hall, 1960; served with howitzer elements, 82d Artillery, 1st Cavalry Division, in Korea, 1960–1961; was promoted to temporary and permanent captain, December 1961 and June 1964; attended artillery officer advanced course at the Air Defense School, Fort Bliss, 1961–1962; served with XVIII Airborne Corps Artillery, 1962–1963; was an exchange officer with the British 7th Royal Horse Artillery (Parachute), 16th Parachute Group, in England, 1963–1965; was promoted to temporary major, August 1965; was team chief, Fire Support Coordination Element, VII Corps Artillery, United States Army, Europe, 1965–1966; was executive officer, 1st Battalion, 7th Artillery, 1st Infantry Division, in Vietnam, 1966–1967; attended the Marine Command and Staff College, Quantico, 1967–1968; was promoted to temporary lieutenant colonel, August 1968; was personnel management officer, Field Artillery Branch, Officer Personnel Directorate, U.S. Army, 1968–1970; was executive officer, 1st Cavalry Division Artillery, in Vietnam, 1970; was promoted to permanent major, June 1971; was commander, 1st Battalion, 77th Artillery, 1st Cavalry Division, in Vietnam, 1970–1971; was operations research/systems analyst, Office of the Vice Chief of Staff, U.S. Army, 1971–1972; was executive officer, Office of the Project Manager for Reorganization of the Army, Office of the Chief of Staff, 1972; attended the Army War College, 1972–1973; was chief, Budget Division, Office of the Deputy Chief of Staff for Personnel, U.S. Army, 1973–1975; was promoted to temporary colonel, February 1974; was commander, 82d Airborne Division Artillery, 1975–1976; was executive to the chief of staff, U.S. Army, 1976–1977; was promoted to temporary brigadier general, January 1977, and permanent lieutenant colonel, June 1978; was assistant division commander, 1st Infantry Division, 1977–1979; was deputy chief of staff for combat developments, United States Army Training and Doctrine Command, 1979–1981; was promoted to temporary major general, July 1980, permanent colonel, June 1981, and permanent major general, January 1982; was commanding general, 8th Infantry Division, United States Army, Europe, 1981–1983; was deputy commanding general, United States Army Training and Doctrine Command, and commanding general, United States Army Combined Arms Center, 1983–1985; was promoted to temporary lieutenant general, June 1983; was deputy chief of staff for operations and plans, U.S. Army, 1985–1986; was promoted to permanent general, July 1986; was commanding general, United States Army Training and Doctrine Command, 1986–1987; was chief of staff of the United States Army, 23 June 1987–21 June 1991; provided leadership to the Army through a period of great challenge and change that included the end of the Cold War, increasingly friendly relations with the Soviet Union, Army operations in Panama to restore the legal government there, and operations in Southwest Asia to free Kuwait from Iraqi occupation; retired from active service, June 1991.

The Artist

Ned Bittinger (1951–) has been a full-time painter since 1982. He pursued his art education and training at Denison University in Granville, Ohio, and at George Washington University in Washington, D.C. He has received numerous awards and participated in many exhibitions around the world, including an exhibition of Washington and Moscow painters at the Tretyakov Gallery in Moscow, 1990–1991. His portrait of General Carl E. Vuono is reproduced from the Army Art Collection.

Carl Edward Vuono
By Ned Bittinger
Oil on canvas, 46" x 36," 1991

GORDON RUSSELL SULLIVAN was born in Boston, Massachusetts, on 25 September 1937; was commissioned a second lieutenant through the Reserve Officers Training Corps at Norwich University, where he graduated in 1959; entered active duty and attended the officer basic course at the U.S. Army Armor School, Fort Knox, 1959–1960; served with the 1st Battalion, 66th Armor, 2d Armored Division, 1960–1961; was promoted to temporary and permanent first lieutenant, May 1961 and November 1962, respectively; served with 3d Battalion, 40th Armor, 1st Cavalry Division, in Korea, 1961–1962; was assistant Civil Guard/Self-Defense Corps adviser, 21st Infantry Division, Military Assistance Advisory Group, Vietnam, 1962–1963; was promoted to temporary captain, November 1963; was executive assistant to the assistant chief of staff, J–2 (Intelligence), Military Assistance Command, Vietnam, 1963–1964; graduated from armor officer advanced course, 1965; married Miriam Gay Loftus, 1965; was promoted to permanent captain, November 1966; served with 3d Battalion, 32d Armor, 3d Armored Division, United States Army, Europe, 1965–1966; served with the Military Personnel Division, Office of the Deputy Chief of Staff for Personnel, United States Army, Europe, 1966–1967; was promoted to temporary major, September 1967; graduated from the U.S. Army Command and General Staff College, Fort Leavenworth, 1969; was personnel services officer, Plans and Operations Division, G–1 (Personnel), Headquarters, I Field Force, Vietnam, 1969–1970; was personnel management officer, Personnel Actions Section, Armor Branch, Office of Personnel Operations, 1970–1973; was promoted to permanent major, November 1973; attended University of New Hampshire to earn a master of arts in political science, 1973–1974; was promoted to temporary lieutenant colonel, May 1974; commanded 4th Battalion, 73d Armor, 1st Infantry Division (Forward), United States (Operations), VII Corps, United States Army, Europe, 1980–1981; was promoted to temporary colonel, July 1980, and permanent lieutenant colonel, November 1980; was commander, 1st Brigade, 3d Armored Division, United States Army, Europe, 1981–1983; was promoted to permanent colonel, March 1982; was chief of staff, 3d Armored Division, United States Army, Europe, 1983; was assistant commandant of the Armor School, 1983–1985; was promoted to permanent brigadier general, October 1984; was deputy chief of staff for support, Central Army Group, Europe, 1985–1987; was deputy commandant, United States Army Command and General Staff College, 1987–1988; commanded the 1st Infantry Division (Mechanized), 1988–1989; was promoted to temporary lieutenant general, July 1989; was deputy chief of staff for operations and plans, United States Army, 1989–1990; was promoted to temporary general, June 1990; was vice chief of staff of the United States Army, 1990–1991; was chief of staff of the United States Army, 21 June 1991–20 June 1995; led the Army through fundamental transformation after the liberation of Kuwait, which included force reductions and base closures accompanied by doctrinal change, successes in peacekeeping, emphasis on new ways of war, and experiments that moved the Army into the information age; retired from active service, June 1995.

The Artist

Ned Bittinger (1951–), a native Washingtonian, is an award-winning portrait painter whose *alla prima* technique gives his paintings energy and immediacy. Also to his credit, he was commissioned by Scholastic, Inc., to paint the illustrations for two of its books—one for children on the Passover seder, the other on the Civil War. He has painted the portraits of prominent figures, including James A. Baker, Shirley MacLaine, Nancy M. Kissinger, and many others. His portrait of General Gordon R. Sullivan is reproduced from the Army Art Collection.

Gordon Russell Sullivan
By Ned Bittinger
Oil on canvas, 40" x 32," 1995

DENNIS JOE REIMER was born 12 July 1939 and grew up in Medford, Oklahoma; graduated from the United States Military Academy, 1962; was commissioned a second lieutenant and attended artillery officer basic course at the Artillery and Missile School, Fort Sill, 1962; married Mary Jo Powers, 28 December 1962; completed ranger and airborne training, Fort Benning, 1962–1963; served as assistant executive officer and executive officer, 20th Artillery, 5th Infantry Division, 1963–1964; promoted to temporary first lieutenant, December 1963; served as assistant battalion adviser, Advisory Team 60, United States Military Assistance Command, Vietnam, 1964–1965; promoted to permanent first lieutenant and temporary captain, June 1965 and November 1965; attended artillery officer advanced course at the Air Defense School, Fort Bliss, 1965–1966; commanded Company C, 11th Battalion, 3d Brigade, U.S. Army Training Center, Fort Benning, 1966–1967; served as aide-de-camp to the commandant, Armed Forces Staff College, Norfolk, 1967–1968; promoted to temporary major and permanent captain, September 1968 and June 1969; served as executive officer and S–3 (Operations), 2d Battalion, 4th Artillery, 9th Infantry Division, in Vietnam, 1968–1970; was instructor at the Field Artillery School, Fort Sill, 1970; attended the Command and General Staff College, Fort Leavenworth, 1970–1971; was personnel management officer, Assignment Section, Field Artillery Branch, Office of Personnel Operations, Wash., D.C., 1971–1972; served in Office of the Chief of Staff as assistant executive officer and aide to General Creighton W. Abrams, Jr., 1972–1974; served as executive officer and S–3, 4th Infantry Division Artillery, Fort Carson, 1975–1976; promoted to temporary lieutenant colonel and permanent major, June 1975 and June 1976; commanded 1st Battalion, 27th Artillery, 4th Infantry Division, Fort Carson, 1976–1978; was commandant of the Training Command, 4th Infantry Division, Fort Carson, 1978; attended the Army War College, 1978–1979; received a master of arts in public administration from Shippensburg State College, 1979; promoted to temporary colonel, August 1979; served as deputy commander and later special assistant to the commander, V Corps Artillery, United States Army, Europe, 1979–1980; commanded 8th Infantry Division Artillery, United States Army, Europe, 1980–1982; promoted to permanent colonel, March 1982; served as chief of staff, 8th Infantry Division, United States Army, Europe, 1982–1983; was deputy assistant commandant, Field Artillery Center and School, Fort Sill, 1983–1984; promoted to permanent brigadier general, September 1984; was commanding general, III Corps Artillery, Fort Sill, 1984–1986; served as chief of staff, U.S. Army Element, Combined Field Army, in Korea, 1986; was assistant chief of staff, C–3/J–3, Republic of Korea/U.S. Combined Forces Command, 1986–1988; promoted to major general, September 1987; commanded 4th Infantry Division, Fort Carson, 1988–1990; promoted to permanent lieutenant general, July 1990; was deputy chief of staff for operations and plans, U.S. Army, and senior Army member, Military Staff Committee, United Nations, Wash., D.C., 1990–1991; promoted to general, June 1991; was vice chief of staff of the United States Army, 1991–1993; served as commanding general, United States Army Forces Command, Fort McPherson, 1993–1995; was chief of staff of the United States Army, 20 June 1995–20 June 1999; revamped the Army personnel system to accommodate modernization and technical diversity; redesigned force structure based upon extensive analyses labeled Division XXI; led the Army during a period of high-tempo deployments, including peacekeeping in Bosnia-Herzegovina and Kosovo; retired from active service, August 1999.

The Artist

Christine Conniff Sheahan (1940–) was born in Los Angeles, California. She majored in art at Marymount College in New York, where she later worked first as an illustrator/graphic designer and then as a magazine publisher while simultaneously fulfilling many commissions as a portrait painter. Well known in New York, she has painted the portraits of prominent personalities, including actress Susan Lucci, and also a number of business and community leaders. Her portrait of General Dennis J. Reimer is reproduced from the Army Art Collection.

Dennis Joe Reimer
By Christine Conniff Sheahan
Oil on canvas, 44" x 33," 1999

ERIC KEN SHINSEKI was born in Lihue on the island of Kauai, Hawaii, on 28 November 1942; graduated from the United States Military Academy and was commissioned a second lieutenant of Artillery, 1965; married Patricia "Patty" Yoshinobu, 26 June 1965; served as forward observer with Battery B, 2d Battalion, 9th Artillery, in Vietnam, and was wounded in action, 1965–1966; served as assistant secretary and then secretary to General Staff, U.S. Army, Hawaii, Schofield Barracks, 1967–1968; transferred to Armor and attended armor officer advanced course at the Armor School, Fort Knox, 1968–1969; commanded Troop A, 3d Squadron, 5th Cavalry, in Vietnam, and was wounded in action, 1970; served as personnel staff officer in Headquarters, United States Army, Pacific, 1971–1974; received a master of arts in English from Duke University, 1976; taught English at the United States Military Academy, 1976–1978; graduated from the Command and General Staff College, Fort Leavenworth, 1979; served as regimental adjutant and then squadron executive officer with 3d Armored Cavalry, Fort Bliss, 1979–1981; served in Office of the Deputy Chief of Staff for Operations and Plans, U.S. Army, 1981–1982; commanded 3d Squadron, 7th Cavalry, 3d Infantry Division, United States Army, Europe, 1982–1984; was the division's assistant chief of staff, G–3 (Operations), 1984–1985; graduated from the National War College, 1986; served as chief, Institutional Training Division, Office of the Deputy Chief of Staff for Operations and Plans, U.S. Army, 1986–1987; served in Europe as commander of 2d Brigade, 3d Infantry Division, 1987–1989, assistant chief of staff, G–3, VII Corps, 1989–1990, deputy chief of staff (support), Allied Land Forces Southern Europe, 1990–1992, and assistant division commander, 3d Infantry Division, 1992–1993; served as director of training, Office of the Deputy Chief of Staff for Operations and Plans, U.S. Army, 1993–1994; commanded 1st Cavalry Division, Fort Hood, 1994–1995; appointed as assistant deputy chief of staff for operations and plans, U.S. Army, 1995; became deputy chief of staff for operations and plans, 1996; served simultaneously as commanding general, United States Army, Europe, and Seventh Army, commanding general, NATO Land Forces, Central Europe, and commander of the NATO-led Stabilization Force, Bosnia-Herzegovina, 1997–1998; was vice chief of staff of the United States Army, 1998–1999; was chief of staff of the United States Army, 22 June 1999–11 June 2003; initiated the Army Transformation campaign to address both the emerging strategic challenges of the early twenty-first century and the need for cultural and technological change in the Army; following the 11 September 2001 terrorist attacks, led the Army during Operations ENDURING FREEDOM and IRAQI FREEDOM; integrated the pursuit of the Global War on Terrorism with Army Transformation, enabling the Army to continue to transform while at war; retired from active service, August 2003.

The Artist

John Boyd Martin (1936–) was born in Ottawa, Kansas. He majored in art at the University of Kansas School of Fine Arts, after which he went on to establish himself as an accomplished portrait artist around the world. His distinctive style, achieved through the use of a broad brush and a palette of rich diversified colors, captures not only a strong, vibrant, accurate likeness but also the essence of each subject. His commissions have crossed the sports, educational, business, and political arenas. He has painted the portraits of many distinguished personalities, including Joe DiMaggio, Arnold Palmer, University of North Carolina Chancellor Christopher Fordham, AT&T Chief Executive Officer Robert Allen, Brookings Institution President Bruce McLaury, and Secretary of the Army Louis Caldera. His portrait of General Eric K. Shinseki is reproduced from the Army Art Collection.

Eric Ken Shinseki
By John Boyd Martin
Oil on canvas, 46" x 36," 2003

PETER JAN SCHOOMAKER was born on 12 February 1946 in Michigan, and was raised in an Army family; was commissioned a second lieutenant through the Reserve Officers Training Corps at the University of Wyoming upon graduation in 1969; entered active duty and attended armor officer basic course at the Armor School, Fort Knox, 1969; completed airborne and ranger training, Fort Benning, 1969; served as reconnaissance platoon leader, 2d Battalion, 4th Infantry, Fort Campbell, 1970–1971; promoted to first lieutenant, June 1970; commanded Company C, 2d Battalion, 4th Infantry, United States Army, Europe, 1970–1972; promoted to captain, June 1971; served as assistant S–3 (Operations) and later as S–4 (Logistics), 1st Squadron, 2d Armored Cavalry, United States Army, Europe, 1972–1973; commanded Troop C, 1st Squadron, 2d Armored Cavalry, United States Army, Europe, 1973–1974; served as assistant inspector general, 2d Infantry Division, in Korea, 1974; served as S–3, 1st Battalion, 73d Armor, 2d Infantry Division, in Korea, 1974–1975; attended the Marine Amphibious Warfare School, Quantico, 1975–1976; served as assignment officer, United States Army Military Personnel Center, Wash., D.C., 1976–1978; received a master of arts in management from Central Michigan University, 1977; commanded a squadron in 1st Special Forces Operational Detachment D, 1978–1981; promoted to major, July 1979; married Cynthia A. "Cindy" Petroski, 14 January 1980; attended the Command and General Staff College, Fort Leavenworth, 1981–1982; served as executive officer, 2d Squadron, 2d Armored Cavalry, United States Army, Europe, 1982–1983; served as J–3, Joint Special Operations Command, Fort Bragg, 1983–1985; promoted to lieutenant colonel, July 1985; served in various command positions in 1st Special Forces Operational Detachment D, 1985–1988; attended the National War College, 1988–1989; commanded 1st Special Forces Operational Detachment D, 1989–1992; promoted to colonel, June 1990; served as assistant division commander, 1st Cavalry Division, Fort Hood, 1992–1993; promoted to brigadier general, January 1993; served as deputy director for operations, readiness, and mobilization, United States Army, Wash., D.C., 1993–1994; commanded Joint Special Operations Command, Fort Bragg, 1994–1996; promoted to major general, March 1996; commanded United States Army Special Operations Command, Fort Bragg, 1996–1997; promoted to lieutenant general, August 1996, and general, October 1997; served as commander in chief, United States Special Operations Command, MacDill Air Force Base, 1997–2000; retired from active duty, December 2000; returned to active duty and became chief of staff of the United States Army, 1 August 2003.

The Photographer

Scott E. Davis (1956–) is from San Antonio, Texas. He began his career in photography in 1977 as an Army photojournalist. After his military service, he worked for the U.S. Army Visual Information Center in the Pentagon, Washington, D.C., photographing ceremonies and visiting dignitaries for the Army and the Office of the Secretary of Defense. He then left government service and moved to Atlanta, Georgia, where he was a freelance photographer for five years. In 1993 he returned to the Army Visual Information Center as the Army's official portrait photographer at the Pentagon. In addition to the Army chief of staff, he has photographed the secretary of defense, the chairman of the Joint Chiefs of Staff, and the secretary of the Army.

Peter Jan Schoomaker
By Scott E. Davis
Photographic Portrait, 2003

Appendices
and
Bibliographies

Appendix A

Chronological List of Chief Executive Authorities, Departmental Secretaries, and Senior Officers

Executive Agency	Presiding Official	Commanding General
Continental Congress	———— 1775–1776	George Washington 15 Jun 1775–
Board of War and Ordnance	John Adams 1776–1777	George Washington
Board of War	Horatio Gates (president) Timothy Pickering Richard Peters 1777–1781	George Washington
War Office	Benjamin Lincoln (secretary at war) 1781–1783	George Washington –23 Dec 1783
	Joseph Carleton (acting) 1783–1785	Henry Knox 23 Dec 1783–20 Jun 1784
	Henry Knox 1785–1789	John Doughty 20 Jun 1784–12 Aug 1784
		Josiah Harmar 12 Aug 1784–

President	Secretary of War	Commanding General
George Washington 30 Apr 1789–3 Mar 1797	Henry Knox 12 Sep 1789–31 Dec 1794	Josiah Harmar –4 Mar 1791
		Arthur St. Clair 4 Mar 1791–5 Mar 1792
	Timothy Pickering 2 Jan 1795–10 Dec 1795	Anthony Wayne 13 Apr 1792–15 Dec 1796
	James McHenry 27 Jan 1796–	James Wilkinson 15 Dec 1796–13 Jul 1798
John Adams 4 Mar 1797–3 Mar 1801	James McHenry –13 May 1800	George Washington 13 Jul 1798–14 Dec 1799
	Samuel Dexter 13 May 1800–31 Jan 1801	Alexander Hamilton 14 Dec 1799–15 Jun 1800
		James Wilkinson 15 Jun 1800–
Thomas Jefferson 4 Mar 1801–3 Mar 1809	Henry Dearborn 5 Mar 1801–	James Wilkinson

Chronological List of Chief Executive Authorities, Departmental Secretaries, and Senior Officers—Continued

President	Secretary of War	Commanding General
James Madison 4 Mar 1809–3 Mar 1817	Henry Dearborn –7 Mar 1809	James Wilkinson
	William Eustis 7 Mar 1809–13 Jan 1813	James Wilkinson –27 Jan 1812
	John Armstrong 13 Jan 1813–27 Sep 1814	Henry Dearborn 27 Jan 1812–
	James Monroe 27 Sep 1814–2 Mar 1815	Henry Dearborn –15 Jun 1815
	William H. Crawford 1 Aug 1815–22 Oct 1816	Jacob J. Brown 15 Jun 1815–
James Monroe 4 Mar 1817–3 Mar 1825	John C. Calhoun 8 Oct 1817–	Jacob J. Brown
John Quincy Adams 4 Mar 1825–3 Mar 1829	John C. Calhoun –7 Mar 1825	Jacob J. Brown
	James Barbour 7 Mar 1825–23 May 1828	Jacob L. Brown –24 Feb 1828
	Peter B. Porter 26 May 1828–	Alexander Macomb 29 May 1828–
Andrew Jackson 4 Mar 1829–3 Mar 1837	Peter B. Porter –9 Mar 1829	Alexander Macomb
	John H. Eaton 9 Mar 1829–18 Jun 1831	Alexander Macomb
	Lewis Cass 1 Aug 1831–5 Oct 1836	Alexander Macomb
Martin Van Buren 4 Mar 1837–3 Mar 1841	Joel R. Poinsett 7 Mar 1837–	Alexander Macomb
William H. Harrison 4 Mar 1841–4 Apr 1841	Joel R. Poinsett –5 Mar 1841	Alexander Macomb
	John Bell 5 Mar 1841–	Alexander Macomb
John Tyler 6 Apr 1841–3 Mar 1845	John Bell –13 Sep 1841	Alexander Macomb –25 Jun 1841
	John C. Spencer 12 Oct 1841–3 Mar 1843	Winfield Scott 5 Jul 1841–
	James M. Porter 8 Mar 1843–30 Jun 1844	Winfield Scott
	William Wilkins 15 Feb 1844–4 Mar 1845	Winfield Scott
James K. Polk 4 Mar 1845–3 Mar 1849	William L. Marcy 6 Mar 1845–4 Mar 1849	Winfield Scott
Zachary Taylor 5 Mar 1849–9 Jul 1850	George W. Crawford 8 Mar 1849–	Winfield Scott

President	Secretary of War	Commanding General
Millard Fillmore 10 Jul 1850–3 Mar 1853	George W. Crawford –23 Jul 1850	Winfield Scott
	Charles M. Conrad 15 Aug 1850–	Winfield Scott
Franklin Pierce 4 Mar 1853–3 Mar 1857	Charles M. Conrad –7 Mar 1853	Winfield Scott
	Jefferson Davis 7 Mar 1853–	Winfield Scott
James Buchanan 4 Mar 1857–3 Mar 1861	Jefferson Davis –6 Mar 1857	Winfield Scott
	John B. Floyd 6 Mar 1857–29 Dec 1860	Winfield Scott
	Joseph Holt 18 Jan 1861–	Winfield Scott
Abraham Lincoln 4 Mar 1861–15 Apr 1865	Joseph Holt –5 Mar 1861	Winfield Scott –1 Nov 1861
	Simon Cameron 5 Mar 1861–14 Jan 1862	George B. McClellan 1 Nov 1861–11 Mar 1862
	Edwin M. Stanton 20 Jan 1862–	Henry W. Halleck 23 Jul 1862–9 Mar 1864
		Ulysses S. Grant 9 Mar 1864–
Andrew Johnson 15 Apr 1865–3 Mar 1869	Edwin M. Stanton –28 May 1868	Ulysses S. Grant
	John M. Schofield 1 Jun 1868–	Ulysses S. Grant –4 Mar 1869
Ulysses S. Grant 4 Mar 1869–3 Mar 1877	John M. Schofield –13 Mar 1869	William T. Sherman 8 Mar 1869–
	John A. Rawlins 13 Mar 1869–6 Sep 1869	William T. Sherman
	William W. Belknap 25 Oct 1869–2 Mar 1876	William T. Sherman
	Alphonso Taft 8 Mar 1876–22 May 1876	William T. Sherman
	James D. Cameron 22 May 1876–3 Mar 1877	William T. Sherman
Rutherford B. Hayes 4 Mar 1877–3 Mar 1881	George W. McCrary 12 Mar 1877–10 Dec 1879	William T. Sherman
	Alexander Ramsey 10 Dec 1879–	William T. Sherman
James A. Garfield 4 Mar 1881–19 Sep 1881	Alexander Ramsey –5 Mar 1881	William T. Sherman
	Robert T. Lincoln 5 Mar 1881–	William T. Sherman
Chester A. Arthur 20 Sep 1881–3 Mar 1885	Robert T. Lincoln	William T. Sherman –1 Nov 1883
		Philip H. Sheridan 1 Nov 1883–

Chronological List of Chief Executive Authorities, Departmental Secretaries, and Senior Officers—Continued

President	Secretary of War	Commanding General
Grover Cleveland 4 Mar 1885–3 Mar 1889	Robert T. Lincoln −5 Mar 1885	Philip H. Sheridan −5 Aug 1888
	William C. Endicott 5 Mar 1885–	John M. Schofield 14 Aug 1888–
Benjamin Harrison 4 Mar 1889–3 Mar 1893	William C. Endicott −5 Mar 1889	John M. Schofield
	Redfield Proctor 5 Mar 1889–5 Nov 1891	John M. Schofield
	Stephen B. Elkins 17 Dec 1891–	John M. Schofield
Grover Cleveland 4 Mar 1893–3 Mar 1897	Stephen B. Elkins −5 Mar 1893	John M. Schofield −29 Sep 1895
	Daniel S. Lamont 5 Mar 1893–	Nelson A. Miles 5 Oct 1895–
William McKinley 4 Mar 1897–14 Sep 1901	Daniel S. Lamont −5 Mar 1897	Nelson A. Miles
	Russell A. Alger 5 Mar 1897–1 Aug 1899	Nelson A. Miles
	Elibu Root 1 Aug 1899–	Nelson A. Miles
Theodore Roosevelt 14 Sep 1901–3 Mar 1909	Elihu Root	Nelson A. Miles −8 Aug 1903

President	Secretary of War	Chief of Staff
	Elihu Root −31 Jan 1904	Samuel B. M. Young 15 Aug 1903–8 Jan 1904
	William H. Taft 1 Feb 1904–30 Jun 1908	Adna R. Chaffee 9 Jan 1904–14 Jan 1906
	Luke E. Wright Jul 1908–	John C. Bates 15 Jan 1906–13 Apr 1906
		J. Franklin Bell 14 Apr 1906–
William H. Taft 4 Mar 1909–3 Mar 1913	Luke E. Wright −11 Mar 1909	J. Franklin Bell
	Jacob M. Dickinson 12 Mar 1909–21 May 1911	J. Franklin Bell −21 Apr 1910
	Henry L. Stimson 22 May 1911–4 Mar 1913	Leonard Wood 22 Apr 1910–

President	Secretary of War	Chief of Staff
Woodrow Wilson 4 Mar 1913–3 Mar 1921	Lindley M. Garrison 5 Mar 1913–10 Feb 1916	Leonard Wood –20 Apr 1914
	Newton D. Baker 9 Mar 1916–4 Mar 1921	William W. Wotherspoon 21 Apr 1914–15 Nov 1914
		Hugh L. Scott 16 Nov 1914–21 Sep 1917
		Tasker H. Bliss 22 Sep 1917–18 May 1918
		Peyton C. March 19 May 1918–
Warren G. Harding 4 Mar 1921–2 Aug 1923	John W. Weeks 5 Mar 1921–	Peyton C. March –30 Jun 1921
		John J. Pershing 1 Jul 1921–
Calvin Coolidge 3 Aug 1923–3 Mar 1929	John W. Weeks –13 Oct 1925	John J. Pershing –13 Sep 1924
	Dwight F. Davis 14 Oct 1925–	John L. Hines 14 Sep 1924–20 Nov 1926
		Charles P. Summerall 21 Nov 1926–
Herbert C. Hoover 4 Mar 1929–3 Mar 1933	Dwight F. Davis –5 Mar 1929	Charles P. Summerall
	James W. Good 6 Mar 1929–18 Nov 1929	Charles P. Summerall
	Patrick J. Hurley 9 Dec 1929–3 Mar 1933	Charles P. Summerall –20 Nov 1930
		Douglas MacArthur 21 Nov 1930–
Franklin D. Roosevelt 4 Mar 1933–12 Apr 1945	George H. Dern 4 Mar 1933–27 Aug 1936	Douglas MacArthur –1 Oct 1935
	Harry H. Woodring 25 Sep 1936–20 Jun 1940	Malin Craig 2 Oct 1935–31 Aug 1939
	Henry L. Stimson 10 Jul 1940–	George C. Marshall 1 Sep 1939–
Harry S. Truman 12 Apr 1945–20 Jan 1953	Henry L. Stimson –21 Sep 1945	George C. Marshall –18 Nov 1945
	Robert P. Patterson 27 Sep 1945–18 Jul 1947	Dwight D. Eisenhower 19 Nov 1945–
	Kenneth C. Royall 19 Jul 1947–	Dwight D. Eisenhower
	Secretary of the Army	
	Kenneth C. Royall –27 Apr 1949	Dwight D. Eisenhower –7 Feb 1948
	Gordon Gray 20 Jun 1949–12 Apr 1950	Omar N. Bradley 7 Feb 1948–16 Aug 1949
	Frank Pace, Jr. 12 Apr 1950–20 Jan 1953	J. Lawton Collins 16 Aug 1949–

Chronological List of Chief Executive Authorities, Departmental Secretaries, and Senior Officers—Continued

President	Secretary of the Army	Chief of Staff
Dwight D. Eisenhower 20 Jan 1953–20 Jan 1961	Robert T. Stevens 4 Feb 1953–21 Jul 1955	J. Lawton Collins –5 Aug 1953
		Matthew B. Ridgway 16 Aug 1953–30 Jun 1955
	Wilber M. Brucker 21 Jul 1955–19 Jan 1961	Maxwell D. Taylor 30 Jun 1955–30 Jun 1959
		Lyman L. Lemnitzer 1 Jul 1959–30 Sep 1960
		George H. Decker 1 Oct 1960–
John F. Kennedy 20 Jan 1961–22 Nov 1963	Elvis J. Stahr, Jr. 24 Jan 1961–30 Jun 1962	George H. Decker
	Cyrus R. Vance 5 Jul 1962–	George H. Decker –30 Sep 1962
		Earle G. Wheeler 1 Oct 1962–
Lyndon B. Johnson 22 Nov 1963–20 Jan 1969	Cyrus R. Vance –21 Jan 1964	Earle G. Wheeler –2 Jul 1964
	Stephen Ailes 28 Jan 1964–1 Jul 1965	Harold K. Johnson 3 Jul 1964–
	Stanley R. Resor 2 Jul 1965–	Harold K. Johnson –2 Jul 1968
		William C. Westmoreland 3 Jul 1968–
Richard M. Nixon 20 Jan 1969–9 Aug 1974	Stanley R. Resor –30 Jun 1971	William C. Westmoreland
	Robert F. Froehlke 1 Jul 1971–14 May 1973	William C. Westmoreland –30 Jun 1972
		Bruce Palmer, Jr. (acting) 1 Jul 1972–11 Oct 1972
		Creighton W. Abrams, Jr. 12 Oct 1972–
	Howard H. Callaway 15 May 1973–	Creighton W. Abrams, Jr. –4 Sep 1974
Gerald R. Ford 9 Aug 1974–20 Jan 1977	Howard H. Callaway –3 Jul 1975	Fred C. Weyand 3 Oct 1974–
	Martin R. Hoffmann 5 Aug 1975–	Fred C. Weyand –30 Sep 1976
		Bernard W. Rogers 1 Oct 1976–

President	Secretary of the Army	Chief of Staff
Jimmy (James E.) Carter 20 Jan 1977–20 Jan 1981	Martin R. Hoffmann –13 Feb 1977	Bernard W. Rogers –21 Jun 1979
	Clifford L. Alexander, Jr. 14 Feb 1977–20 Jan 1981	Edward C. Meyer 22 Jun 1979–
Ronald W. Reagan 20 Jan 1981–20 Jan 1989	John O. Marsh, Jr. 21 Jan 1981–	Edward C. Meyer –21 Jun 1983
		John A. Wickham, Jr. 23 Jun 1983–23 Jun 1987
		Carl E. Vuono 23 Jun 1987–
George Bush 20 Jan 1989–20 Jan 1993	John O. Marsh, Jr. –13 Aug 1989	Carl E. Vuono
	Michael P. W. Stone 14 Aug 1989–19 Jan 1993	Carl E. Vuono –21 Jun 1991
		Gordon R. Sullivan 21 Jun 1991–
William J. Clinton 20 Jan 1993–20 Jan 2001	Togo D. West, Jr. 22 Nov 1993–5 May 1998	Gordon R. Sullivan –20 Jun 1995
		Dennis J. Reimer 20 Jun 1995–
	Louis E. Caldera 2 Jul 1998–20 Jan 2001	Dennis J. Reimer –20 Jun 1999
		Eric K. Shinseki 22 Jun 1999–
George W. Bush 20 Jan 2001–	Thomas E. White 31 May 2001–9 May 2003	Eric K. Shinseki –11 Jun 2003
	Les Brownlee (acting) 10 May 2003–3 Dec 2004	Peter J. Schoomaker 1 Aug 2003–
	Francis J. Harvey 19 Nov 2004–	Peter J. Schoomaker

Appendix B

Chronological List of Senior Officers of the United States Army

Rank[1]	Name	Date of Birth	Date Took Office	Age Yrs/Mos	Left Office	Tour Yrs/Mos	Date of Death	Age Yrs/Mos
Gen[2]	George Washington	22 Feb 1732	15 Jun 1775	43/4	23 Dec 1783	8/6	14 Dec 1799	67/10
Maj Gen	Henry Knox	25 Jul 1750	23 Dec 1783	33/5	20 Jun 1784	0/6	25 Oct 1806	56/3
Capt	John Doughty	25 Jul 1754	20 Jun 1784	29/11	12 Aug 1784	0/2	16 Sep 1826	72/2
Bvt Brig Gen	Josiah Harmar	10 Nov 1753	12 Aug 1784	30/9	4 Mar 1791	6/7	20 Aug 1813	59/9
Maj Gen	Arthur St. Clair	23 Mar 1736[3]	4 Mar 1791	55/0	5 Mar 1792	1/0	31 Aug 1818	82/5
Maj Gen	Anthony Wayne	1 Jan 1745	13 Apr 1792	47/3	15 Dec 1796	4/8	15 Dec 1796	51/11
Brig Gen	James Wilkinson	circa 1757	15 Dec 1796	39/0	13 Jul 1798	1/7	28 Dec 1825	68/0
Lt Gen	George Washington	22 Feb 1732	13 Jul 1798	66/5	14 Dec 1799	1/5	14 Dec 1799	67/10
Maj Gen	Alexander Hamilton	11 Jan 1757	14 Dec 1799	42/11	15 Jun 1800	0/6	12 Jul 1804	47/6
Brig Gen	James Wilkinson	circa 1757	15 Jun 1800	43/0	27 Jan 1812	11/7	28 Dec 1825	68/0
Maj Gen	Henry Dearborn	23 Feb 1751	27 Jan 1812	60/11	15 Jun 1815	3/5	6 Jun 1829	78/3
Maj Gen	Jacob J. Brown	9 May 1775	15 Jun 1815	40/1	24 Feb 1828	12/8	24 Feb 1828	52/9
Maj Gen	Alexander Macomb	3 Apr 1782	29 May 1828	46/2	25 Jun 1841	13/1	25 Jun 1841	59/3
Bvt Lt Gen	Winfield Scott	13 Jun 1786	5 Jul 1841	55/1	1 Nov 1861	20/4	29 May 1866	79/11
Maj Gen	George B. McClellan	3 Dec 1826	1 Nov 1861	34/11	11 Mar 1862	0/4	29 Oct 1885	58/11
Maj Gen	Henry W. Halleck	16 Jan 1815	23 Jul 1862	47/6	9 Mar 1864	1/7	9 Jan 1872	56/11
Gen[2]	Ulysses S. Grant	27 Apr 1822	9 Mar 1864	41/10	4 Mar 1869	5/0	23 Jul 1885	63/3
Gen[2]	William T. Sherman	8 Feb 1820	8 Mar 1869	49/1	1 Nov 1883	14/8	14 Feb 1891	71/0
Gen[2]	Philip H. Sheridan	6 Mar 1831	1 Nov 1883	52/8	5 Aug 1888	4/9	5 Aug 1888	57/5
Lt Gen	John McA. Schofield	29 Sep 1831	14 Aug 1888	56/11	29 Sep 1895	7/1	4 Mar 1906	74/5
Lt Gen	Nelson A. Miles	8 Aug 1839	5 Oct 1895	56/2	8 Aug 1903	7/10	15 May 1925	85/9
Lt Gen	Samuel B. M. Young	9 Jan 1840	15 Aug 1903	63/7	8 Jan 1904	0/5	1 Sep 1924	84/9
Lt Gen	Adna R. Chaffee	14 Apr 1842	9 Jan 1904	61/8	14 Jan 1906	2/0	1 Nov 1914	72/7
Lt Gen	John C. Bates	26 Aug 1842	15 Jan 1906	63/4	13 Apr 1906	0/3	4 Feb 1919	76/5
Maj Gen	T. Franklin Bell	9 Jan 1856	14 Apr 1906	50/3	21 Apr 1910	4/0	8 Jan 1919	63/0
Maj Gen	Leonard Wood	9 Oct 1860	22 Apr 1910	49/6	20 Apr 1914	4/0	7 Aug 1927	66/10
Maj Gen	William W. Wotherspoon	16 Nov 1850	21 Apr 1914	63/5	15 Nov 1914	0/7	21 Oct 1921	70/11
Maj Gen	Hugh L. Scott	22 Sep 1853	16 Nov 1914	61/1	21 Sep 1917	2/10	30 Apr 1934	80/7
Gen	Tasker H. Bliss	31 Dec 1853	22 Sep 1917	63/8	18 May 1918	0/8	9 Nov 1930	76/10
Gen	Peyton C. March	27 Dec 1864	19 May 1918	53/5	30 Jun 1921	3/1	13 Apr 1955	90/4
Gen[2]	John J. Pershing	13 Sep 1860	1 Jul 1921	60/9	13 Sep 1924	3/2	15 Jul 1948	87/10
Maj Gen	John L. Hines	21 May 1868	14 Sep 1924	56/3	20 Nov 1926	2/2	13 Oct 1968	100/4
Gen	Charles P Summerall	4 Mar 1867	21 Nov 1926	59/8	20 Nov 1930	4/0	14 May 1955	88/2
Gen[2]	Douglas MacArthur	26 Jan 1880	21 Nov 1930	50/9	1 Oct 1935	4/11	5 Apr 1964	84/2
Gen	Malin Craig	5 Aug 1875	2 Oct 1935	60/1	31 Aug 1939	3/11	25 Jul 1945	69/11
Gen of Army	George C. Marshall	31 Dec 1880	1 Sep 1939	58/8	18 Nov 1945	6/2	16 Oct 1959	78/9
Gen of Army	Dwight D. Eisenhower	14 Oct 1890	19 Oct 1945	55/1	7 Feb 1948	2/2	28 Mar 1969	78/5

Rank[1]	Name	Date of Birth	Date Took Office	Age Yrs/Mos	Left Office	Tour Yrs/Mos	Date of Death	Age Yrs/Mos
Gen[2]	Omar N. Bradley	12 Feb 1893	7 Feb 1948	54/11	16 Aug 1949	1/6	8 Apr 1981	88/1
Gen	J. Lawton Collins	1 May 1896	16 Aug 1949	53/3	5 Aug 1953	4/0	12 Sep 1987	91/4
Gen	Matthew B. Ridgway	3 Mar 1895	16 Aug 1953	58/5	30 Jun 1955	1/10	26 Jul 1993	98/4
Gen	Maxwell D. Taylor	26 Aug 1901	30 Jun 1955	53/10	30 Jun 1959	4/0	19 Apr 1987	86/4
Gen	Lyman L. Lemnitzer	29 Aug 1899	1 Jul 1959	59/10	30 Sep 1960	1/3	12 Nov 1988	89/3
Gen	George H. Decker	16 Feb 1902	1 Oct 1960	58/7	30 Sep 1962	2/0	6 Feb 1980	77/11
Gen	Earle G. Wheeler	13 Jan 1908	1 Oct 1962	54/8	2 Jul 1964	1/9	18 Dec 1975	67/11
Gen	Harold K. Johnson	22 Feb 1912	3 Jul 1964	52/4	2 Jul 1968	4/0	24 Sep 1983	71/7
Gen	William C. Westmoreland	26 Mar 1914	3 Jul 1968	54/3	30 Jun 1972	4/0	18 Jul 2005	91/4
Gen	Bruce Palmer, Jr.[4]	13 Apr 1913	1 Jul 1972	56/2	11 Oct 1972	0/3	10 Oct 2000	87/6
Gen	Creighton W. Abrams, Jr.	15 Sep 1914	12 Oct 1972	58/1	4 Sep 1974	1/10	4 Sep 1974	59/11
Gen	Frederick C. Weyand	15 Sep 1916	3 Oct 1974	58/0	30 Sep 1976	2/0		
Gen	Bernard W. Rogers	16 Jul 1921	1 Oct 1976	55/2	21 Jun 1979	2/8		
Gen	Edward C. Meyer	11 Dec 1928	22 Jun 1979	50/6	21 Jun 1983	4/0		
Gen	John A. Wickham, Jr.	25 Jun 1928	23 Jun 1983	57/0	23 Jun 1987	4/0		
Gen	Carl E. Vuono	18 Oct 1934	23 Jun 1987	52/8	21 Jun 1991	4/0		
Gen	Gordon R. Sullivan	25 Sep 1937	21 Jun 1991	53/9	20 Jun 1995	4/0		
Gen	Dennis J. Reimer	12 Jul 1939	20 Jun 1995	55/11	20 Jun 1999	4/0		
Gen	Eric K. Shinseki	28 Nov 1942	22 Jun 1999	56/7	11 Jun 2003	4/0		
Gen	Peter J. Schoomaker	12 Feb 1946	1 Aug 2003	57/6				

[1]Rank indicated, whether permanent or temporary, is the highest rank held while in office.

[2]Lack of uniformity in upper-level military rank and title throughout Army history negates attempts to draw comprehensive comparisons and establish true seniority. In early years high rank was bestowed temporarily upon individuals rather than permanently through the grade structure. Variations in title and organization make it difficult to equate individuals and positions of one generation with those of another, and there has often been confusion between title and rank. From 1775 to 1783 George Washington was general and commander in chief of the Continental Army. When he was recalled in 1798, the Congress passed legislation that would have made him General of the Armies of the United States, but his services were not required in the field and the appointment was not made until the Bicentennial in 1976, when it was bestowed posthumously as a commemorative honor. After the Civil War Ulysses S. Grant, William T. Sherman, and Philip H. Sheridan all held the grade of general, specified as General of the Army of the United States; but, unlike the more modern practice, the word *General* represented grade while the rest of the phrase denoted title—a style that extended to lower levels in similar titles of lieutenant general of the Army and, earlier, major general of the Army. In 1919 the rank of General of the Armies of the United States was given to John J. Pershing, who chose, however, to continue wearing four stars. Present-day formality entered the picture in 1944, when the temporary grade of General of the Army, identified by five stars and limited to four recipients, was established. It was made permanent for those holding it in 1946: George C. Marshall, Douglas MacArthur, Dwight D. Eisenhower, and Henry Arnold. The subsequent transfer of General of the Army Arnold to the Air Force opened the way for the promotion of General Omar N. Bradley to the vacated space.

[3]St. Clair's date of birth conforms to the old style, or Julian calendar. Under the new style, or Gregorian calendar, the date would be 3 April 1736.

[4]Palmer provided key managerial continuity during the Westmoreland-Abrams interregnum, and therefore is included in the list of Army chiefs of staff.

General Bibliography

As the Army's past is a substantive element of American history, its uniformed heads are, perforce, national as well as institutional figures. A knowledge of their roles and of the part played by their branch of the service in the events of the times is thus important to an understanding of both national and international affairs.

The literature of an institution and its leaders over an extended period of time is bound to be uneven. Not all senior officers are destined to be prominent figures during their tenures, nor is every era likely to see the Army in the forefront of American life. The ebb and flow of events, as well as the personality and style of an official, inevitably influence the degree of attention accorded an institution or an individual at any given time.

This general bibliography includes works on national defense, the Army, the departmental headquarters, the civil administration and selected civilian department heads, the General Staff, and the broad details of the organization and operation of the department.

Allard, C. Kenneth. *Command, Control, and the Common Defense.* Rev. ed. Washington, D.C.: Center for Advanced Concepts and Technology, National Defense Univ., 1996.

American State Papers: Documents, Legislative and Executive, of the Congress of the United States. . . . Class 5. Military Affairs. 7 vols. Washington, D.C.: Gales and Seaton, 1832–61.

Ball, Harry P. *Of Responsible Command: A History of the U.S. Army War College.* Rev. ed. Carlisle Barracks, Pa.: Alumni Assoc. of the United States Army War College, 1994.

Beaver, Daniel R. *Newton D. Baker and the American War Effort, 1917–1919.* Lincoln: Univ. of Nebraska Press, 1966.

Bell, William Gardner. *Secretaries of War and Secretaries of the Army: Portraits and Biographical Sketches.* Rev. ed. Washington, D.C.: Center of Military History, United States Army, 2003.

Bernardo, C. Joseph, and Eugene H. Bacon. *Military Policy: Its Development Since 1775.* Harrisburg, Pa.: Military Service, 1955.

Borklund, Carl W. *Men of the Pentagon: From Forrestal to McNamara.* New York: Praeger, 1966.

———. *The Department of Defense.* New York: Praeger, 1968.

Brock, Peter. *Pacifism in the United States From the Colonial Era to the First World War.* Princeton: Princeton Univ. Press, 1968.

Brown, Alvin. *The Armor of Organization: A National Plan of Organization for the Armed Forces and . . . Inquiry Into the Origins of Existing Military Organization.* New York: Hibbert, 1953.

Caraley, Demetrios. *The Politics of Military Unification: A Study of Conflict and the Policy Process.* New York: Columbia Univ. Press, 1966.

Coffman, Edward M. *The Old Army: A Portrait of the American Army in Peacetime, 1784–1898.* New York: Oxford Univ. Press, 1986.

———. *The Regulars: The American Army, 1898–1941.* Cambridge, Mass.: Harvard Univ. Press, 2004.

———. *The War To End All Wars: The American Military Experience in World War I.* 1968. Reprint, with new preface, Lexington: Univ. Press of Kentucky, 1998.

Cole, Alice C.; Alfred Goldberg; Samuel A. Tucker; and Rudolph A. Winnacker, eds. *The Department of Defense: Documents on Establishment and Organization, 1944–1978.* Washington, D.C.: Office of the Secretary of Defense, 1979.

Cooling, B. Franklin, ed. *The New American State Papers. Military Affairs.* 19 vols. Wilmington, Del.: Scholarly Resources, 1979.

Cosmas, Graham A. *An Army for Empire: The United*

States Army in the Spanish-American War. 2d ed. Shippensburg, Pa.: White Mane, 1994.

Crackel, Theodore J. *West Point: A Bicentennial History*. Lawrence: Univ. Press of Kansas, 2002.

Cullum, George W. *Biographical Register of the Officers and Graduates of the United States Military Academy.* . . . Vols. 1–3. 3d ed. Boston: Houghton, Mifflin, 1891. Vols. 4–9. Assoc. of Graduates, U.S. Military Academy, 1901–50.

Dawson, Joseph G., III, ed. *Commanders in Chief: Presidential Leadership in Modern Wars*. Lawrence: Univ. Press of Kansas, 1993.

Eberstadt, Ferdinand. *Report to Hon. James Forrestal, Secretary of the Navy, on Unification of the War and Navy Departments and Postwar Organization for National Security*. Prepared for U.S. Senate, Committee on Naval Affairs, 79th Cong., 1st sess. Washington, D.C.: Government Printing Office, 1945.

Ekirch, Arthur A., Jr. *The Civilian and the Military*. New York: Oxford Univ. Press, 1956.

Feaver, Peter. *Armed Servants: Agency, Oversight, and Civil-Military Relations*. Cambridge, Mass.: Harvard Univ. Press, 2003.

Fisher, Louis. *Presidential War Powers*. 2d ed. Lawrence: Univ. Press of Kansas, 2005

Gabriel, Richard A., and Paul L. Savage. *Crisis in Command: Mismanagement in the Army*. New York: Hill and Wang, 1978.

Ganoe, William Addleman. *The History of the United States Army*. New York: Appleton, 1924.

Gavin, James M. *War and Peace in the Space Age*. New York: Harper, 1958.

Goodpaster, Andrew J. *For the Common Defense*. Lexington, Mass.: Heath, Lexington Books, 1977.

Hammond, Paul Y. *Organizing for Defense: The American Military Establishment in the Twentieth Century*. Princeton: Princeton Univ. Press, 1961.

Hattaway, Herman, and Archer Jones. *How the North Won: A Military History of the Civil War*. 1983. Reprint, Urbana: Univ. of Illinois Press, 1991.

Heitman, Francis B. *Historical Register and Dictionary of the United States Army, 1789–1903*. Washington, D.C.: Government Printing Office, 1903.

Herspring, Dale R. *The Pentagon and the Presidency: Civil-Military Relations From FDR to George W. Bush*. Lawrence: Univ. Press of Kansas, 2005.

Hewes, James E., Jr. *From Root to McNamara: Army Organization and Administration, 1900–1963*. Special Studies. Washington, D.C.: Center of Military History, United States Army, 1975.

Hittle, James D. *The Military Staff: Its History and Development*. Harrisburg, Pa.: Military Service, 1944.

Huntington, Samuel P. *The Soldier and the State. The Theory and Politics of Civil-Military Relations*. Cambridge, Mass.: Harvard Univ. Press, Belknap, 1957.

Ingersoll, Lurton D. *A History of the War Department of the United States With Biographical Sketches of the Secretaries*. Washington, D.C.: Mohun, 1880.

Jacobs, James Ripley. *The Beginnings of the U.S. Army, 1783–1812*. Princeton: Princeton Univ. Press, 1947.

Janowitz, Morris. *The Professional Soldier: A Social and Political Portrait*. Glencoe, Ill.: Free Press, 1960.

Jessup, Philip C. *Elihu Root*. 2 vols. New York: Dodd, Mead, 1938.

Just, Ward S. *The Military Men*. New York: Knopf, 1970.

Kemble, Robert C. *The Image of the Army Officer in America: Background for Current Views*. Westport, Conn.: Greenwood, 1973.

Killigrew, John W. *The Impact of the Great Depression on the Army*. New York: Garland, 1979

Kitfield, James. *Prodigal Soldiers: How the Generation of Officers Born of Vietnam Revolutionized the American Style of War*. 1995. Reprint, Washington, D.C.: Brassey, 1997.

Klare, Michael T. *War Without End: American Planning for the Next Vietnams*. New York: Knopf, 1972.

Kohn, Richard H. *Eagle and Sword: The Beginnings of the Military Establishment in America*. New York: Macmillan, Free Press, 1964.

Kolodziej, Edward A. *The Uncommon Defense and Congress, 1945–1963*. Columbus: Ohio State Univ. Press, 1966.

Korb, Lawrence J. *The Fall and Rise of the Pentagon: American Defense Policies in the 1970s*. Westport, Conn.: Greenwood, 1979.

———. *The Joint Chiefs of Staff: The First Twenty-five Years*. Bloomington: Indiana Univ. Press, 1976.

Masland, John W., and Laurence I. Radway. *Soldiers and Scholars: Military Education and National Policy*. Princeton: Princeton Univ. Press, 1957.

Matloff, Maurice, ed. *American Military History*. American Historical Series. Rev. ed. Washington, D.C.: Office of the Chief of Military History, United States Army, 1973.

May, Ernest R., ed. *The Ultimate Decision: The President as Commander in Chief*. New York: Braziller, 1960.

Meneely, Alexander Howard. *The War Department, 1861: A Study in Mobilization and Administration*. Studies in History, Economics, and Public Law, no. 300. New York: Columbia Univ. Press, 1928.

Millett, Allan R., and Peter Maslowski. *For the Common Defense: A Military History of the United States of America*. Rev. ed. New York: Free Press, 1994.

Millis, Walter. *Arms and Men: A Study in American Military History*. New York: Putnam, 1956.

Morison, Elting E. *Turmoil and Tradition: A Study of the Life and Times of Henry L. Stimson*. Boston: Houghton Mifflin, 1960.

Chaffee, Adna R.

Carter, William Harding. *The Life of Lieutenant General Chaffee.* Chicago: Univ. of Chicago Press, 1917.

Collins, J. Lawton

Collins, J. Lawton. *Lightning Joe: An Autobiography.* Baton Rouge: Louisiana State Univ. Press, 1979.

———. *War in Peacetime: The History and Lessons of Korea.* Boston: Houghton Mifflin, 1969.

Dearborn, Henry

Coffin, Charles, comp. *The Lives and Services of Major General John Thomas, Colonel Thomas Knowlton, Colonel Alexander Scammell, Major General Henry Dearborn.* New York: Egbert, Hovery and King, 1845.

Dearborn, Henry. *Revolutionary War Journals of Henry Dearborn, 1775–1783.* Edited by Lloyd A. Brown and Howard H. Peckham. New York: Caxton, 1939.

Erney, Richard Alton. *The Public Life of Henry Dearborn.* New York: Arno, 1979.

Eisenhower, Dwight D.

Ambrose, Stephen E. *Ike, Abilene to Berlin: The Life of Dwight D. Eisenhower. . . .* New York: Harper, 1973.

———. *Eisenhower: Soldier and President.* New York: Simon and Schuster, 1983.

Childs, Marquis W. *Eisenhower, Captive Hero: A Critical Study of the General and the President.* New York: Harcourt, Brace, 1958.

Clarfield, Gerard H. *Security With Solvency: Dwight D. Eisenhower and the Shaping of the American Military Establishment.* Westport, Conn.: Praeger, 1999.

D'Este, Carlo. *Eisenhower: A Soldier's Life.* New York: Holt, 2002.

Eisenhower, David. *Eisenhower at War: 1943–1945.* New York: Random House, 1986.

Eisenhower, Dwight D. *Crusade in Europe.* Garden City, N.Y: Doubleday, 1948.

———. *The Eisenhower Diaries.* Edited by Robert H. Ferrell. New York: Norton, 1981.

———. *The Papers of Dwight David Eisenhower.* Vols. 7–9, edited by Louis Galambos. Baltimore: Johns Hopkins Univ. Press, 1978.

Eisenhower, John S. D. *General Ike: A Personal Reminiscence.* New York: Free Press, 2003.

Hatch, Alden. *General Ike: A Biography of Dwight D. Eisenhower.* New York: Holt, 1944.

Lyon, Peter. *Eisenhower: Portrait of a Hero.* Boston: Little, Brown, 1974.

Grant, Ulysses S.

Badeau, Adam. *Grant in Peace: From Appomattox to Mount McGregor.* Hartford: Scranton, 1887.

Catton, Bruce. *Grant Moves South.* Boston: Little, Brown, 1960.

———. *Grant Takes Command.* Boston: Little, Brown, 1969.

———. *U. S. Grant and the American Military Tradition.* Boston: Little, Brown, 1954.

Fuller, John Frederick Charles. *The Generalship of Ulysses S. Grant.* New York: Dodd, Mead, 1929.

Grant, Ulysses S. *Memoirs and Selected Letters: Personal Memoirs of U. S. Grant, Selected Letters 1839–1865.* New York: Library of America, 1990.

———. *The Papers of Ulysses S. Grant.* Edited by John Y. Simon. Vols. 10–19. Carbondale: Southern Illinois Univ. Press, 1982–95.

———. *Personal Memoirs of U. S. Grant.* 2 vols. New York: Webster, 1885–86.

Hyman, Harold M. "Johnson, Stanton, and Grant: A Reconsideration of the Army's Role in the Events Leading to Impeachment." *American Historical Review* 66 (October 1960): 85–100.

Lewis, Lloyd. *Captain Sam Grant.* Boston: Little, Brown, 1950.

Perret, Geoffrey. *Ulysses S. Grant: Soldier & President.* New York: Random House, 1997.

Smith, Jean Edward. *Grant.* New York: Simon and Schuster, 2001.

Halleck, Henry.

Ambrose, Stephen E. *Halleck: Lincoln's Chief of Staff.* Baton Rouge: Louisiana State Univ. Press, 1962.

Halleck, Henry W. *Elements of Military Art and Science. . . .* New York: Appleton, 1846.

———. *International Law, or Rules Regulating the Intercourse of States in Peace and War.* New York: Van Nostrand, 1861.

Marszalek, John F. *Commander of All Lincoln's Armies: A Life of General Henry W. Halleck.* Cambridge, Mass.: Harvard Univ. Press, 2004.

Hamilton, Alexander

Cooke, Jacob E. *Alexander Hamilton.* New York: Scribner, 1982.

Chernow, Ron. *Alexander Hamilton.* New York: Penguin, 2004.

Hacker, Louis M. *Alexander Hamilton in the American Tradition.* New York: McGraw-Hill, 1957.

Hamilton, Alexander. *Alexander Hamilton and the Founding of the Nation.* Edited by Richard B. Morris. New York: Dial, 1957.

———. *The Works of Alexander Hamilton.* Edited by Henry Cabot Lodge. 9 vols. New York: Putnam, 1885–86.

McDonald, Forrest. *Alexander Hamilton: A Biography.* New York: Norton, 1979.

Miller, John C. *Alexander Hamilton: Portrait in Paradox.* New York: Harper, 1959.

Walling, Karl-Friedrich. *Alexander Hamilton on War and Free Government.* Lawrence: Univ. Press of Kansas, 1999.

Harmar, Josiah

Harmar, Josiah. *Outpost on the Wabash, 1787–1791: Letters of Brigadier General Josiah Harmar. . . .* Edited by

Gayle Thornbrough. Indianapolis: Indiana Historical Society, 1957.

Peckham, Howard H. "Josiah Harmar and His Indian Expedition." *Ohio State Archeological and Historical Quarterly* 55 (1946): 227–41.

Johnson, Harold K.

McMaster, H. R. *Dereliction of Duty: Lyndon Johnson, Robert McNamara, the Joint Chiefs of Staff, and the Lies That Led to Vietnam.* New York: HarperCollins, 1997.

Sorley, Lewis. *Honorable Warrior: General Harold K. Johnson and the Ethics of Command.* Lawrence: Univ. Press of Kansas, 1998.

Knox, Henry

Brooks, Noah. *Henry Knox: A Soldier of the Revolution. . . .* New York: Putnam, 1900.

Callahan, North. *Henry Knox: General Washington's General.* New York: Rinehart, 1958.

Carter, Michael D. "Nationbuilding and the Military: The Life and Career of Secretary of War Henry Knox, 1750–1806." Ph.D. diss., West Virginia Univ., 1997.

Drake, Francis S. *Life and Correspondence of Henry Knox, Major General in the Revolutionary Army.* Boston: Drake, 1873.

Lonergan, Thomas J. *Henry Knox: George Washington's Confidant, General of Artillery, and America's First Secretary of War.* Rockport, Me.: Picton, 2003.

Thompson, John Mark. "Citizens and Soldiers: Henry Knox and the Development of American Military Thought and Practice." Ph.D.diss., Univ. of North Carolina, 2000.

MacArthur, Douglas

James, Dorris Clayton. *The Years of MacArthur.* 3 vols. Boston: Houghton Mifflin, 1970–85.

Lisio, Donald J. *The President and Protest: Hoover, MacArthur, and the Bonus Riot.* 2d ed. New York: Fordham Univ. Press, 1994.

Lowitt, Richard, comp. *The Truman-MacArthur Controversy.* Chicago: Rand McNally, 1967.

MacArthur, Douglas. *Reminiscences.* New York: McGraw-Hill, 1964.

Perret, Geoffrey. *Old Soldiers Never Die: The Life of Douglas MacArthur.* New York: Random House, 1996.

Petillo, Carol Morris. *Douglas MacArthur: The Philippine Years.* Bloomington: Indiana Univ. Press, 1981.

Macomb, Alexander

Macomb, Alexander. *The Practice of Courts Martial.* New York: Coleman, 1840.

Richards, George H. *Memoir of Alexander Macomb, the Major General Commanding the Army of the United States.* New York: McElrath, Bangs, 1833.

March, Peyton C.

Coffman, Edward M. *The Hilt of the Sword: The Career of Peyton C. March.* Madison: Univ. of Wisconsin Press, 1966.

March, Peyton C. *The Nation at War.* Garden City, N.Y.: Doubleday, Doran, 1932.

Marshall, George C.

Cray, Ed. *General of the Army: George C. Marshall, Soldier and Statesman.* New York: Norton, 1990.

Frye, William. *Marshall: Citizen Soldier.* Indianapolis: Bobbs-Merrill, 1947.

Larrabee, Eric. *Commander in Chief: Franklin Delano Roosevelt, His Lieutenants, and Their War.* 1987. Reprint, Annapolis, Md.: Naval Institute Press, 2004.

Marshall, George C. *Memoirs of My Services in the World War, 1917–1918.* Boston: Houghton Mifflin, 1976.

———. *The Papers of George Catlett Martshall.* Edited by Larry I. Bland and Sharon R. Stevens. Vols. 2–5. Baltimore: Johns Hopkins Univ. Press, 1981–2003.

Parrish, Thomas. *Roosevelt and Marshall: Partners in Politics and War.* New York: Prentice-Hall, 1951.

Payne, Robert. *The Marshall Story: A Biography of General George C. Marshall.* New York: Prentice-Hall, 1951.

Pogue, Forrest C. *George C. Marshall.* 3 vols. New York: Viking, 1963–73.

———. *George C. Marshall Interviews and Reminiscences for Forrest C. Pogue.* Lexington, Va.: George C. Marshall Research Foundation, 1991.

Stoler, Mark A. *George C. Marshall: Soldier-Statesman of the American Century.* Boston: Twayne, 1989.

U.S. War Department. General Staff. *Biennial Report of the Chief of Staff of the United States Army, July 1, 1943 to June 30, 1945, to the Secretary of War.* Washington, D.C., 1945.

McClellan, George B.

Beatie, Russel H. *Army of the Potomac.* Vol. 2, *McClellan Takes Command, September 1861–February 1862.* Cambridge, Mass.: Da Capo, 2005.

Hassler, Warren W., Jr. *General George B. McClellan: Shield of the Union.* Baton Rouge: Louisiana State Univ. Press, 1957.

McClellan, George B. *The Armies of Europe.* Philadelphia: Lippincott, 1861.

———. *The Civil War Papers of George B. McClellan: Selected Correspondence, 1860–1865.* Edited by Stephen W. Sears. New York: Ticknor and Fields, 1989.

———. *McClellan's Own Story: The War for the Union. . . .* New York: Webster, 1887.

Sears, Stephen W. *George B. McClellan: The Young Napoleon.* New York: Ticknor and Fields, 1988.

Miles, Nelson A.

DeMontravel, Peter R. *A Hero to His Fighting Men: Nelson A. Miles, 1839–1925.* Kent, Ohio: Kent State Univ. Press, 1998.

Johnson, Virginia Weisal. *The Unregimented General: A Biography of Nelson A. Miles.* Boston: Houghton Mifflin, 1962.

Miles, Nelson A. *Personal Recollections and Observations.* . . . Chicago: Werner, 1896.

———. *Serving the Republic: Memoirs of the Civil and Military Life of Nelson A. Miles.* New York: Harper, 1911.

Wooster, Robert. *Nelson A. Miles and the Twilight of the Frontier Army.* Lincoln: Univ. of Nebraska Press, 1993.

Palmer, Bruce, Jr.

Palmer, Bruce, Jr. *The 25-Year War: America's Military Role in Vietnam.* Lexington: Univ. Press of Kentucky, 1984.

Pershing, John J.

Palmer, Frederick. *John J. Pershing, General of the Armies: A Biography.* Harrisburg, Pa.: Military Service, 1948.

Pershing, John J. *My Experiences in the World War.* 2 vols. New York: Stokes, 1931.

Smythe, Donald. *Guerrilla Warrior: The Early Life of John J. Pershing.* New York: Scribner, 1973.

———. *Pershing, General of the Armies.* Bloomington: Indiana Univ. Press, 1986.

Vandiver, Frank E. *Black Jack: The Life and Times of John J. Pershing.* 2 vols. College Station: Texas A&M Univ. Press, 1977.

Ridgway, Matthew B.

Bacevich, A. J. "The Paradox of Professionalism: Eisenhower, Ridgway, and the Challenge to Civilian Control, 1953–1955." *Journal of Military History* 61 (April 1997): 303–34.

Ridgway, Matthew B. *The Korean War: How We Met the Challenges.* . . . Garden City, N.Y.: Doubleday, 1967.

———. *Soldier: The Memoirs of Matthew B. Ridgway.* New York: Harper, 1956.

Soffer, Jonathan M. *General Matthew B. Ridgway: From Progressivism to Reaganism, 1895–1993.* Westport, Conn.: Praeger, 1998.

Rogers, Bernard W.

Rogers, Bernard William. *Cedar Falls–Junction City: A Turning Point.* Vietnam Studies. Washington, D.C.: Department of the Army, 1974.

Schofield, John M.

Connelly, Donald B. " Political Soldier John M. Schofield and the Politics of Generalship." Ph.D. diss., Univ. of Houston, 2003.

Schofield, John M. *Forty-six Years in the Army.* New York: Century, 1897.

Scott, Hugh L.

Harper, James W. "Hugh Lenox Scott, Soldier-Diplomat." Ph.D. diss., Univ. of Virginia, 1968.

Scott, Hugh L. *Some Memories of a Soldier.* New York: Century, 1928.

Scott, Winfield

Eisenhower, John S. D. *Agent of Destiny: The Life and Times of General Winfield Scott.* New York: Free Press, 1997.

Elliott, Charles Winslow. *Winfield Scott: The Soldier and the Man.* New York: Macmillan, 1937.

Johnson, Timothy D. *Winfield Scott: The Quest for Military Glory.* Lawrence: Univ. Press of Kansas, 1998.

Long, Laura. *Fuss 'n' Feathers: A Life of Winfield Scott.* New York: Longmans, Green, 1944.

Mansfield, Edward D. *The Life of General Winfield Scott.* New York: Barnes, 1846.

Peskin, Allan. *Winfield Scott and the Profession of Arms.* Kent, Ohio: Kent State Univ. Press, 2003.

Scott, Winfield. *Memoirs of Lieut.-General Scott, LL.D.* New York: Sheldon, 1864.

Sheridan, Philip H.

Hutton, Paul Andrew. *Phil Sheridan and His Army.* Norman: Univ. of Oklahoma Press, 1999.

Sheridan, Philip H. *Personal Memoirs of P. H. Sheridan, General, United States Army.* 2 vols. New York: Webster, 1888.

Sherman, William T.

Andrews, Richard Allen. "Years of Frustration: William T. Sherman, the Army, and Reform, 1869–1883." Ph.D. diss., Northwestern Univ., 1968.

Athearn, Robert G. *William Tecumseh Sherman and the Settlement of the West.* Norman: Univ. of Oklahoma Press, 1956.

Fellman, Michael. *Citizen Sherman: A Life of William Tecumseh Sherman.* New York: Random House, 1995.

Kennett, Lee. *Sherman: A Soldier's Life.* New York: HarperCollins, 2001.

Lewis, Lloyd. *Sherman: Fighting Prophet.* New York: Harcourt, Brace, 1932.

Liddell Hart, Basil Henry. *Sherman: Soldier, Realist, American.* New York: Dodd, Mead, 1929.

Marszalek, John F. *Sherman: A Soldier's Passion for Order.* New York: Free Press, 1993.

Merrill, James M. *William Tecumseh Sherman.* Chicago: Rand McNally, 1971.

Miers, Earl Schenck. *The General Who Marched to Hell: William Tecumseh Sherman and His March to Fame and Infamy.* New York: Knopf, 1951.

Sherman, William T. *Memoirs of General William T. Sherman.* 2 vols. New York: Appleton, 1875.

St. Clair, Arthur

St. Clair, Arthur. *A Narrative of the Manner in Which*

the Campaign Against the Indians, in the Year 1791, Was Conducted, Under the Command of Major General St. Clair. 1812. Reprint, New York: Arno, 1971.

————. The St. Clair Papers: The Life and Public Service of Arthur St. Clair. . . . Edited by William Henry Smith. 2 vols. 1882. Reprint, New York: Da Capo, 1971.

Wilson, Frazer Ells. Arthur St. Clair, Rugged Ruler of the Old Northwest: An Epic of the American Frontier. Richmond, Va.: Garrett and Massie, 1944.

Sullivan, Gordon R.

Sullivan, Gordon R., ed. Portrait of an Army. Washington, D.C.: Center of Military History, United States Army, 1991.

Sullivan, Gordon R., and Michael V. Harper. Hope Is Not a Method: What Business Leaders Can Learn From America's Army. New York: Random House, 1996.

Taylor, Maxwell D.

Kinnard, Douglas. The Certain Trumpet: Maxwell Taylor and the American Experience in Vietnam. Brassey, 1991.

Taylor, John M. General Maxwell Taylor: The Sword and the Pen. Garden City, N.Y.: Doubleday, 1989.

Taylor, Maxwell D. Precarious Security. New York: Norton, 1976.

————. Responsibility and Response. New York: Harper, 1967.

————. Swords and Plowshares: A Memoir. New York: Norton, 1972.

————. The Uncertain Trumpet. New York: Harper, 1959.

Washington, George

Flexner, James Thomas. George Washington. 4 vols. Boston: Little, Brown, 1965–72.

————. Washington: The Indispensable Man. Boston: Little, Brown, 1974.

Freeman, Douglas Southall. George Washington: A Biography. 7 vols. New York: Scribner, 1948–57.

Kwasney, Mark V. Washington's Partisan War, 1775–1783. Kent, Ohio: Kent State Univ. Press, 1996.

Marshall, John. The Life of George Washington, Commander in Chief of the American Forces . . . and First President of the United States. 5 vols. Philadelphia: Wayne, 1804–07.

Washington, George. The Diaries of George Washington, 1748–1799. Edited by John C. Fitzpatrick. 4 vols. Boston: Houghton Mifflin, 1925.

————. The Writings of George Washington . . . , 1745–1799. Edited by John C. Fitzpatrick. 39 vols. Washington, D.C.: Government Printing Office, 1931–44.

Wayne, Anthony

Boyd, Thomas Alexander. Mad Anthony Wayne. New York: Scribner, 1929.

Gaff, Alan D. Bayonets in the Wilderness: Anthony Wayne's Legion in the Old Northwest. Norman: Univ. of Oklahoma Press, 2004

Knopf, Richard C., ed. Anthony Wayne, A Name in Arms: Soldier, Diplomat, Defender of Expansion Westward of a Nation. Pittsburgh: Univ. of Pittsburgh Press, 1959.

Nelson, Paul David. Anthony Wayne: Soldier of the Early Republic. Bloomington: Indiana Univ. Press, 1985.

Preston, John Hyde. A Gentleman Rebel: The Exploits of Anthony Wayne. New York: Farrar and Rinehart, 1930.

Tucker, Glen. Mad Anthony Wayne and the New Nation: The Story of Washington's Front-line General. Harrisburg, Pa.: Stackpole Books, 1973.

Wildes, Harry Emerson. Anthony Wayne: Trouble Shooter of the American Revolution. New York: Harcourt, Brace, 1941.

Westmoreland, William C.

Furguson, Ernest B. Westmoreland: The Inevitable General. Boston: Little, Brown, 1968.

U.S. Department of the Army. General Staff. Report of the Chief of Staff of the United States Army, 1 July 1968 to 30 June 1972. Washington, D.C., 1977.

Westmoreland, William C. A Soldier Reports. Garden City, N.Y.: Doubleday, 1976

Zaffiri, Samuel. Westmoreland: A Biography of General William C. Westmoreland. New York: Morrow, 1994.

Wickham, John Adams, Jr.

Wickham, John Adams, Jr. Korea on the Brink: A Memoir of Intrigue and Military Crisis. 1999. Reprint, Washington, D.C.: Brassey, 2000.

Wilkinson, James

Hay, Thomas Robson, and Morris Robert Werner. The Admirable Trumpeter: A Biography of General James Wilkinson. Garden City, N.Y.: Doubleday, Doran, 1941.

Jacobs, James Ripley. Tarnished Warrior: Major General James Wilkinson. New York: Macmillan, 1938.

Shreve, Royal Ornan. The Finished Scoundrel: General James Wilkinson. . . . Indianapolis: Bobbs-Merrill, 1933.

Wilkinson, James. Wilkinson: Soldier and Pioneer. New Orleans: Rogers, 1935.

————. Memoirs of My Own Times. Philadelphia: Small, 1816.

Wood, Leonard

Hagedorn, Hermann. Leonard Wood: A Biography. 2 vols. New York: Harper, 1931.

Lane, Jack C. Armed Progressive: General Leonard Wood. San Rafael, Calif.: Presidio, 1978.

Wood, Leonard. Our Military History: Its Facts and Fallacies. Chicago: Reilly and Britton, 1916.

Wotherspoon, William W.

Birtle, Andrew J. "The U.S. Army's Pacification of

Marindugue, Philippine Islands, April 1900–April 1901." *Journal of Military History* 61 (April 1997): 255–82.

Wotherspoon, William Wallace. *The Training of the Efficient Soldier.* Philadelphia: American Academy of Political and Social Science, 1905.

PIN: 052512–000